Listening, Playing, Creating

Listening, Playing, Creating

Essays on the Power of Sound

Edited by

Carolyn Bereznak Kenny

State University of New York Press

Published by
State University of New York Press, Albany

For information, address State University of New York Press,
State University Plaza, Albany, N.Y. 12246

Production by M. R. Mulholland
Marketing by Theresa A. Swierzowski

Library of Congress Cataloging-in-Publication Data

Kenny, Carolyn.
  Listening, playing, creating : essays on the power of sound /
edited by Carolyn Bereznak Kenny.
      p.   cm.
  Includes bibliographical references (p.) and index.
  ISBN 0-7914-2285-2. — ISBN 0-7914-2286-0 (pbk.)
  1. Music therapy. 2. Music—Physiological effect. 3. Music.
Influence of. I. Title.
ML3920.K38 1995
615.8'5154—dc20   94-4920
                                                                  CIP
                                                                  MN

10 9 8 7 6 5 4 3 2 1

This book is dedicated to bridgebuilders and mapmakers all

Contents

Figures

Acknowledgments

First and foremost, I want to thank all of the contributors who have written such beautiful work for this collection. They have been patient and endured the long wait from the initiation of this project three years ago to its completion. Some who read the manuscript say that the collection sounds more like a symposium of good friends and colleagues sitting together around the fire. Of course, this is what we all wish.

There have been many others who have contributed throughout the years to enrich and inspire me but for one reason or another are not represented here. I thank them, as well. You know who you are.

I would also like to thank Antioch University Santa Barbara for support in this project. In particular, Chairman of the Graduate Clinical Psychology Program, Terrence Keeney, and Chairman of the Undergraduate Liberal Studies Program, Richard Whitney, and our Academic Dean, Laurien Alexandre, as well as the staff of the university.

My research assistant, Jessie Stone-Phennicie, has been a wonderful companion in the final stages of preparation, as well as an enthusiastic participant in both technical and creative aspects of gathering our materials for the State University of New York Press.

Thanks to Carola F. Sautter, our editor at SUNY for supporting this project.

And last, but certainly not least, I would like to thank Jack Crane for personal inspiration and valuable editorial counsel. Now it begins. . . .

Part I

THE BEGINNING

Introduction to Part One

In 1969 I began my work as a music therapist. In 1994 I will celebrate 25 years in the profession. Recently, I have been filled with gratitude to have had work so rich, so full, so inspiring and meaningful both day-to-day and over time. I have had opportunities to serve a range of clients in varied states of being and a wide range of age, from three years to 102. I have had the great privilege of training hundreds of music therapists in both Canada and the United States and to work collaboratively to design music therapy training programs. I have been invited to speak about music therapy in Canada, the United States, and Europe. And I have had the good fortune to produce several written documents describing the beauty of our work.

This kind of rich work life is never done in isolation. There have been many companions on my way. And of all my blessings, one of the most sacred is the work friendships I have made—the relationships. This volume is a collection of prose, poems, case studies, stories, essays, and articles by people who are my friends. They are the ones who have inspired me. They have sometimes challenged me. They have disagreed with me. And in many cases agreed. Often we have shared laughter and tears and, always, we have shared a love of our work, even in moments of seeming despair.

It is a privilege and an honor to share my friends with you, the reader. In these works you will find something profound, something playful, something inspiring. Many of the works are what I would call transformative in nature. So be prepared for deep personal change, even as you read. Some are intellectually stimulating. So be prepared to think and learn. Some are more like music than words. So be prepared to dream.

You will find variety of style, texture, form, and tone. This is a varied and rich world. Each contribution is an original work written expressly for this collection in the spirit of listening, playing, creating, and the power of sound.

In many ways this book has been my world and I would like to tell you a little about the topography of this place. At the center of this world is music therapy. Sixteen of the contributors are professional music therapists and five others use music as therapy in some form. There are four performers, two philosophers, and two anthropologists. Twelve women and twelve men are represented in this volume. There are fifteen Americans, though eight of these have chosen lifestyles which often find them in Europe or Mexico. There are six Canadians, one Dane, one Norwegian, and one Israeli. The two geographic centers most represented in this volume are Vancouver, British Columbia, and New York, though you will find California, Quebec, Israel, France, Norway, Denmark, and other places, as well.

As you read, you will find one of the striking features of this book to be a kind of walking between worlds and a creative process of new maps. For all of the people writing here are interdisciplinarians. Though they may function primarily in one field, they are dedicated to the bridge-building process. In some cases, it is quite remarkable that one or the other can have such an intense focus on one field, yet be open to something new from "the outside." Therefore you will find a theme to be one of opening and closing—defining what is discrete to a field, yet expanding to learn from "the outsiders" of a defined realm, from a mystery, a non sequitur, a question, an implication. These people are not afraid. Because, in this sense, they are free to be unbound by specialization and the determinism of categories, they help us to expand. And that is what they have done for me.

Often, in the introductions to each piece, you will notice a reference to the Children's Spontaneous Music Workshops. This group developed serendipitously in the early 1970s in Vancouver, British Columbia. Several members of this original group have made contributions here including Michael Fles, John Marcus, Nancy McMaster, myself, and, vicariously, Christopher Tree. In my life the experiences with the Children's Spontaneous Music Workshops have continued to be a source of great inspiration, even though many years have passed. In a sense, it is a cultural influence. The members of this group were children of the 60s. The 60s were our time and we were all affected by the events of the time. This was our bond.

As a child, I did not learn, but rather spontaneously came upon, my tendency to do open improvisation. I would spend hours at the piano or with voice, creating tunes and lyrics, or merely gravitating to the music to express deep emotion, which seemed impossible or inappropriate to express in my world with words. In the Children's Spontaneous Music Workshops, this natural tendency became formalized and shared with others, in our group, and in the community at large. It seemed like a noble experiment to us. And it was certainly a commitment to the power of sound.

Another reference you will often find in the preludes or introductions is the New York Music Therapy Community and the Phonecia Music Therapy Retreat Group. This group was formed from the vision of Barbara Hesser, of New York University. She had an idea to create a different kind of professional community, in which spirituality would be at the center of our dialogs and our approach. I have seldom met a person with such a clear and strong sense of community as Barbara. This is demonstrated in the music therapy training programs she has created at New York University, her vision for the Phoenecia Music Therapy Retreat Group, and her ability to pull together international gatherings such as the *1982 Symposium on Music in the Life of Man: Toward a Theory of Music Therapy*, another significant event often mentioned in these introductory texts. There are many contributors who are part of this community on a regular or occasional basis. They include Barbara Hesser, Gillian Stephens Langdon, Kenneth Bruscia, Dorit Amir, David Burrows, Lisa Summer, David Marcus, Even Ruud, Benedikte Scheiby, Kenneth Aigen, and myself.

Joanne Crandall, Frances Smith Goldberg, Penelope Nichols-Rothe, and Jeremy Shapiro are generally in California, that is to say, a lot of my experience with them has been in California. Jillian and Robin Ridington and Peter O'Loughlin are Vancouver folk.

Connie Isenberg-Grzeda and I have shared our work in Montreal. Joseph Moreno is a music therapist with whom I have not shared a geographic place, but rather an intellectual space of mutually shared interests, meeting occasionally at conferences throughout the United States, Canada, and Europe. Paul Lauzon and I have worked together in both Canada and the United States.

I invited all of these friends to make a contribution to a book entitled *Listening, Playing, Creating: Essays on the Power of Sound*. I provided little direction, hoping that the title was provocative and inspiring enough to stimulate and activate them, each in their own way. I trusted that there was something implied by our experience together over the years which would blossom and be created through the suggestion of these words, and the title was selected with exactly this possibility in mind. It represents the essence of what we have shared. In my invitation, I did set a phenomenological tone and provided a quote from Don Idhe's (1973) *Sense and Significance*:

Phenomenology is a revolution in man's understanding of himself and his world. But the newness and radicality of this revolution is faced with a problem, the same problem which arises in the epiphany of any new phenomenon. What phenomenology has to say must be made understandable—but what it has to say is such that it cannot be said easily in a language already sedemented and accommodated to a perspective quite different than that taken by the revolutionary. What eventually may be said must first be "sung." One only gradually learns to hear what sounds forth from the "song." (p. 162)

I hope this book will be a revolution and you will hear "the song," and it will touch your life and your work and inspire you. It is a revolution about sound, about music and about the place of the aesthetic experience in our daily lives. Many of the works describe therapeutic and healing environments, which are merely a reflection of our own possible gravest state. How can we forget to imagine? In the end does not a spiritual approach suggest that our lives are inextricably linked, each to the other, no matter the difference in our circumstances? In these pages you will find both explicit and implicit clues about the path of connection and change.

Another feature of the collection is my own personal commitment to acknowledging the importance of social context, represented here in a professional community, or more accurately, in a work community, because many of the contributors are not so-called "professionals," as society would have it.

For myself, I have developed a work which was primarily outside of the mainstream. It has been extremely important for me to gather a set of colleagues in which I would find support and inspiration—people who I could trust and listen to, even if we disagreed. This kind of gathering is fundamentally based on caring.

I needed a community, a secure base from which to develop my work, and colleagues I could trust and respect. The contributors to this book represent many of the people whom I have gathered (and who have gathered me, and who have sometimes, as you will soon learn, been serendipitously gathered for "us"). This type of gathering creates an environment in which listening, playing, and creating can occur. This rich social context is the soil upon which so much has grown.

This collection, I hope, tells the story of a profound connection between love and work. Some of the contributors here are lifelong friends, some I barely know. But with everyone, this feeling of caring and trust and respect is present.

The format of the text is a brief introduction to each contributor describing how we met, where we met, and some of the experiences we have shared over time. I do not attempt to explain, interpret, or critique any of the works. The collegial and interdisciplinary dance we have done over the years is a dance you will not do. Yet, I hope you will find your own movement within these pages, your own "sound." My contributions to the collection are impressionistic even to the last.

This is a tribute and a thanks to those who have offered me so much, and who will offer you a great deal if you listen to "the song."

Reference

Idhe, D. (1973) *Sense and Significance*. N.J.: Humanities Press.

Part II

LISTENING

1

The Silent Source

John Marcus

Prelude to John Marcus

Johnny arrived on the Vancouver scene at some point in time, early on, and became a part of the Children's Spontaneous Music Workshops, along with Michael, Shelley, Nancy (also a contributor), Charles, Sandy, Thea, Clark, various others, and me. From the beginning, for me, John embodied the Muse. In the music he was free, and his facility with sound was enough to inspire and transport. In spirit, he was Pan. In the flesh, he was another tortured soul, just like the rest. And this aspect of his existence he expressed through quoting Blake, Shelley, Yeats, and the occasional Thoreau, Emerson, and various other naturalists and pantheists. He always wanted to play music in the forest, even at Laural House, when we worked with autistic children. And of course, the children responded well to the interplay of gentle wind, flutes, chimes, and bells, glimpses of sun beneath shady Douglas firs in the backyard of the treatment facility. And they responded well to John. His contact with the children was impressive, to say the least. He was not afraid.

Once when a famous Canadian film maker got a grant from the National Film Board of Canada to make a color film about our work, we all became enraptured with the new possibility of film commentary on the work. The images the filmmaker created were fantastic and we were allowed to view and approve them. However, when we read the script, we were appalled. It portrayed us as a band of dedicated young folk who took mercy on slobbering retarded or culturally deprived children and sacrificed ourselves to spend time with them. In our beings, the relationships with the kids were mutually inspired. It did not matter if they had 30 I.Q.s or were blind or dirty, or even if they had broken the law. In the sound there was a communication between souls that rose above human context, yet in some ways celebrated our human condition. John proposed that we write a letter to the Canadian Government attempting to ban the film, stating that it misrepresented our work. Michael applauded. It seemed a little bold to some of us in the group—but right. So we did. And to this day, there is a beautiful film about the Children's Spontaneous Music Workshops which sits on a shelf somewhere, unviewed by the public eye.

At some point our community disbanded. John went to Chiapas and then France with Michael. They both continued the work with the sound, and added light in collaboration with John's Mexican/Mayan wife, Carmen. In the south of France they stayed close to the land, building a home from stone ruins in a remote rural setting. I figured they had left North America because, for them somehow, living on a constant creative edge, creativity had died here, or was at least in a hiatus. Then twenty years later I received a letter from John from Southern California. He had returned and had read my name in a music therapy journal article. He was studying music therapy at California State University, Northridge. What a reunion this was, if you can imagine. Subsequently John and Carmen and I began a new collaboration in the form of performance art which integrated sound, light, color, and poetry. This collaboration continues intermittently as permitted by the overriding chaotic tone of the Southern California lifestyle and the fundamental paradoxes of the human condition. For two summers, John came to New York and participated in the Phoenecia Music Therapy Community Retreat.

Of himself John says: "Music has been a major theme in my life, bringing me a wealth of inner experiences and a few outward accomplishments. I have worked creatively with Michael Fles and Carolyn Kenny with Spontaneous and Therapeutic Music and have searched for the Lost Chord in Mexico, Europe, and the Middle East. Currently, I am a school teacher for the L.A. School District and am listening to the harmonies and dissonances that are thereby being added to my inner hearing."

John lives with his wife, Carmen, and three children in Sylmar, California. They live on the edge of the world and in the center of it, and certainly in the center of the sound.

Music has always been a source of joy, of sharing, of renewal, and some form of music is part of almost everyone's life. Music seems to be a universal human need, although why this is so is seen as a mystery.

There is, however, a certain experience of music which seems to be occurring more and more frequently. It is a very personal experience, one difficult to put into words, and is experienced most often, on a conscious level at least, in a very individual way, and in the most private of moments. It is an experience which sheds some light on the mystery of music.

If one approaches a musical experience with a greater inner quietness and spontaneity—this would involve laying aside not only one's "work-a-day" concerns, but also any previous musical constructs one might have—and enters, with this particular attentiveness, deeply into the pure experience of tone (and indeed into the process of its generation), one may feel quite an extraordinary transformation occur. No longer is the musical tone a symbol or gesture—it becomes, in itself, full of meaning and palpable to some newly-emerging inner touch. No longer does the music speak through conventions, cultural, rhetorical, or mental constructs—it seems to speak a new language, as if one were hearing the inner voice of nature sing a new song. As multicolored rays of warmth and love, the tones of this transformed music shine within us, illuminating and blessing the invisible reaches of our being. Indeed, might it not happen that it may touch our very inner core, and whisper to us the Silent Source, so that we realize that we, too, are another chord in the Cosmic Harmony?

2

The Unbidden Song

Frances Smith Goldberg

Prelude to Fran Goldberg

Unlike the others, it is difficult for me to remember the exact moment I met Fran. She came as a person whom I began to notice at music therapy conferences when I first moved to California in 1980. She seemed to always be part of a team. I liked her, but she was on the edge of my world. We both lived in California, though one north and one south. I always wished that we had had more time together. I heard her speak and was impressed by the integrity and depth of her words, her natural intelligence, her originality.

Then much later, in 1989, we found ourselves working together at the Bonny Foundation: A Center for Music-Centered Therapies. Helen Bonny, Barbara Hesser, and I served as the founding members of this organization. We three gathered in Kansas for several months to build a home for The Bonny Method of Guided Imagery and Music (GIM). Fran and Lisa Summer were the two primary GIM trainers at the Foundation. As the organizer of the practical matters for these trainings, I had several opportunities to work with Fran and to participate tangentially in one of her trainings. My respect for her deepened. I came to know what I had sensed, that her work did have an integrity, which combined beautifully the consciousness element of GIM and the intellectual component of the psychoanalytic tradition. Her years of clinical experience informed her formation of theory. And when she spoke about music and emotion, one knew that she had been a compassionate witness and imaginative companion for many "travelers."

Several years later, when I had an opportunity to design a Music Therapy Symposium in Santa Barbara for the Santa Barbara Symphony, I thought of Fran immediately and invited her to be one of our presenters. Of course her presentation was excellent. But more important for me, personally, was an intense connection we two made in discussing our cultural histories—the walking between worlds—African-American, Native American, White, personal, and professional. In our talk, it seemed to me that the rest of the social context, the outdoor garden party, fell away, only to reveal a sister, true and clear. One prays for moments like these in a life. There was a bond. Much was unknown. But, for me, the sense of recognition was deep.

Since then I have felt a clear and pure connection to Fran and it does not matter what we discuss, or where we are. I am just glad she is there. She is inspiring to me. And she is one of those I think of in moments of despair and doubt. We are connected, and through connection, there is hope for going on. Our worlds meet and know. This is our way.

Fran lives in San Francisco and is a licensed psychotherapist and music therapist. She conducts a private practice and is Associate Clinical Professor, Psychiatry, at the University of California School of Medicine where she supervises group therapy. She is a Fellow of the Association for Music and Imagery and continues her work as one of the primary trainers at the Bonny Foundation, teaching Guided Imagery and Music both in Europe and the United States. She has presented numerous workshops and papers at national and international conferences, has published several articles and book chapters, and serves on the editorial boards of *The Arts in Psychotherapy, Music Therapy Perspectives* and *The Journal of the Association for Music and Imagery.*

Prelude

This is a description of group and individual experiences with one song. Rather than a formal phenomenological analysis, this represents an effort to record the essence of the experiences as they unfolded and their meaning in my life.

The Song

It is just a simple song. Twelve bars. Major key. Margie is teaching the song to our group of twelve women. Margie's bright eyes sparkle as her rich soprano voice soars with the melody, a capella. The women struggle to learn this simple song. Its simplicity is deceiving. I struggle, too. The words are familiar—an old Scottish saying. But the melody is new to me and its form is irregular. Nothing repeats. Finally we know the song well enough to add the dance.

Margie patiently demonstrates the steps, moving gracefully to the accompaniment of her beautiful voice. Holding hands we move in a circle singing, "May the road rise to meet you. . . ." Facing a partner, ". . . May the wind be always at your back." Framing our partners' faces with our hands, ". . . May the sun shine warm upon your face; may the rain fall softly on your fields." Partners embracing warmly, ". . . Until we meet again may God hold you in the hollow of her hand."

We sing it over and over, changing partners with each new rendition, each woman embracing each woman in turn. My voice is strong; it feels good to sing and embrace each of these women. Then my voice falters. I am crying. We are all crying; crying and singing, singing and crying and hugging.

We have had an intense week together. Images flood through my mind. Images of pain and hurt, of joy and triumph. We have been nudged, shoved, and pushed, held, caressed, and filled to the brim by the music of Mozart, Mahler, Bach. And we have laughed, cried, and sung together as we laugh, cry, and sing together now. My voice is completely choked. I hear the voices around me; this song says what I feel in my heart.

As I fly home, the song reverberates in my head. A tear escapes. Going about my regular routine, the song continues in my head.

"This is the perfect goodbye song," I say. "We must teach it." We do. We sing and cry. And over the weeks, the song keeps singing in my head. I sing it aloud when I am alone.

"We have to learn this song for our closure." Sarah has it on a cassette?! Here?! And we sing. Filled with the joy of having shared the hearts and souls of these men and women through the archetypal beauty of the music of great masters, I find, once again, this little song is perfect. Goodbye to old friends I just met.

I continue to hear the song, sing the song, wherever I am, whatever I am doing. Day in, day out, many times each day.

"Gerri, you're going to love this song. Let's figure out the chords so we can sing it at the end." We're not quite satisfied with the chords, but they will do. I am elated! Gerri's guitar makes it much easier for these women to learn. Two years we have been working together and now our group has come to an end. We sing and we cry.

I sit at my piano. I must find the right chords, the right key. I feel obsessed by this little song. As I softly play and sing I feel sadness all through my being. It turns to gospel. I sing out with strength and with joy. It becomes a prayer. I sing for my elderly aunt who has just died. I sing for my father—her brother. I sing for all of my father's sisters. I sing for my grandmother, my grandfather. I sing for my great grandmothers, my great grandfathers. They are all gone now. *All gone now.* Tears stream down my face as I sing goodbye to my father and his family. Three generations who lived in the family home in that small town—all gone now. I hear the piano, bold and strong, slow and sad, faster, slower, changing with each time through. I hear my voice assuring them all that I remember, that I hold each of them in my heart. ". . . Until we meet again may God hold you in the hollow of her hand."

Postlude

This time of my life was filled with goodbyes. I had just left a job after 20 years. I learned that my 91-year-old aunt was sick about the same time that I had my first encounter with the song. A diagnosis of cancer came a month or so later. I flew out to arrange for her care and to begin to close the home that my great grandfather had built over one hundred years ago. She died a few weeks later.

At first, I thought this unbidden song was related to leaving the job. Only when I sat down at the piano, allowing myself to be fully in the music and to experience the incredible synergistic energy of the music and my state of being, did I come face to face with my grief and begin to understand the deeper meaning of this song.

3

Entering the World of Tones

David Marcus

Prelude to David Marcus

My primary connection with David Marcus over the last few years has been through our work on *Music Therapy*, the Journal of the American Association for Music Therapy. He serves as the Editor-in-Chief and I am a member of the editorial board. In this way we share the task, in collaboration with others, of shaping the presentation of music therapy to practitioners and others interested in our work. This is a rich and meaningful task, and one which David approaches with a finely-tuned and conscientious spirit. His ear is simultaneously tuned to the professional, the social, the political, and the philosophical/scientific realms. He knows the beauty of our relationships with clients. And he knows the power of tone and sound.

I realized this several years prior to our work together on the journal. One summer, when I was in New York working with and visiting my friend Barbara Hesser, David called and asked if we could meet. He came over to Barbara's apartment and presented me with a manuscript entitled "Entering The World of Tone." He said that this was a work-in-progress and that he would appreciate my reviewing the manuscript and offering my impressions.

So many of us talk about the importance of an intimate relationship with music. As music therapists, this is the territory and unless we have been and are receptive to sound and music, unless we have in some way given ourselves over to the intricacies of this world, the power and complexity, the territory remains unknown.

After spending time with David's manuscript, I knew that David understood this territory in an intensely personal sense. He had made his own journey into the world of tone. His work touched me deeply and I admired his courage and commitment to discovery. I was impressed with his surrender, his capacity to take risks, his connection to the sound. He did not feign complexity, rather he embraced it. He stood on the edge of the world and said to the sound, "come to me." Because of his willingness to participate, the relationships he established were deep. I had no impressions to offer David. I was only moved. The phrase "an intimate relationship with music" meant something different now, something I had not even imagined.

David had taken the time and had endured tenaciously in the World of Tone. We can all benefit from his journey.

In this article, he summarizes what he has learned, what he knows about tone—a deeply moving personal account and one which can touch us all. The words merely connote his direct experience and because of his mastery of the implied, with David, we can enter the World of Tone and be changed by it.

Of himself David says: "I am a musician and music therapist who lives, works, and plays in the New York City area."

> But these things cannot be really felt and understood unless we make it clear to ourselves that the experience of music is not related to the ear in the manner usually assumed. Musical experience is something which concerns the whole human being, and the ear has here a function that is quite different form the one usually ascribed to it. Nothing is more false than the statement: I hear a tone or melody with my ears. This is quite wrong. The tone or melody or any kind of harmony is really experienced by the whole human being.
>
> —Rudolf Steiner

Introduction

Anyone who ventures with an open mind in search of reportorial evidence of the power of music, sound, and tone will find an abundance of relevant information. There are mythological, historical, and Biblical references. There is much description of ancient and modern religious, spiritual, and occult practice. There are anthropological studies of shamanic and ritual practice involving music in many cultures. There is a growing music therapy literature which reports the use of music in healing with a diversity of orientations. Throughout this varied and widely scattered literature, many events and outcomes, ranging from the intimate to the cataclysmic, the healing to the destructive, are attributed to the power of music, sound, and tone and their apparent masters. Detailed and plausible explanations for such occurrences and achievements are generally in short supply. However, the preponderance of such claims and their consistency through history and across cultures give them a certain credibility.

It is not my purpose here to recount, classify, or analyze events or methods that have been reported previously. Rather, it is to add to my own personal experience the briefest of contemporary footnotes to the ancient and ongoing saga of the power of music. Some years ago, I sought to consciously enter what I have come to call the world of tones, and to experience and understand what I could of the powers or forces that I might encounter. My search might be best described as taking the form of that combination of curiosity, ingenuity, and faith known as an experiment. The procedures and results of that experiment are what I wish to share at this point. In order to do that fully, I will also discuss some of the concerns that preceded the experiment as well as some of the ways in which the results have influenced my subsequent thinking and practice in the fields of music and music therapy.

This experimentation took place at a time "between theory and practice." That is, it occurred after I had finished my formal academic preparation in the field of music therapy, and prior to the time when I actually began clinical work as a music therapist. This interval was lengthened and deepened according to my own determination not merely to plunge ahead into the practical without pausing to contemplate something of what I had encountered of the theoretical. Thus the experiment served both as a gesture of faith and as a search for understanding. It was done with the faith that what was true in myth, in history, and in distant cultures would also be true for me in the present: that I, too, could experience in some limited but significant sense the power of music that I had read and heard so much about; not only this, but the faith that the experience would enhance my understanding of the medium that I would be using in the service of others, and perhaps enhance my understanding of myself.

With these hopes in mind, I began to think about exactly what I would study, and exactly what procedures I would use. The power of music, as I saw it, involved two very complicated things. One was the music itself, the production and interaction of sounds in a myriad of combinations. A second was the human being, an exceedingly complex organism, whose various reactions and responses to outside stimuli were not always easy to understand. One of my primary objectives in preparation and execution of the experiment was to simplify as much as possible the task of dealing with these two complexities.

Music and Personality

What makes a music therapist, a performer, a shaman, effective?

If I employed the same music as another therapist, would I achieve the same results? If I played the same repertoire as another musician, would I receive the same reception? If I performed the same ritual as another shaman, would it have the same effects? Or is each practitioner unique, and each relationship formed with music as a basis of a highly individual manifestation of those involved in its formulation? Are the finest practitioners those who are best able to manifest, through whatever medium and method they choose, their own compelling identities?

What is the effect of music as the basis of a relationship—no matter the duration? Is it merely the stereotypical "non-threatening means of communication" which, through its seductive innocence, involves even the most fearful or withdrawn? Or is music also a transformational force, never fully the creature of creator or perceiver, which, more than merely establishing a relationship, also works ineffably to galvanize and organize somehow the energies which inevitably cause change, transiently or permanently, for better or for worse?

Ah, sweet speculation! Although in my limited experience I could not even begin to formulate answers to such questions clearly when there was more than one person present, it was often difficult to extricate the musical from the interpersonal influences. Since my interest was in the effect of musical and not interpersonal influences, I decided that there would be only one person involved in the experiment. I myself would be creator and observer. This might give rise to concerns regarding the general applicability of result, but it would limit the interpersonal influences that could bias strictly musical phenomena. And since the anticipation of applicable results seemed like optimism verging on conceit at the time, such a trade-off appeared to be a good one.

Music and Tones

What to listen to? What to experience?

Again, the complexities of the alternatives were formidable. The simplest piece of music might consist of a multiplicity of tones, of actual and/or implied intervals and chords, of some sense of tempo and meter. Each of these elements could be controlled or altered: melodies transposed, harmonies simplified, enriched, or inverted, tempi accelerated or retarded, meters changed. What were the influential factors, the salient features? Where did the power reside?

Radical simplification seemed a preferable alternative to confusion. If I chose to listen to anything that was normally considered music, I might indeed experience something, but I had the strongest premonition that I would never be able to single out any element or aspect to which I could attribute a particular effect. I would never be able to sort things out. The alternative was to break down the agglomeration to which we normally apply the singular "music" into its elements, and listen to, or otherwise experience, a single one. Tones, single tones, seemed like an attractive candidate here.

In considering this alternative, the concerns voiced previously about excessive complexity were now turned on their heads. Would reduction of music to the single element of tone reduce its effects to imperceptibility?

I thought not. Rather, I thought—and hoped—that tone, in its apparent simplicity and purity, would produce *something*, an orienting phenomenon, which would guide both my perceptions and the course of the experiment. Perhaps this element was not an insignificant speck, but the microcosm of a greater entity. Perhaps this building block would furnish some clue as to the effects of the magnificent, ephemeral edifices constructed through its inspired agglomeration.

Intention

As my conception of the experiment I was about to undertake became more and more concrete, I realized that a mental approach was going to be an important factor in the work. This would be true because in choosing to work alone (and thereby reducing the interpersonal complications that were pervasive in many situations in which music was made and perceived) I had taken on two functions which did not easily cohere in the same individual: I was both the experimenter and the subject of the experiment.

As the conceiver and the designer of the experiment, I might be expected to have an adequate background knowledge of the area or discipline in which I worked. I might be expected to have a particular hypothesis which I was trying to test, and might also be expected to be looking for certain information or results which would tend either to support or refute that hypothesis.

As a subject in the research that was being undertaken, knowledge of its background and conception, the particular hypothesis being tested, and the particular response or information that was being sought would in many cases have to be considered a disadvantage. In fact, it might bias me to the point of disqualification as a subject. Surely the possibility that I could be a fresh or objective observer would diminish if I had prior awareness of what the significance of my observations or lack of observations might be.

This uneasy simultaneity of the roles of experimenter and subject created a certain tension as well as a great concern about intention. Ultimately, the only way I could bring the experiment from its conception to its conclusion was to alternate in the roles, making every mental effort to take the appropriate role for the particular stage the experiment had reached and to abandon totally any mental vestige of the role previously held.

As experimenter, I conceived the basic purposes and concerns of the experiment, designed the procedures, and selected the materials. I then assumed the role of the subject. As subject, I observed the effects of tone and recorded them as best I could. I had no preconception or intention with regard to the nature of the results I sought. I made no attempt to analyze, understand, or anticipate results as they accumulated. In fact, as the subject of the experiment, I would have been perfectly happy had there been no result whatsoever.

As long as I was able to separate the roles and mindsets, and maintain the appropriate one, I could continue. When I tried to plan a new procedure with the mindset of the subject, I became confused. The subject, after all, had no concern with the possible significance of past results or the design of new procedures. The subject memory observed and recorded, observed and recorded. When I tried to observe with the mind of the experimenter, I also became confused. The experimenter wanted to know, in fact, though, that he had some premonitional understanding of each phenomenon, each experience, each perception. Each observation was the basis of profound new speculation or the basis for the refutation of all previous profundities.

To assume either role completely and to the exclusion of the other was the ideal, and it turned out to be one that could barely be reached, much less sustained. I could not conceive and plan the experiment and then observe totally without expectation or intention. Each succeeding set of observations brought new speculations and the anticipation of what the next set of results might be. In fact, the whole experiment has some merit as an exercise in observation of the workings of one human mind.

However, I digress. What is best remembered is that a mind totally open and alert, and clear of any preconception or expectation that would distort perception, was the ideal to which I aspired and continually reoriented myself as I sat, solitary, and prepared to enter the world of tones.

Materials and Procedures

To generate the tones I listened to, I chose a set of tuning forks. The full set consisted of 13 forks, ranging chromatically in pitch from middle C to the C above middle C on the piano. They were bluish in color and came with no indication as to exactly what metal or metals they were made of. They were coated with a transparent, plastic-like substance, which may have been applied to resist oxidization. They ranged in length from 6 1/2 inches for the low (middle) C to 5 1/4 inches for the high C. Their exact vibration rates were as follows:

C—261.6 cycles per second (cps)
C#—277.2 cps
D—293.7 cps
D#—311.1 cps
E—329.6 cps
F—349.2 cps
F#—370 cps
G—392 cps
G#—415.3 cps
A—440 cps
A#—466.2 cps
B—493.9 cps
C—523.3 cps

Actual listening was done in sessions ranging from 10-15 minutes in some of the exploratory periods, to 45-60 minutes in the most strenuous phases. Listening sessions were undertaken during the quietest part of the day, from four to six AM.

Once begun, the experience of listening itself suggested different ways in which the listening could be systemized to achieve different purposes. Throughout the entire course of the experiment, which took some months, a total of five different procedures were employed. These were as follows, in the order in which they were initiated:

I. Exploratory listening: Forks were chosen at random and listened to. Some forks were listened to more than once, others not at all. Different ways of striking the forks, and different ways of "presenting" the forks, that is, holding them near different parts of the body other than the ear, were explored. I remained open to different reactions as possible orientations for future listening.

II. Systematic listening: Each of the 13 forks was listened to individually, one in each day's session, and the results of each listening session were noted.

III. Blind listening (first round): The forks were "masked" and placed in a random order, so that neither by relative size nor by visual examination would I be able to know the pitch to which I was listening. The pitches were then listened to systematically, with each pitch presented to the ear, and to each of the "centers" (described below and in Figure 3.1) that had become apparent in earlier phases of listening.

IV. *Blind listening (second round):* With the forks still masked, each of the 13 forks were presented to a single area (ear or center) in a session.

V. *Interval listening:* The different intervals available through listening to two of the forks simultaneously (minor second through perfect octave) were listened to systematically.

The Process of Listening and Its Results

The overall process of listening breaks down fairly naturally into subdivisions. First, there is a natural subdivision between single tone listening and interval listening. There was a significant period between the end of single tone listening and the commencement of interval listening which gave the two periods a sense of separation. Also, the results of the latter were qualitatively different from those of the former and are best described and discussed separately.

Within the period of single tone listening, the process breaks down into four phases. These phases *do not* correspond in onset and completion with the different techniques and procedures for single tone listening described in the previous section. Rather, there was an interplay between procedure and result, with each influencing the other. The results of employing a certain listening technique would suggest the need for an alternation in procedure. The realization that a different procedure was desirable or necessary often came some time before the new procedure was actually initiated. A change of procedure often resolved an intellectual concern, or reflected a different orientation toward what was being perceived.

Overarching all phases of single tone listening was a growing intensity of experience which was noted to be continuous through all procedural and orientational adjustments.

Single Tone Listening

Phase I: Exploratory listening. The key issues at the beginning of this phase of listening involved the efficacy of the methodology itself. The concern was that the tuning might not produce sound of sufficient intensity and duration to make using them worthwhile. During this period, this concern quickly proved to be unfounded.

Another issue addressed during exploration was the issue of presentation, that is, where and how to direct the sound being reproduced by the forks. Obviously, the ear was one place to direct the sound, since it is generally held that music is perceived and has its effect through listening. However, another aspect of the exploration undertaken during this initial period of listening involved presenting the fork to areas of the body other than the ear. Thus, in addition to presenting a fork to the ear and listening to it, the same fork was also moved around and presented to areas up and down the length of the body and head to see if some response occurred through such a method of presentation. The fork was also presented to particular areas that I had come to think of as "centers," places in the body that had special significance. At the time of my listening, I had little detailed information about the centers (also known by their Sanskrit name, "chakras," or "wheels"). I did not know of their exact locations, nor did I know about how they were thought to function. I knew about them largely through hearing others talk about them, and through references in reading that I had done. The presentation of the tones to the centers at this early point was done as much out of untutored curiosity as it was out of experimental design.

The exploratory period of listening passed pleasantly but without major event for the better part of two weeks. I quote from session notes of the time:

> The experience has been a pleasant one so far, not unlike meditation of a sort. I have concentrated on the tone, when presented to my ear, almost to the exclusion of anything else. It has been relaxing. I have not had any strong reactions of any kind to any tone. In response to trying to affect the centers with the forks, results have been minimal. In response to running the fork over the length of the body, I did notice a feeling of energy, of emanation, almost as if I had been "tuned up" somehow. This was a very good feeling, but how or if it relates to the fork I do not know.

Soon after the above summary was recorded, a session occurred which marked both an apparent intensification of the responses to the forks, and the beginning of a sense of orientation concerning the observations I was making.

> On the present occasion, I listened to F (above middle C) with the tuning fork at my ear for some time. The note seemed to be of particularly long duration.

> At one point, I had the feeling on my stomach of something "coming alive." I moved the fork to this area with little or no local

result. But as I did this, I noticed a tightness in my throat area. This was a definite and growing feeling—it felt something like a constriction, a faint choking sensation, and something like the skin at the throat being stretched as well. At its height, it felt somewhat like a collar extending around to the back of the neck as well.

"I must recheck this sensation," I concluded.

There followed the question that was to result in the orientation which guided the research to its conclusion: *"Is it possible that I am dealing with the phenomena that are audible, but whose importance lies in their other aspects and effects?"*

As if to answer the question posed above, the next few days' sessions produced a replication and an itensification of the phenomena observed previously.

Seeking to "replicate" some of yesterday's findings, I took the F fork and held it near the throat area. I thought I felt some of the tension I had felt yesterday, but not to the same degree. My mind was extremely active, due, I think, to a period of emotional and personal doubt, and perhaps that served to dissipate the response somehow. I don't know.

Remembering the spot on my stomach area that had "come alive" previously, I applied the fork to that area. At this point I felt the throat again, but in a different way. It was a combination pulsation/rotation. This is a very difficult sensation to describe. At times it felt like a spinning—like a damp towel in a laundromat dryer—not symmetrical or uniform, but spinning nonetheless. At times it felt like it might be something like my own peristalsis, the pulsation/convulsion at the top of my digestive tract. At times it felt like an exterior phenomenon—coming from the fork and impinging on the skin like a slow breaking of waves. I just don't see how the fork itself could produce this slow wave phenomenon.

These sessions marked the end of the exploratory period of listening. Although the ongoing process was still, strictly speaking, exploratory in nature, the phenomena experienced gave the work a sense of orientation—to the "other aspects and effects" of audible sound—which was quite in contrast to the sense of randomness and openness which had typified its commencement. A very exciting new phase of the experiment now began.

Phase II: Awakening. If the phenomena experienced at the end of the exploratory period of listening constituted a stirring, a circumscribed hint of life, then the phenomena of the period which followed represented a full-fledged awakening. Under the gentle prodding of the sound of forks, I felt a sensation so soft as to be imperceptible at any significant distance, area after area of my body yawned, stretched, and "came to life," spinning, rotating, pulsating or just passively "glowing" as if in response to a greeting. I was still making my choice of which fork to listen to in a particular day's session randomly, having yet to institute the procedure of systematic listening. Even working in this almost haphazard way produced a new area of response almost daily.

In short order, I experienced a pulsation centered in the genital/urinary area in direct response to the note G; a rotation/pulsation at a point midway vertically between the navel and the heart area and centered horizontally in response to the note A; a definite pulsation at the navel in response to the note D; a rhythmic feeling of pulsation in the center of the forehead as well as some reaction in the heart area in response to the middle C; and a pulsation on the top of the head that felt "more like a flapping than a spinning" in response to the note E.

These intense phenomena produced an array of reactions and no little conflict, related in part to the dual roles I had taken in regard to them. As the subject of the experiment, there was a sense of wonder at what was beginning to happen. It was as if in the middle of the night, an area hitherto indistinguishable from the blackness that surrounded it had been illuminated, and a whole network of structures had been revealed. There was an elation at the presence of these structures, and a fascination with the experience of becoming aware of them for the first time.

As the experimenter who set out originally to find out what the responses to the forks might be, there was a great deal of questioning, both of the experience itself and of the methodology that helped produce it. It was at this point that I instituted the systematic listening procedure (one session devoted to each of the 13 forks), and that I made a full summary of my observations in the sessions to date. I questioned how much suggestion and intent were responsible for the continuous awakening that I was experiencing, and how much could be attributed solely to the influence of the tones themselves. I found, in fact, that once I was aware of the existence of an area through awakening it with sound, I could then produce pulsation in that area through mental suggestion, without the presence of sound. I was slowly becoming aware that I might have definite concerns and hopes regarding the direction the future results of the listening might take, and began to contemplate a period of "blind" listening, during which I would have no awareness of which fork I was actually listening to.

A single session served as the culmination of the period of awakening. I was brought face to face with the articulated, crystallized content of my expectations for the phenomena I was experiencing, and simultaneously I realized that the ever-intensifying awakening going on inside me had already far outstripped anything that I had been able to anticipate.

> While listening, I am very much aware of bodily reactions. I feel the tightness in the throat that I have come to expect from F, but also reaction from other areas—pulsations—until I feel that wherever among the areas I turn my attention there is a pulsation to be felt. It is not a matter of the particular area reacting to the particular tone—today it seems as if they are all reacting and it is merely a matter of where I will turn my attention, where my awareness is directed, because that is where I will sense activity.

> Is it then the sound that provokes activity in response (tone? vibration?)—or is it my attention which provokes or organizes the activity into a discrete response? What is the nature of this *attention*? Physical? I am not consciously aware of my toe (for example) all the time, and yet when I want to be, I can really get a much better sense of it (by directing my attention toward it). All of this activity in response to one tone is somewhat disconcerting, and in the reaction I can see an expectation—namely—EACH TONE WILL CAUSE A REACTION FROM A SINGLE CENTER, *AND FROM NO OTHER CENTER.* This is definitely not so today.

Phase III: A Subtle Anatomy. The experiences and realizations which concluded the period of awakening had a profound and immediate effect. I had to acknowledge that I did not understand the relationship between the tones I was generating and the responses I observed. I had to acknowledge that I had little knowledge and no understanding of the "centers" which seemed to be coming alive under the influence of the tones. I had to acknowledge that I had the desire and expectation that what I would experience would be a coherent, orderly, comprehensible set of phenomena (one tone, one center). I had to acknowledge that what had developed did not seem to conform to this or any other order, and that my expectations, far from clarifying my perceptions and experiences, might very well be biasing them in ways which I could not fully account for. To repeat a phrase that I employed in my initial report of these results, "I was both troubled by my ignorance and committed to my ignorance at the same time."

My decision in confronting these difficulties was to remain ignorant. I resolved to remain in the role of the subject rather than reassume the role of the experimenter and seek new background information, or alter the basic techniques and procedures being employed. After finishing the systematic round of listening (of which the session concluding the phase of awakening was the sixth) I started the first of two rounds of blind listening. I cleared my mind as best as I could of previously held assumptions, expectations, and speculations, and continued the experiment in much the same manner as it has begun. Curiosity and lack of understanding remained, almost as an occupational disease, an ever-present itch or ache the side effects of whose direct treatment I had deemed to be more dangerous than the disease itself.

The period of listening which followed this decision was one of consolidation more than one of new experiences. The particular areas of response that had been awakened during previous phases could now be labeled and located rather securely. In addition to the clearest ones, the navel, heart, throat, forehead, and top of head, two others, the "stomach," which was midway between the heart and navel centers, and the "genital," which was in the genital/urinary area, were also fully discerned. A complete diagram of the location of these areas of response, or "centers," is given in Figure 3.1.

The blind listening which began after the completion of the systematic listening was more rigorous than its predecessors in a few ways. At each session, the particular fork to be used was held to the ear for a period, and then presented to each center or area of response in turn starting from the lowest (genital) and rising to the highest (top of head). The fork was struck a number of times (usually seven) before proceeding to the next area for presentation.

The blind listening was typified by an overall growth in the subtlety, number, and intensity of the experiences. There were the familiar pulsations and rotations in the various centers, but there were also other newer sensations. These included "auric" feelings, as if an area in or around a center was surrounded with an aura, or halo of energy. Also, I began to sense waves, or tides of energy which moved upward or downward in the body. Overall, there was a feeling of a general heightening of the experiences occurring, and a concurrent feeling that I was becoming a more aware and sensitive observer. The cumulative effect of this growth in awareness was the sense that I was beginning to apprehend, accept, include as a part of an enhanced sense of self, a "subtle anatomy," a whole body-within-the-body which came alive in the energy of the tones I presented.

FIGURE 3.1

The Sonic Centers As Perceived in Single Tone Listening

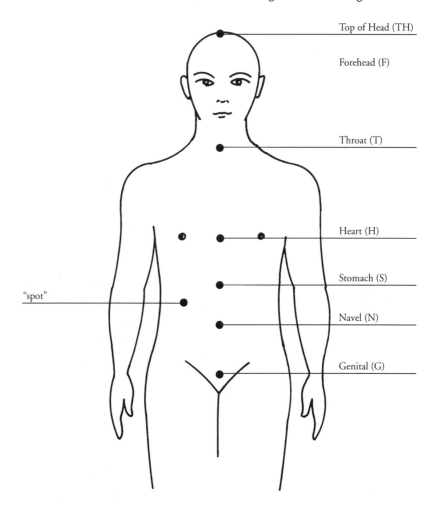

Toward the end of the first blind round of listening, I began to be aware of a phenomenon unlike any I had yet experienced. When I held the fork near some centers, it began to feel as if the fork was moving in my hand. This was a phenomenon that started almost imperceptibly, but soon grew to the point that it was the subject of much attention and an almost startled, incredulous reaction, as is illustrated below from session notes.

Movement of the fork in something approaching a regular motion at times. Beginning to accept the motion of the fork. Why does it move?

Steady pulsation in the forehead felt in/against fork and in steady corresponding motion of fork. Something in my forehead is pushing against the fork in my hand, making the fork feel like it moves slightly—pendulum fashion. I can't see it—dark, eyes closed—LOOK!"

Stronger but more erratic movements of the fork—fatigue from position?—pulsation of the forehead—LOOK!

Phase IV: The Body Answers. The phenomenon which concluded the subtle anatomy phase of listening was in many ways the least anticipated and the most difficult to accept or explain of any that I had experienced to date. Responses observed to this point were clearly felt to be "internal" in nature, only slightly below the physical surface of the body. Now it seemed as if a qualitatively different response had developed. The body, awakened by tone, was "answering," pushing beyond what would normally be considered its limits with forces felt impinging against the objects around it, the very objects that had caused it to respond in the first place.

Initially, the sensation of motion felt in the forks was a very weak one, a slight fluttering. It felt like the play of small magnets, which can be felt to attract and repel each other when held and manipulated in the hands. The fork, held away from the body, was repelled or attracted, pushed or pulled. Sometimes the rapid alternation of attraction and repulsion produced a fluttering sensation. At other times, the pulsation felt in a nearby center was also felt against the fork, so that it appeared that the center moved the fork.

The movement felt in the fork, as pressure against the fingers of the hand, was never so pronounced that it could easily be distinguished visually. This was because my hand that held the fork was never observed to be fully still. There was always a slight trembling of the hand that led, necessarily, to movement of the fork which was grasped in it. Thus it was impossible to distinguish on a strictly visual basis between the motion of the forks that I felt as being caused by the emanation of forces from the body and the motion of the forks that I perceived as a consequence of the apparently natural and constant motion of my hand. I could feel the emanation from the body that moved the forks and distinguish the movements caused by this energy based on a combination of internal, kinesthetic perception and visual perception. It was also my distinct impression that the largest movements caused by the body's responses to sound were larger than those caused by trembling.

In the course of the daily sessions, the movement of the fork became another of the phenomena that were routinely experienced and recorded. As with all the others, it seemed to increase in intensity and also became more regular in its onset and its perceived effect over time. When this phenomenon was its most intense, the vibrating fork was perceived as being suspended between opposing forces, one emanating from the fork being held away from the body, the other projecting outward from the body itself. The fork stood between these forces.

In addition to the strengthening of the fork phenomenon, the older responses continued to gain in frequency and strength. I became much more aware of the passage of energy throughout the "subtle anatomy" and was able to distinguish discrete pathways along which energy seemed to travel. Here there seemed to be a "dorsal" route which went through the spine area, and a more "frontal" route which went from center to center. Energy could pass either up or down along these paths.

The result of the appearance of new phenomena and the continued strengthening of the phenomena already observed was a taxing of my ability to keep abreast of everything. This is apparent from session notes at the end of the first blind round of listening: "There is almost too much happening in most presentations—reactions in several places at once—sequences of reactions—reactions in the hand/fork/body. Attention is almost not great enough to be aware of it all, much less record it."

With the commencement of the second blind round of listening (presentation of all the forks to a single center in a day's session), the length of time needed for each session expanded dramatically. Remarks such as "long haul" and "fatigue" began to appear in my notes as these sessions wore on. On one occasion, a session had to be concluded before all forks were presented. What had begun as a pleasant, energizing experience had evolved into a draining test of endurance. After what would have been the second-to-last session, the presentation of all forks to the navel center, I fell quite ill. The last session was never attempted.

After a hiatus of two months, interval listening commenced.

Interval Listening

Interval listening was not viewed as a simple and direct continuation of single tone listening. This was in part because, given the materials chosen (the 13 forks), interval listening had more varied and complex possibilities. Instead of dealing with 13 tones, there were now 156

(13×12) combinations of two tones to consider. The prospect of extended months of daily session, or of long sessions that were more tests of endurance than perception, was not appealing. In the end, the decision was made to begin by exploring with the hope that an orientation would arise from the initial phenomena observed.

Phase I: Exploratory Listening. My experience using the forks made this second period of exploration much less tentative than the initial period of single tone listening. My first impulse was to listen to intervals by striking each fork and holding one to each ear. Thus the first effects I noticed in my listening were "acoustic" effects. When listening to an interval of a major third, I could sometimes hear the fifth above the lower note, completing the major triad. I also felt, incidentally, the phenomena that had been the points of orientation during the single tone listening: forces emanating from my body and pushing or pulling gently at the forks held to my ears, and the stirrings of energy and pulsation at the centers. These were apparent immediately and without the necessity of any long period of awakening.

It was a technique attempted more for the sake of convenience than awareness which led to the discovery of the orienting phenomenon of interval listening. Rather than holding a fork in each hand and having to continuously be restriking one or the other to maintain the balance of resonance between the two notes of the interval, I began to strike and hold both forks in a single hand. This new technique, once mastered, produced a more "centered" tone. The interval became more of a single entity, rather than two separate tones held apart physically and integrated through listening and perception. Soon after the commencement of this technique, while holding two forks that made up the interval of a major sixth in different areas of the body, I felt a distinct sensation in my thigh. It felt as if something had awakened in that particular area, a tingling that soon organized itself into a particular feeling or flow. A gentle wave of energy passed from the knee area to the hip area and back again. The visual analogy that best expresses the perception I had is that of a liquid between two barriers. A wave of energy would wash in one direction until it hit the barrier of the knee and then it would be deflected back in the opposite direction until it met the barrier of the hip. The energy would flow in this way as long as the two forks containing the major sixth were held in the area of the thigh. When the forks were removed, the waves would no longer be apparent, only the tingling feeling that preceded the awakening of the area would remain.

A new orientation had been found, and a new and highly productive phase of listening had begun.

Phase II: A Second Awakening. The discovery of the "waves-within-barriers" phenomenon led to a second period of awakening in the overall experiment. There were differences and similarities between this awakening and the first one—the awakening that occurred during single tone listening—which are noteworthy. The broad sense of a gradual intensifying of the phenomena observed was true of this period as it had been of the past one. On the other hand, the responses observed were much more discrete and "orderly," although no more comprehensible, than the initial awakening of the centers had been. This led to the now familiar intellectual/emotional reaction to such experiences: wonder and pleasure that they were occurring, and disturbance and doubt that they could not be understood.

What I began to find in the course of the second awakening was that each interval seemed to have a particular place in the body, an area where it produced the identical awakening and "waves-within-barriers" responses I first felt in connection with the major sixth. This aspect of the subtle anatomy is diagrammed in Figure 3.2. The minor sixth produces this response in the calf area, between the knee and the ankle, I discovered. The fifth produces that response over the length of the foot itself between the ankle and the toes.

The smaller intervals work in the arm and hand in a way similar to that in which the large intervals work in the leg and the foot. The fourth produces a response in the upper arm between the shoulder and the elbow. The major third produces the response in the forearm between the wrist and the elbow. The minor third produces the response in the length of the hand, and the seconds produce the response in the fingers, and the major second in the area nearest the palm of the hand, and the minor second in the fingertip.

Further experimentation revealed that the minor seventh produced the familiar "waves-within-barriers" response in the upper area of the body, between the genital area and the top of the head. The major seventh produces the same sensation over an area extending downward from the genital area through the legs to the feet. The octave gives rise to the same phenomenon in a majestic fashion, waves washing slowly over the entire length of the body, head to foot. The motion of the waves here seems decidedly slower than that perceived with the other intervals, but the effect is clearly present.

A place for tritone was never found.

A period of checking and rechecking produced no substantial changes in the nature of any of these phenomena. The only alteration noticed was a gradual intensification and lengthening of the responses.

FIGURE 3.2

The Locations of Interval Sensations As Perceived in Interval Listening

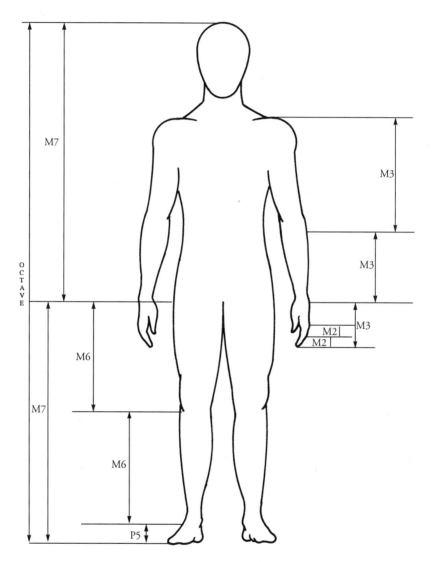

What had come alive in the presence of the intervals seemed to become stronger and more durable over time.

This concluded the period of listening undertaken for the purposes of this experiment.

Discussion and Conclusions

After finishing the listening, I attempted to analyze and draw conclusions from my experiences. The basis for these conclusions included my own session notes and recollections of the experiences, and reading and research done subsequent to the actual experiment. These will be summarized in the first section below.

It is also of interest to note the ways in which the experiences recounted here have influenced my beliefs, thinking, and practice in the areas of music therapy over the ensuing years, and how I regard these experiences now that some time has elapsed since their conclusion. These present ruminations will conclude this presentation.

Conclusions at the Time of the Experiment

One of the important questions that I attempted to answer in reporting the results of this experiment was, "What in me responded to the tones?" I wondered, more specifically, whether the particular, defined areas of response that had come alive during the single tone listening were in fact the chakras, the energy centers that I had heard and read about prior to the actual experiment.

The answer was a tentative affirmative. It was tentative because my research indicated disagreements among those supposed experts who discussed the chakras as to where and even how many there were. Therefore, while there was substantial agreement between areas of response to single tones that I had observed and the location of the chakras as portrayed in the relevant literature, my account did not fully agree with any of the accounts that I consulted. Five centers (top of head, forehead, throat, heart, and navel) that I observed were in agreement with the other accounts. Two centers (genital and stomach) were at some variance, with the genital center in particular a source of conflict in the accounts of the experts.

I also noted that the passageways for energy that I felt in single tone listening and especially in interval listening bore more than a superficial resemblance in location and apparent function to the *nadis*, the system of channels associated with the chakras which distribute energy throughout the body, and also with the *meridians* of Chinese medicine (acupuncture) through which vital energy (Ki) is said to pass.

Thus, the "subtle anatomy" which came into sharper and sharper focus during the listening process appeared to have similarities to anatomical and medical models that had some acceptance in other cultures. This was a reassuring realization at the time. I have noted over the years more references to such terms as "chakras," "centers," and the passage and blockage of energy among practitioners whose methods are collectively coming to be known as "alternative medicine."

In discussing the tones themselves and the particular qualities which might have lead to the responses I observed, I tended to discount the influence of particular pitches. My early and initially unacknowledged expectation was that a single pitch would produce a particular response in a certain area, and this was not borne out with the procedures I employed. There are a few factors which make the discounting of pitch also, of necessity, a tentative conclusion. First, it must be considered that the scale formed by the pitches of the forks I used was, to the best of my knowledge, an even-tempered one. It is not beyond the realm of possibility that a series of pitches based on a single fundamental, and more in accordance with the overtone series, might produce different results. A related possibility is that each body, each subtle anatomy, has its own fundamental and overtone series which will produce more discrete, orderly, and perhaps powerful responses to single tones than I observed. Finally, it may be that on such subtle levels it is impractical to talk of single tones at all, since all pitches produce overtones which, even though inaudible, may elicit subtle responses.

With the influence of pitch called into question, I tended to think that *energy itself* and not the particular pitches was responsible for the awakening of the subtle energy system and the strengthening of response over time. Indeed, it was this constant strengthening that was crucial to my understanding of the whole process, tentative though it was. Whereas I initially might have attributed each new perception, each passage from phase to phase of the listening process, to the increasing subtlety of my discrimination, upon reflection I had to abandon this hypothesis. The plain fact was that the strongest responses, the responses which actually "left the body" and were felt in relation to the forks held outside of what are ordinarily considered its confines, were also among the last responses to become apparent. If perception were a matter of increasing discrimination and improved powers of observation, then *the most subtle and delicate effects would be the ones to be observed last, and the most powerful ones would be the ones to be observed first.* In my experience, this was not the case. Therefore, I came to look at the broad sweep of responses, particularly those experienced in single tone listening, as being, despite my ability to separate and categorize them, different degrees of the same response, manifestations of the same subtle energy. Some energy, or power, intensified during the course of the listening from the point of imperceptibility to the point where it could be manifested outside the body's confines.

I pointed out that the strengthening and free passage of energy in the body was often related to wellness—to an optimum level of functioning. Such a manifestation of energy is also related to subtle and so-called "spiritual" development of many kinds, including the development of psychic powers. My experience in many of the briefer sessions was of pleasant sensations and a feeling of well-being, both physically and emotionally. Long sessions, with much energy expended, produced feelings of fatigue which were ultimately followed by a period of illness.

Thus, although the primary results of the experiments were clearly of an educational and relevatory nature, it is also true that the techniques employed and the knowledge gained appeared to have clinical and therapeutic implications.

Present Ruminations

Almost immediately upon submission of the results of my experiment, I began the clinical practice of music therapy. I did not become a single tone therapist, or an interval therapist, or even a tuning fork therapist. I became what I had trained to be: a *music* therapist.

This meant that I plunged fully into the great complexity that we call, with understated simplicity, "music." I became engaged and engaged others, in the creation and re-creation of sometimes sinuous and highly ornamented melodies, handfuls and clusters of notes simultaneously resounding, energizing and occasionally thunderous rhythm. I became a practitioner inseparable from the creative and created products of the practice.

How, then, do I look back upon my experiment? What have I carried forth from that interval of quiet listening and concentration?

I have carried with me the experience of the long and continuous awakening, and the gradual coming into awareness of a vast network of centers and passageways for energy whose existence I had barely suspected. This awareness represented knowledge of the most compelling kind: noninferential, nonreferential, "knowledge without thought," based entirely on experience: unshakable, irrefutable. I carry forth from the experience an appreciation of human beings more miraculous, more divinely subtle and wondrous than I had ever thought them to be, and more of all these things in the presence of sound than in its absence.

I have carried with me the recollection of the conflicts between my roles as experimenter and subject, between the necessity to experience and the desire to understand. I remember the almost pernicious desire for order and comprehensibility that sprang up as indefatigably as a hearty weed and had to be cleared with great vigilance from the fertile seed bed of perception. This is a need which may well be stronger in me than in others, but it seems that awareness of its intensity and its effects is of surpassing importance. For experience indicates that in fixating on the predictable, one may overlook the miraculous. The ideal of clarity of perception, and the attempt to eliminate preconceptions or biases that might distort perception—of tones or of people—is something that has remained with me.

Most influential, perhaps, of the things carried forth from my experiment, was the idea that music could be a "way" for inquiry and increased awareness. Just as sound created the breathtaking awakenings that were the results of my experiments, sound and music and the responses and realizations they bring forth can be a source of further revelation. Thus, although I have yet to return to the methods and procedures discussed in previous sections, I have continued to ponder and process my experiences and observations as a musician and therapist. The legacy of past experiment and inquiry has current application.

I am more and more convinced that a profound study of music—as art, as craft, as therapeutic medium, as manifestation of energy—must involve the examination of the most subtle and subjective responses and effects. Those who experience music in the broadest variety of its applications are the living laboratories in which to conduct this research. The best vantage point from which to observe is the time and place music begins or ends. The significance of this moment is often overlooked, since it occurs with great frequency and is marked by no greater ceremony or ritual than the pushing of a button. But as bias and preconception are abandoned and perception clears, the imperceptible line between music and no music becomes a chasm, and the transformation that occurs as it is traversed appears miraculously complete. I am more and more convinced that a profound study of humanity is a musical study. Sound and feeling are a perfect equipoise to vision and thus in developing a fully rounded awareness of humanity and the universe we inhabit.

And the road to that awareness passes through the world of tones.

4

The Power of Sound and
Music in Therapy and Healing

Barbara Hesser

Prelude to Barbara Hesser

I have known Barbara Hesser for many years now, since 1982. And she has become, through these years, like a sister to me. When I consider the important connection between love and work, Barbara immediately comes to mind.

We first met at the 1982 New York Symposium on *Music in the Life of Man: Toward a Theory of Music Therapy*. I have no idea how I came to be invited to this rather prestigious event. The symposium was a vision of Barbara's. She had mobilized New York University and the Musicians Emergency Fund to co-sponsor a gathering of 32 academics and professionals from 20 different countries to come together for five days and dialogue about music therapy. She claimed as her inspiration an earlier such conference in Herdecke. The symposium in New York was a turning point in my life and the friends I made there have remained near and dear to me ever since.

Barbara impressed me as a New York kind of gal—in the fast lane. I could only observe her from the edge of my world, as a participant in a conference which she had planned.

Then about a year and a half later, I got a phone call from her. She wanted to come to California and visit me in Ojai. Ojai was a place I had gone to retreat. How could I be discourteous to a person whose vision I so admired? After all, I had received so much from the New York meetings. So I said "fine."

At the time I had more or less decided to leave music therapy. I had not intended to leave the work, but I did intend to leave the field, in terms of my professional identity. I was redefining myself. I was taking a Ph.D. in Human Development and calling my work "human development through the arts." I had received a devastating blow in 1982 after publishing my first book, *The Mythic Artery*. A lot of people in music therapy were angry about what I had done, my approach of looking at ancient healing systems, using the lens of anthropology, and having the audacity to mention the word "spirit." The good story is the one about how I got called "a pagan witch."

After the high of the NYU Symposium, I figured I had met some interesting, open-minded people, with whom I could meet or correspond. I would go underground, where I belonged.

Lo and behold Barbara landed. She came around my peaceful abode with stories about a new kind of gathering in which people like me could feel nurtured rather than attacked. I kept saying: "Nice story. Good luck. Isn't it time for you to go back to the big city now?" I even left my own house—I left it to Barbara for a few days to go on with business, developing my "new" identity. But she would not go away with her dreams.

Several months later I received an invitation to join a small group of music therapy folk in the Catskill Mountains for five days of "Retreat" for conversation and improvisation. I was eating my doubtful words as in June, 1984, I was flying out of the ashes of the Ojai fire, still recovering from surgery to get my "old" identity to Phoenicia in the Catskill Mountains as fast as I could. So in a sense, Barbara saved my life.

Since then, we have created many stories together. We have traveled not only to the mountain, but also to the desert and the prairie. In Kansas we collaborated with Helen Bonny as co-founders of the Bonny Foundation.

Barbara Hesser has been, in my regard, one of the most important people in the field of music therapy. The reason for this is not because she has written or lectured extensively, although she has. It is not because she has an important position of leadership at an important university, although she does. It is not even necessarily because she has stood up for advanced graduate training and created two of the best graduate music therapy training programs in the world. She is important in my mind and in my heart because she has instilled in us "a sense of community." This is her gift. And she has shared this gift in every aspect of the work, whether in the privacy of her home, on the international scene, or in the intimacy of the Phoenecia Music Therapy Community, which met every year for seven years in the Catskills.

Barbara Hesser is a friend I hope I will have for life. She is an innovator, a pioneer, a politician. And yet, to me, she is a friend who can laugh and cry and joke over our silly human situations. She can play and dream. She is a woman of the heart.

Of herself, Barbara says: "Presently I serve as the Coordinator of the Music Therapy training at New York University including a master's and doctorate of the arts degree programs. I also work as the Project Director for the Nordoff/Robbins Music Therapy Clinic and Program Liason for the Guided Imagery and Music Training Institute in New York. I am a GIM Fellow and work with private clients in Guided Imagery and Music."

Opening

When I tell people that I am a music therapist and that I use music in therapy and healing there is an immediate intuitive understanding and recognition that this is an important profession. Most people will share an anecdote of how the power of music has helped them or someone they know.

We all recognize the power of music in our lives. Whether we are an avid listener, a singer, or play a musical instrument, we are touched and moved by the power of music. We may not understand intellectually exactly what it is about music that moves us so deeply, but we still spend a great deal of time listening to and making music. The enormity of the music entertainment business with its voluminous sales of audio equipment, records, tapes, and compact discs shows that people are involved with music in large numbers. We no longer need to leave our home to hear music and yet large groups of people still attend live music concerts of all kinds.

I have practiced music therapy for many years and have observed how powerfully music can affect our bodies, move and express our emotions, and allow access to the spiritual part of our beings. I see this demonstrated again and again in the sessions of the clients who come to me for therapy.

One day some years ago, I came upon a book in a bookstore which had a profound effect on me as a music therapist. I was transfixed as I paged through and marveled at the pictures I was seeing and the far-reaching implications that I felt they had concerning the power of sound and tone on man. This book, entitled *Cymatics*, was written by a Swiss physicist named Dr. Hans Jenny. The pictures show the various geometric shapes that are created when a tone is introduced to vibrate a liquid or solid substance on a laboratory plate. Different tones create different forms, and when a tone is discontinued the form ceases to be. Before my eyes I saw familiar shapes and forms I had so often seen in pictures taken inside the human body, pictures of outer space and views seen from the windows of airplanes. These included mountains and oceans, human cells, and galaxies in outer space. Truly, tone and vibration have a powerful effect on matter.

In the Bible, it says: "In the beginning was the Word." Some sources say that "Word" in this sentence can also be translated as Sound or Vibration. Could it really be that sound, audible and inaudible, actually creates form?

This book revealed visually the deepest connection between mankind and sound. My commitment to working with sound and music was strengthened and somehow validated. My experience with *Cymatics* scientifically confirmed for me the intuitive feeling that we live in a universe of moving and dancing particles and that all life is vibration manifested in different forms. Each person has a unique pattern of vibration which can be called his "music." It follows that each group, community, and nation has its own unique music as well.

Music can be defined as humanly organized sound. All human beings are born with an innate sensitivity to tone and rhythm. Music making is concerned with expression, communication, and relationships between and among people. A person who can open her consciousness to this activity can derive benefit from it. Music is not healing or harmful in and of itself, but rather its effect is derived from the conscious intention of the creator, performer, and listener.

Verbal expression and musical expression offer the individual quite different opportunities. The concrete aspects of language help us to articulate our rational, intellectual thoughts, and the abstract nature of music allows for a deep expression of the emotional and transpersonal aspects of life.

Music Therapy

Music therapy is the conscious use of the power of sound and music for therapy and healing. I define music therapy broadly in an effort to be inclusive rather than to create fixed guidelines about the potential and varied uses that music can have. The music therapist's work is to tap this unique potential of sound and music for the health and well-being of the clients. The music therapist is an artist who sensitively and creatively moves with and guides the process of music therapy.

Music therapy is a process that can allow for the expression of the whole person—mind, body, and spirit. Ideally, in a group, music can be an opportunity for the self-expression of individuals to be recognized and nurtured in the collective consciousness of the community.

Unlike a medicine, with a particular music prescribed for a particular symptom, I view music therapy as more of an art, the music and music activity selected spontaneously in the moment-to-moment flow of the therapeutic relationship. The client and therapist bring their unique experience and needs to the session where they meet for the purpose of enhancing the client's well-being. As the relationship unfolds, the musical activity (listening, playing, composing) emerges from the therapeutic work taking place at that moment. The therapist has a wide range of possible techniques and uses of music, but it is my belief that they are not effective unless the resonance between the client and therapist is well established.

All of our clients are already "healthy," for this is our natural state of being. When we experience health we are in harmony and balance within ourselves and in relationship to others. Music can reach into and express the healthy part in each of us. This state is difficult to experience if mental, physical, or emotional problems stand in the way, and music can offer an opportunity to work with these problems. This does not mean that it is always possible to eliminate the physical, mental, and emotional problems. The goal is to assist clients to live as healthy a life as possible given their particular challenges in that moment in time. Throughout life we all meet with problems whether they be mental retardation, emotional difficulties, chronic illness, or the natural physical losses of aging. Therefore, we can all benefit from music therapy at some point in our lives.

All their lives musicians develop personal qualities that are useful in therapy. They begin to take a deeper interest in music because of their sensitivity to vibration, tone, and rhythm. As they play music, this sensitivity is developed and their capacity to listen expands. Making music requires an increased willingness to express one's own emotions and those of others. This experience brings a deeper understanding and sensitivity to the human condition and prepares the musician to work with others.

Music therapists need to spend time making music, listening to music, and exploring the uses of sound and music for their own particular growth and transformation. In this way, therapists find the ways that are most natural for them to work with music and that suit the needs of the client with whom they work.

The Process of Music Therapy

Clinical improvisation, one of many approaches to using music in therapy, is here-and-now experience where the music of the session is improvised based on the person or persons present in the session. Each individual and group will respond to this task differently. Many percussive and melodic instruments from around the world are made available to the clients and can be played successfully without previous training. These instruments tap the innate potential of all people to make and respond to music. Singing and sounding, instrument playing, dancing and moving are all interwoven into the unique expression of the group.

Each music therapy group becomes a miniature society. The definition of music and the uses of music for healing and therapy will be organically discovered by the members of that particular community, just as this has happened in every society since the beginning of history. Each therapy group is an exciting discovery of the deep meaning and potential of music in our lives.

In a therapy session, a person selects an instrument or instruments that he/she is drawn to and begins to play, one tone after another, one beat after another. This spontaneous, improvised music making allows the client to express him/herself in the moment and to hear and observe the creation as it unfolds. Sometimes the client will be supported musically in this effort by the therapist or other group members. The music allows for expression of emotion and thoughts as they arise and subside. The use of many instruments, and elements of music (rhythm, pitch, etc.) allow for the elaboration and expansion of expression.

At the beginning it is the goal of therapy for each client to attempt to express him/herself as fully as possible through sound and music. Although this is a natural experience for humans, we have lost the ability to freely improvise as civilization has developed and so it may be the first such experience for the client.

As we allow the expression of our inner being to come into sound, we can then observe it as it unfolds from moment to moment. This stage of therapy requires a quality of gentleness and acceptance. The complete acceptance of all the client's expressions by the therapist helps him/her to become less self-critical in this process. We need to allow into awareness all aspects of the self, both the positive aspects and the negative aspects. Through time, the client becomes comfortable expressing his/her individual experience in music.

This experience of self-discovery through music is a powerful and moving one. Through this process, clients become more deeply aware of their feelings, actions, and thoughts. The music therapy session can become a creative working environment where the clients feel safe to express and explore all facets of their selves. This increased awareness of their expression gives them a fuller awareness of who they are. As a client feels safe enough, new aspects of his or her personality can be discovered. This can lead to an expanded and more satisfactory self-image.

When individuals become comfortable with their own unique forms of self-expression, they are ready to enter into healing relationships with other members of the therapy group. Many clients experience a lack of intimate and fulfilling relationships in their lives. Playing music with another person can allow a deep exploration of intimate relationships. The music allows more dimensions of the person to emerge and to be observed than are often seen through ordinary verbal communication. Individually, each person has learned to express him or herself in the music and now there is the opportunity to communicate this essence to another and to receive response to it. The music evolves slowly with each person consciously attempting to express him/herself deeply in the moment and then the meeting places and interplay between the two people emerge. This allows a relationship to evolve and be explored as it evolves. This exploration is a unique and often difficult experience, for with others we often are not able to be who we truly are.

Playing music in a group provides an opportunity to explore and more deeply understand relationships in the community, and the changing dynamics of groups as they grow and develop. It is also a chance for each individual to explore the expression of his uniqueness in relation to the community. At times, we can feel the oneness of all group members when we make music and dance together. This consonance can be supportive and healing. At times the differences and variety in the individuals within the community are expressed. It is a challenge to learn to make music together in a group and to allow the dissonances to exist.

In a music therapy group one major theme is how members can get their own needs met while continuing to relate to others in the group in a caring and giving way. If one constantly gives up one's needs there is the possibility of becoming out of touch with who one is. On the other hand, it is impossible to always have one's needs met in a relationship or group. To find a way to maintain the unity of the group and still work on one's own needs is a challenge for group members. This same challenge also can apply to most groups and communities.

Finding the harmonious balance of consonance and dissonance among group members is a goal of the music therapy process. One of the wonderful aspects of music is that consonance and dissonance can be woven together in a beautiful and deeply satisfying way. To organically find this musical balance among group members takes a great deal of conscientious work. Leading up to this stage are many preliminary stages of growth and development. In groups that attain this rare phenomenon, however, there is a new sense of intimacy, acceptance, and support. Finding this balance is possible in highly developed and mature groups and requires each individual to be willing to hear and accept a new kind of music than perhaps they are used to. The therapist is always present to help with the exploration of these issues and to offer support to the group members during this process.

Conclusion

It would be good if the nations of our world were willing to play a new kind of music together that allows for the beauty of each unique player to remain while creating a unified and harmonious piece that has room for us all. As in a music therapy group, we need a new understanding of individuality within the community. Some societies suppress individuality for the collective good, while others allow expression of individuality to the point of chaos. A better balance must be found.

Music therapy has a great deal to offer to the lives of all people. It offers all of us an opportunity to explore self-expression, intimate relationships, and more satisfying community. The power of sound and music can offer us a unique opportunity for growth and transformation.

5

On Sound, Music, Listening, and Music Therapy

Dorit Amir

Prelude to Dorit Amir

I had seen Dorit in various gatherings of the NYU Music Therapy Community over the years. But my memory of our first encounter is our experience at one of the Music Therapy Renewal Workshops, led by Barbara Hesser and myself. Dorit played a piano improvisation which communicated a substance and depth which I came to know throughout the years as the essential feature of her being. During the workshop, when she began to play, I lay under the grand piano so that the sound would flow into me completely. It was magnificent and I never wanted to forget it. I remember saying to Barbara at the time: "Only an Israeli woman could play that sound." Dorit was expressing herself as an individual, as a woman, but also as an Israeli, full of passion, depth, sorrow, and mystery.

Throughout the years we have found ourselves having intense conversations in various places around NYU—Greenwich Village coffee bars, Soho restaurants, friends' apartments, on the campus of NYU, at Phoenecia. We speak as women, mothers, music therapists, people with a strong cultural identity. Often Dorit has said: "You should come to Israel. You'd love it. So would Shannon [my daughter]."

I have had the privilege of serving as a consultant in Dorit's dissertation prccess. She produced an outstanding document, one of the great contributions to music therapy research, entitled: "Awakening and expanding the self: Meaningful moments in the music therapy process as experienced and described by music therapists and music therapy clients." In this manuscript she demonstrated intellectual acuity and impeccable research skills in the tradition of phenomenology. Her heartfelt commitment to searching for a language which honors rather than diminishes our experience with clients is formidable. Her commitment to integrate her substance and depth into all of her endeavors is a wonder to behold and a joy to experience. She has been challenged many times in this endeavor and remains constant.

Of herself Dorit says: "I am an Advanced Certified Music Therapist (ACMT) by the American Association for Music Therapy and a Certified Music Therapist by the Israeli Association for Creative Art Therapies. I am the head of the music therapy program at Bar Ilan University in Israel, a program I initiated in 1982. I received my masters and doctorate in music therapy at New York University and have worked as a professional music therapist for 16 years as clinician, educator, and supervisor. I recently have created the first Israeli creative arts therapy journal: *Therapy through the Arts* and serve as co-editor. I have also published several articles in Israel and the United States. My interests are in deepening music therapy training and conducting more qualitative research in music therapy in order to build a unique theory for the field and gain a better understanding of the hidden spiritual aspects of music therapy."

Introduction

For many years I have been fascinated with sounds. It started with my interest in exploring the sounds of nature, and continued with my interest in the sounds of human beings. I remember many mornings waking up and listening to the sounds of the birds outside of my window. Many times I would fantasize who the bird behind the sound was and try to figure out what her mood was today: was she happy or sad, joyful or mad. . . . In my work as a music therapist, I became aware that each of my clients had his/her own individual sounds which were organized in their own unique form. Not only that, but each client's sounds and form changed during the course of therapy. The sounds became an indication of the person's state of being. They became an external reality which mirrored the internal reality of the client. Therefore, I became aware that I started to see music therapy as a process in which I assist my client in making music out of the sounds. In other words, music therapy became a process of helping my clients to recognize their own unique sounds and to organize these sounds into a form of meaningful expression. I also realized that the main factor which allowed this process to occur is listening. In music therapy we listen both to our clients and to our own inner sounds. We encourage the clients to listen to their inner sounds and express them vocally and with musical instruments. In this way, the sounds become music.

What is Sound?

Sound is a source of energy that exists within the earth. We live in a vibrating universe. The earth, seas, plants, animals, and human beings all have vibrations. They all have sounds. As Gaston (1968) says, "all share the same kind of building materials: the elements, molecules and atoms. . . . The basic mechanisms of reproduction and transmission of heredity are the common property of all plants and animals. Genes and chromosomes exist in sunflowers, roses, fishes, birds and mammals" (p. 10).

What is Music?

In spite of all the similarities, human beings are different from all other creatures. It is the human spirit that sets human beings apart from the rest of creation. Human beings can organize the sounds that exist within the earth and create music out of them. Music is the essence of humanness. That is why music can be so beautiful and powerful. It comes from the heart. It is the song of the soul.

Each human being is unique. Therefore, each person's sounds are unique. When we make music, we give meaning to the sounds by organizing them. It is the relationship between sounds that gives them meaning.

All human beings are musical entities despite their handicaps, pathologies, and problems. All human beings have inside themselves a musical self no matter where they live or which culture they come from. The musical self is the aesthetic entity in each and every individual. It is the "life spirit" of the person. In the professional world of music, the composer who writes music tries to find ways to express the sounds he hears within himself and in the universe. The performer brings the music to the listener, who listens to the music.

What is Listening?

There are two kinds of listening: external and internal. External listening occurs when the listener opens the door to his heart and allows the tones and rhythms to vibrate into his inner, private world. In this way, music has the capacity to create new forms and new energy fields. External listening can be seen as a movement of music directed from the outside to the inside. In order to allow this listening to take place one needs to be open to receive the music without any judgment or preconceived ideas. This means being fully in the present moment, receiving the music on a moment-to-moment basis. It also requires a total concentration and attention to the music. By that I mean the ability to fully "be with" the music.

Internal listening is tuning into one's own inner sounds and rhythms. It is the listening to inner messages that come from within the self, messages that contain harmonious as well as disharmonious chords, consonances and dissonances. It is "to be with" oneself, to fully experience oneself on various levels. In order to do this kind of listening one has to be still, to let the mind rest and stay passive in order to activate the deeper states of being. In this way one gains an intuitive knowledge about one's own being. This kind of knowledge comes only when the person is open to hear it. Internal listening can be seen as a movement that takes place only inwardly, without letting the outside world interfere. The process of meditation is an example for this kind of listening.

These two kinds of listening can be looked at through the concept of "entrainment."

What is Entrainment?

Goldman (1988) explains that everything that vibrates has a natural tendency to harmonize together. It is the listener's relationship with the music that can "create energy fields of sound which can resonate and entrain others" (p. 33). Entrainment is "a phenomenon of sound in which the powerful rhythmic vibrations of one object will cause the less powerful vibrations of another object to lock in step with the rhythms of the more powerful object and oscillate at this rate" (p. 28).

The Meaning of Listening in Music Therapy

In music therapy we want both kinds of listening to occur. When the client and the therapist allow for both external and internal listening to take place, a new inner state of being is created in each one, a state of being which is still but moving at the same time, relaxed yet stimulated, passive but active. We can try to understand it with the concept of energy. Listening is an energy that goes in all directions at the same time: outside-inside, inside-outside, up-down, down-up, left-right, right-left, and so on. One way to picture it is to imagine a complicated web of relations between the various elements—at least two human beings and their sounds—of a unified whole—the musical experience of the here and now. These elements are energy waves. The two kinds of listening are essential in order to be healed by music. The relationship between these two kinds of listening determines if entrainment can take place. In other words, to be with oneself and at the same time to open one's heart to receive the music that comes from the outside world can cause entrainment. Entrainment can be one of the new concepts to describe the healing power of music.

More on Listening

What is the meaning of listening for music therapists? Listening means to attend, to "give ear to." It is the ability to keep our ears open, to observe, to pay attention, to take notice of what is going on with our clients as well as with ourselves. We listen with our whole selves to the clients' thoughts, feelings, images, sensations, and wants as being expressed musically and verbally. We listen to our inner voices and express them musically and verbally in order to serve our clients. It is important to acknowledge that all listening is geared toward the client. In order to serve, our listening has to be transcendent. It has to go beyond the personal into the transpersonal. Our own goals, interests, and desires on a personal level must be set aside and temporarily forgotten. This allows a clearer vision of the client's needs and purifies our presence and our ability to be with our clients. A transcendent listening comes from the heart. When this listening is connected to our client's inner and outer music, it has the potential of awakening the life spirit within the client, nurturing it, and thus creating new energy fields within him. As I discussed before, inner listening causes intuitive knowledge that comes only when the mind is still. Paying too much attention to rambling thoughts can close us up and make us ineffective. As Shainberg (1983) says, "The endless noise of thought keeps the therapist from being emotionally available for listening to the patient" (p. 175). Listening occurs when the "being" is the "doing." This allows for a new inner state of being to be created in both therapist and client: a state of being which is still but moving at the same time, relaxed yet stimulated, passive but active.

Looking at This from the Point of View of New Physics

This new state of being is impossible to understand if it is seen according to ways of perceiving reality that took place during the 17th, 18th, and 19th centuries. During this period, matter was seen as the basis of all existence. The material world was viewed as "a multitude of separate objects assembled into a huge machine. Like human-made machines, the cosmic machine was thought to consist of elementary parts" (Capra, 1982, p. 32). Yet if we try to understand it from the point of view of modern physics, we can see that this new state of being matches the new discoveries in quantum physics, the theory of atomic phenomena, that started at the beginning of the 20th century. Physicists found out that subatomic particles—electrons, protons, and neutrons—are units of matter that appear sometimes as particles and sometimes as waves. It all depends how we look at them. Physicists like Neils Bohr, Albert Einstein, and Fritjof Capra are among the few that "reached the extraordinary place where the mind could no longer produce data of the content they wanted, and they were in the territory of inspiration where their intuitions accelerated and they knew that there was something more than the realm of time and space and matter, something more than physical life" (Zukav, 1989, p. 12). Zukav believes that these people were motivated by a great vision that transcends the personality.

The Need to Create a New Language in Music Therapy

If we try to look at this new state of being, which is unanimated and animated at the same time, we realize that it is a paradox that cannot be explained in classical terms. Among the great physicists in our generation there is an agreement that we need to find new language and to look into other directions in order to understand the new reality.

We live in a new and exciting era. It is a time of deep change in the perceptions of all aspects of human experience. Music therapists, who live in the depth of their work, experience more than can be expressed in the existing language. Much of the difficulty in addressing and describing the depth of our work is the lack of vocabulary. Any language used to describe the experience of music therapy does not necessarily capture the essence of the actual experience. This is due to the nature of art which is often nonverbal, secretive, and mysterious. As such, it contains elements such as spirituality, emotions, and beauty. Yet it is important to let go of old ways of thinking and pursue an understanding that fits the new era.

In recent years there have been some calls for creating a new language in music therapy. Aigen (1991), Amir (1992), Hesser (1988), and Kenny (1985) are some of the music therapists who emphasized the need to establish new terms and categories in order to be able to describe the essence of music therapy.

Summary

In this article I try to look at the concepts of sound, music, and listening from a new perspective. I borrowed some of the concepts and words used by modern science in order to understand reality. In describing sound and music I used the words energy and vibrations, and in an attempt to describe and explain the concept of listening I borrowed an explanation from quantum theory and used the concept of entrainment.

I, personally, find it very exciting. The new physics views the universe in a holistic way, as "one indivisible, dynamic whole whose parts are essentially interrelated" (Capra, 1982, p. 66). By borrowing some of the concepts and perceptions that are being used in modern physics we can find answers to some of our most profound questions. We can adapt some of these concepts in order to describe the essence of our work and by doing that we see the close connection between music therapy and science. A new connection that does not limit us, but on the contrary expands us and deepens our understanding.

References

Aigen, K. (1991). The Roots of Music Therapy: Towards an Indigenous Research Paradigm. Unpublished Doctoral Dissertation, New York University, New York.

Amir, D. (1992). Awakening and Expanding the Self: Meaningful Moments in the Music Therapy Process as Experienced and Described by Music Therapists and Music Therapy Clients. Unpublished Doctoral Dissertation, New York University, New York.

Capra, F. (1982). *The Turning Point*. London: Flamingo.

Gaston, E. T. (1968). *Music in Therapy*. New York: The Macmillan Co., 1968.

Goldman, J. (1988). Toward a New Consciousness of the Sonic Healing Arts: The Therapeutic Use of Sound and Music for Personal and Planetary Health and Transformation. *Music Therapy* 7(1), pp. 28-33.

Hesser, B. (1988). Creating a Strong Professional Identity. *Journal of the International Association of Music for the Handicapped*, 4(1), pp. 11-14.

Kenny, C. (1985). Music Therapy: A Whole Systems Approach. *Music Therapy* 5(1), pp. 3-11.

Shainberg, D. (1983). Teaching Therapists How to Be With Their Clients. In J. Wellwood (ed.), *Awakening the Heart*. Boston: New Science Library, pp. 163-175.

Zukav, G. (1989). *The Seat of the Soul*. New York: Simon and Schuster.

6

Unsound Medicine

Lisa Summer

Prelude to Lisa Summer

Lisa and I have spent many hours traveling long into the night, into that playful land of imaginative thought. When did it all begin? I cannot say.

But our first real connection, even though we may have met before at various music therapy gatherings, was at Phoenecia. Lisa was one of the original members of the Phoenecia Music Therapy Retreat Group. That first year was powerful as we gathered, meditated, improvised, told stories, and shared our deepest cares and concerns about our work and our worlds. We laughed and we cried. Each year through our retreats in those nestling mountain forests, our friendship has grown.

There were several years in which our experience at Phoenecia and our experience in designing training structures for the Bonny Foundation overlapped.

Lisa was working extensively with *The Field of Play* and curious about how the GIM method could use certain concepts presented in this theory to explain theoretical underpinnings of GIM. There were so many overlaps: consciousness, a musical space, a field of play in the sound. We conducted three level I trainings together through the Bonny Foundation in those years. After each day's work we would retreat to our room and for hours we would discuss our students, our experience of the day, and our ideas.

Lisa's mind was vast. She was not afraid to imagine, to experiment, to connect, to disconnect. These conversations were so inspiring to me. We were silly. We smoked long and elegant slender cigars. We landed on ideas simultaneously or "syncopatedly."

In the daily work, we negotiated our differing styles to find the best complementary approach for our students. We did not always agree, but we learned.

Sometimes I felt like Lisa was my sister, my daughter, or my friend. A striking feature of our relationship was our capacity to switch roles. Sometimes she called me her teacher. Yet she inspired me through her intricacies of thought, her imaginal realm.

When we witnessed our students traveling in the sound, so relaxed, we sometimes found ourselves in a state of combined rapture and gratitude. The process was something to behold—intense, deep, filled with beauty.

Lisa continues her work with the Bonny Foundation as Coordinator of Guided Imagery and Music programs. She leads GIM trainings in the United States and in Europe. She is a board certified registered music therapist, has a master's degree in Creative Arts Therapies and has been a music therapy clinician and educator for 15 years. The focus of her work has been to use classical music for transformation and she has chronicled her work in articles and a textbook entitled *Guided Imagery and Music in the Institutional Setting*. She has recently completed (with her composer husband) a book surveying spurious philosophical and acoustical tenets of current "music healing" techniques.

It is tempting to view the power of sound as a force inherent in the very frequencies and rhythms of the phenomena itself. After all, it is true that light nourishes the planet; that light is the food of the green life which covers this earth; and consequently, the food of that which devours the green life. As much as the ideas might appeal to us, of a life dependent upon sound in similar fashion to its dependence upon light, this conceit does not stand up to scrutiny. Sound is useful, but it does not share the power or primogeniture of light except symbolically. When we fail to recognize that the power of sound is a symbolic and humanistic concept, and mistakenly imbue it with exaggerated physical concrete qualities, we fall into the error of believing our own fiction. This is not without its effects on our philosophies of healing through sound.

Sound has power, but it is a power created and manipulated by human beings when used therapeutically. Its greatest power is in the realm of aesthetics. Those of us who recognize that the greatest power of sound is aesthetic need to accept that it is therefore artificial, man-made. Shorn of human interpretation, music is irrelevant and powerless. Beethoven's Ninth may have more effect on your cat than it does on a colony of ants, but neither the cat nor the colony can experience the sui generis intellectual comprehension and appreciation of music that is unique to humans (in this solar system, at least).

With the exception of some scientifically proven and medically useful sonic therapeutic tools (ultrasound imaging, the use of lasers to destroy kidney stones, etc.), all of sound's power is derived from the aesthetic experience and almost always from music.

A reductionistic trend in approaches to music healing has been occurring. It is a philosophy that denies the importance of human contribution, even human contact, in the healing process. It is a passionless, simplistic pseudoscience that describes itself as holistic and compassionate. It is a philosophy that says that human beings cannot aid other human beings in their progress toward health, and that listening to the Appassionata Sonata is of no ameliorative significance when compared to a mechanical repetition of specific tones.

In "On Composing Medical Music," Kay Gardner relates how O. Skille, a Norwegian researcher, has treated Bechterev's Disease with "44HZ (lowest F), 58 Hz (the fifth), and 88Hz (the octave) and of treating menstrual pain, asthma, and cystic fibrosis with a 50 Hz (G#) root, fifth, octave, root sequence" (1988, p. 13). (Regarding the Bechterev's Disease frequencies, the 58 Hz is not a fifth above 44Hz. Sixty-six Hz is a fifth above 44Hz.) Gardner believes that composers could design "custom made works" to cure diseases by utilizing "low frequency tone sequences as bass drones. These drones would determine the key centers of such compositions. . . . The function of drone, therefore, is to set the listener or patient in sympathetic vibration with the key center thereby touching the body in a specific area" (p. 13). She believes she has succeeded in so doing and gives us an example of her cassette, "A Rainbow Path," in which she uses a tamboura and a "vocal drone . . ." throughout the entire movement on the tonic, meant both musically and medicinally. Stripped to its essentials, Gardner's philosophy is that specific frequencies cure specific ailments apparently regardless of the individual. In her program notes to *Garden of Ecstasy* she describes her composition "Viriditas":

> It was the fight against AIDS and other life-threatening diseases that called me to write "Viriditas." In my years of research on music as a healing force, including how particular tones and key centers affect the human organism, I determined that the composition would be centered around an F# tonic. This pitch, for most people, touches the mid-chest area of the body where the thymus, the "brain" of the immune system is located. . . . It is my hope that "Viriditas" may be of therapeutic assistance for people struggling alone with their dis-eases or for those working in therapy groups or individually with counselors or therapists.

For Gardner, the power of sound can be defined very simply. Physical ailments can be cured or ameliorated by playing specific frequencies. Basically, Gardner is attempting to apply a medical model of treatment to the use of sound in therapy; however, the medical model is based upon rigorous research and testing which Gardner either eschews or ignores. For Gardner to make the claim that F# can benefit AIDS patients, she needs more proof than her statement above. The medical model is an extremely rigid, prescriptive system. A specific diagnosis results in a specific treatment or prescription. However, a medical doctor takes into account variables such as the stage of the illness, the individual's medical history, the current physical state of the individual, and his previous responses to medications in determining a treatment plan. Kay Gardner determines treatment based on only one fact, the illness, believing that all those with a particular illness will respond identically to identical treatment. Criticism of the medical model for therapy normally focuses upon its impersonal approach to illness and its failure to accommodate attitudinal influences upon disease. Gardner's approach to illness is not a step toward a more personal, holistic treatment, nor does it address attitudinal influences any more than the medical model. It is rather a flawed imitation, a simulacrum, of the medical model system.

Howard Richman, a music healer who created the corporation Found Feelings to distribute his tapes, claims to ameliorate conditions of obesity, AIDS, and cancer. Richman is, however, careful to include a medical disclaimer with his products. Richman claims:

> The music that I compose is with [sic] the express intention of bringing about the three qualities of entrainment; 1) to resonate or lock-in with the listener's present feelings; 2) to assist in the transformation of negativity into positivity; and 3) to arrive at a state of liveliness of serenity. (1988, p. 145)

Though Richman claims that he infuses his music with "entrainment" qualities, he neglects to inform us how he can "resonate or lock-in with the listener's present feelings" when he is neither present nor aware of the individual listener's feelings. Richman is presupposing, as does Gardner, that his music will affect all people (or all people with the same illness) identically, and that upon receiving his tape will listen to it in the same state of mind.

A medical doctor does not prescribe a specific drug uniformly to all patients. All cancer patients do not receive chemotherapy. Richman's tape therapy depends upon the medical model of illness diagnosis, but without the prescriptive subtleties and the scientific research inherent in the medical model of treatment. Nor does a physician prescribe a specific drug dosage uniformly to all patients. Even over-the-counter drugs such as aspirin are taken in varied amounts depending upon age and severity of pain. The concept of universally applied musical remedies cannot be a seriously considered use of sound in treatment and the music healer who produces an impersonal musical nostrum is denying his or her listeners the real power of sound for healing purposes.

Steven Halpern, in his *Tuning the Human Instrument*, carries the idea of a systematic objectification of the power of sound one step further in his application of the medical model to specific body parts, rather than to specific diseases. Halpern discusses this system as one which could involve:

> "feeding" pure vibrations, via a tone-frequency generator, into the body. These (tones) could match the actual calculated vibration rates of various organs and muscles, which however, in a state of "disease", were vibrating at other than their proper frequency. So they would pump in the proper frequency ("food") and get things back in tune, as it were. . . . If someone is deficient in the functioning of a liver, for instance, instead of just giving them vitamin A, one might receive a portion of sound vibrations—vitamin A-sharp. Interestingly, these sound stimuli can be transduced directly into the skin, so that there is actually no sound that is heard, by patient or technician. Now, that's far out! And you don't have to be awake to benefit. (1978, p. 26)

Halpern's music treatments involve the judgment that each part or organ of our body should be "in tune," or vibrating at a certain frequency. In addition, the body as a whole is said to have an identifiable "healthy" frequency, at which it is "in tune" with the earth. Halpern heals an unhealthy organ by supplanting its "unhealthy" frequency with a healthy one.

Obviously, Halpern is ignoring many basic issues in his prescriptive system. First, how does Halpern know that a liver vibrates at the frequency of "A#" ? How does he know that any organ vibrates? How is it that his patients' livers will all vibrate at the same pitch, when frequency is determined, in part, by the weight of an object? Does he mean to imply that all of his patients have the exact same liver weight? What does he mean by an "in tune vibration"? For example, the pitch A can be many frequencies: from approximately 438 Hz to 446 Hz. Would Halpern mean the 435 Hz "A" or the 445 Hz "A"?

In Halpern's unsound solution to illness lies a denial of the aesthetics of music, of the process of aesthetic perception and its role in healing. In Halpern's view, the power of sound is in its ability to immediately change the physical body upon contact. His musical medicine is a behavioral solution which does not address the individual patient, and does not address their individual illness. The tone/body part healing system is a simple, behavioral solution camoflauged in holistic and musical terminology.

Although it is seductive to ponder upon the possibility of an objective healing system of music or sound, it is the responsibility of every person utilizing music as a healing art to do justice to the subjective, aesthetic nature of music and of the individual she is treating. Musical panaceas lack credibility. Any serious therapeutic application of the power of sound must take into account the human element of compassion. The compassionate music healer is one who looks each client in the eye, hears his/her individual music, and develops a client-centered, holistic, music healing process.

References

Gardner, K. (1989). *Garden of Ecstasy* (cassette recording). Durham, N.C.: Ladyslipper, Inc.

Gardner, K. (1988). On Composing Medical Music In *Proceedings of the Second Annual Music and Health Conference* (pp. 12-20). KY: Eastern Kentucky University.

Halpern, S. (1978). *Tuning the Human Instrument: An Owner's Manual.* Palo Alto, CA: Spectrum Research Institute.

Richman, H. (1988). Music for Stress-release: Responding to the Entrainment Process. In *Proceedings of the Second Annual Music and Health Conference* (pp. 140-152) KY: Eastern Kentucky University.

7

The Power of Silence in Music Therapy

Gillian Stephens Langdon

Prelude to Gillian Stephens Langdon

Gillian and I met through our work on *Music Therapy*, journal of the American Association for Music Therapy. For several years, she was Editor-in-Chief and I served on the editorial board. In 1983, her article, "The Use of Improvisation for Developing Relatedness in the Adult Client," appeared in this journal. I had never read a better description of the musical improvisation experience and felt a kindred spirit. At that time, I was just beginning to formulate my own theoretical thoughts. Although I used different words, I recognized that Gillian also knew a kind of "musical space" with clients and her work provided an inspiration for me.

Later I had an opportunity to meet Gillian when she participated in a Music Therapy Renewal Workshop at New York University, led by Barbara Hesser and myself. This workshop was based on the Phoenecia model. The purpose was to bring practicing music therapists working in New York together for mutual support through improvisation, dialog, and silence.

In the workshop, I had a chance to know something beyond Gillian's thoughts—I experienced her sound, her sensibilities as an improviser and her music which were just as inspiring to me as her ideas. We drummed. We danced. We played. These are the moments when we come together and know that the work we share is a wonder to behold.

Gillian continues to work in music therapy and is currently Director of the Creative Arts Therapies Department at Bronx Psychiatric Center, where she has worked for the past 20 years. Among other positions, she has served as adjunct professor in the Music Therapy Department at New York University and has presented at numerous conferences and workshops throughout the country. Her writings include articles published in *Music Therapy* and a chapter on her work appears in the textbook *Improvisational Models in Music Therapy* by Kenneth Bruscia. She offers private supervision for practicing music therapists.

A music therapist makes many decisions within a session: what music to play, what verbal responses to make, when to be silent, when to initiate music, when to wait for the client, when to support the client musically. It is easier to trace the rationale for some of these decisions than others. It may be based on what is known of a client's history, the strength and limitations of musicianship, and the repertoire of successful past interventions and techniques.

There is another factor not as easy to pin down—intuition. Although a music therapist may have a sense of this intuition from the very beginning, he or she needs to have a foundation of music therapy techniques in order to focus on this area. He or she needs already to be able to observe, support, lead, make musical and verbal interventions skillfully, and generally make it from the beginning to the end of a session with some benefit to the client in order to be ready to go to a deeper level.

It is essential for the music therapist to have developed those skills in order to be able to enter into the music which requires a deep joining with the client, and to be able to be clear about what are the client's issues, what may be one's own, and what are those that merge. If this is not clear, then much of the work may be merely a projection of the music therapist and have little to do with the client's own needs.

Once therapists have developed these skills, they are then ready to work on a deeper level, some of which require that they let go of their usual defenses and boundaries and work from this merged place. It becomes clear that this place is rich with music and maybe even wisdom.

There are several levels to focus on in order to work with intuition. At the very heart of this work is the development of a respect for silence within the music therapy session. If one studies a piece of music carefully, one discovers that it is not simply the notes, rhythms, and harmonies that create the power of the music. It is the rests and pauses— the silences. It is the same in a music therapy session.

Although the types of silence blend into one another from time to time, for the sake of discussion I will divide this silence into four categories: (1) silencing words, (2) active silence, (3) sitting in silence, and (4) silencing the rational mind. I will describe the first two only briefly since they are more concrete and, perhaps, more obvious. My main focus will be on the last two.

The first category refers to movement into the musical mode as opposed to the verbal. Support, conversation, and intervention occur only through the music. Through the musical form the therapist gains insights and moves in a particular direction. The therapist foregoes the temptation to question the client or verbally interpret or encourage the client. This may be used as a part or whole of a session.

The second category refers to the internal dialogue the therapist carries on during the session. Although externally quiet, the therapist may ask him/herself questions such as, Why did he hand me the guitar for this part when I was playing the piano? How does this work connect with the last session? How am I feeling? How shall I respond? etc. It is from this running internal dialogue that musical or verbal interventions are made.

In the third category, "sitting in silence," the therapist begins to make room for the client on a deeper level. For myself, the understanding of this came after I began to meditate. Meditation helped me to become familiar with a depth of silence—a place of connection as opposed to isolation—and feel comfortable there. I found the clients I worked with felt the difference between a silence filled with inner questions as opposed to a calm inner silence. They were never frightened by it. The silence was not a new technique but a new place from which to receive the client and the client's music. Although the silence might be appropriate at the beginning of a session after our usual verbal greetings, more often it would be after playing an improvisation which was very moving. Instead of jumping in and asking, "How did that feel?" I would just sit and soak in the music into an inner empty space.

If the client asked, "What are you thinking?" I would answer honestly how I felt and how I felt during the music. This space is an open space where closing off my personal shared experience for the sake of the "blank screen" is not helpful. Playing music together has already bridged that distance.

In this silence the therapist is also "blank" enough to accept negative feedback. "That sounded terrible." "You're not helping me!" Since this space is not filled with anxiety and personal investment, the therapist can proceed easily to what is next.

In addition, there is room for the existence of pain—pain that joins to the sorrow of the world. In this inner space the pain can exist freely. It is not a place that exists to fix or relieve. It is not a place of catharsis. It is a place of recognition and the place of the heart. Many universal images may be experienced in this open place—the bleeding of the heart as in the image of Christ, the smile of the Buddha, the reflection of the moon on calm waters.

Or perhaps it is the joy the client feels—a joy that does not want limitations or interpretation—a joy that springs from a place of well-being—of hope. From the place of inner silence the therapist can be truly present, accompanying without encircling the client or limiting the feeling with his or her understanding.

In the fourth category, "silencing the rational mind," the therapist not only apprehends from this deep place of silence but also responds from this place. The response may take the form of music, songs, or words.

In my experience, at times what emerges is a song. This occurs usually after a client has played or spoken something very intense for them. An intimate feeling is present in the session and somehow a song comes forth. It often seems to be a universal type of song, for example with words expressing a journey together. In my first experiences with this phenomenon I found myself struggling between, on the one hand, a deep sense that this was the right direction for the session, yet on the other hand my conscious mind was saying, "Why are you singing this song?" "What about the client? Did he ask for this?" "Where are you going with this song? What if you get stuck?" But if I kept going, the words formed for me. "Walking down the road—I keep walking. So tired. So alone. Hear my voice. Hear me calling. Find my way into the morning sun." Sometimes words I did not expect popped out.

I began to talk myself along internally. "Go ahead, sing. That's fine. Don't worry," might be my inner dialogue. This inner dialogue would help push away the rational mind and keep the channel open to this current or well spring.

The songs or music seemed to be right there. It was as if the songs were presented to me. I responded "Yes" with my whole being. The song would emerge out loud. I did not plan the harmonies or the rhythms if there were any. There was also no investment in the outcome or a preconception of where we were going. Instead it would be a pouring out of a universal energy. It felt as if I were traveling with the client, giving him or her the strength to feel, trust, and travel through the experience.

In fact it never seemed as if these songs made me or the client more attached. By nature, they are not mine. This makes it possible.

If I ever tried to force a song out, the client could feel the difference. I remember one group where I was feeling the need to do something to help. The group felt so bad. "There must be something we can do to make them feel better," was my thought. This was not from a centered, open place of inner silence. I was the music therapist trying to make everyone feel good. As I began, the group's laughter drowned me out. The difference was obvious.

Whether it be simply silencing words or active silence, sitting in silence or silencing the rational mind, the development of a respect and sensitivity for the silences in the music therapy session is the way to listen for the deeper messages within a session. Silence can become the place of pure listening. Then the response, whether verbal or musical, rather than coming from the personal or theoretical, comes from the universal.

8

Listening: A Sacred Act

Nancy McMaster

Prelude to Nancy McMaster

Nancy is one of my best friends. We have known each other over a twenty-year period and have shared life and work through many cycles. It would be impossible to describe here the many significant experiences we have had together over time. We have shared both joy and sorrow. We have celebrated success and mourned failure. But mainly, we have reveled in our work. And this shared reveling is our bond.

Nancy and I met through our collaboration in the Children's Spontaneous Music Workshops in the early 1970s in Vancouver. She and I were both members of the serendipitous group which formed to offer musical improvisation experiences to a wide range of clients in the greater Vancouver area. After several years, most of the members of our little group went their separate ways. Nancy went to India to travel and meditate and to London to study both classical music and musical improvisation with Paul Nordoff and Clive Robbins. I went to New Orleans and took my training in music therapy at Loyola University and had a baby, my daughter Shannon.

In the mid-1970s we both found ourselves back in Vancouver, the only remaining members of our group. Whereas we had experienced many differences within the Children's Spontaneous Music Workshops, when we found ourselves together, the only surviving members of our small but strong community, we felt "the same," and immediately began to formulate plans to continue the work we had started with our group, but in our own unique way.

We applied for and received several grants from Health and Welfare Canada and continued the itinerate spontaneous music making at various institutions in Vancouver, with the added component of our new-found skills. These years were tremendously rich and exciting, and both our work and our friendship of mutual inspiration grew steadily. What had appeared to be differences in our early days together now became areas to learn and grow from each other. This was the tone. And in the many miles we traveled across the city, carrying our instruments from place to place, significant moments with clients were equally matched with significant moments of dialog and relationship.

When an opportunity came to establish a music therapy training program at Capilano College, we were thrilled. Our work in the community seemed to have generated enough enthusiasm about music therapy for Capilano College to take a big risk with a new field. The program at Cap was the first music therapy training program in Canada and it was a great example of how grassroots movements can grow over time and offer enduring and substantive education and training to the community. From the Children's Spontaneous Workshops to Health and Welfare Canada Demonstration Projects to the training program at Capilano College, music therapy grew and so did we.

Sometimes we could not believe that we were so blessed to have a work like this—full of love and joy and music and moving experiences with clients and students every day. It was hard work, but good, meaningful work full of connectedness in all of the relationships—between ourselves, our clients and students, the institutions and the community. This sense of connection is one of the ongoing features of the Capilano program, even today.

Once when the members of the Executive Board for the Canadian Association for Music Therapy were gathered in Toronto for intensive meetings to discuss critical issues in the formation of our philosophy and ethical standards, we all needed a break. Nancy began to play the piano. At the time, I was just completing my first book, and had not yet settled on a suitable title. As she played, everyone became very still. When she ended, her music had been so moving that as a group we sighed and someone said: "It's only music that can say it all." As we played with the question of "what is unique about music?" we came up with the image of music as a massive mythic artery, which keeps us connected to the heart and provides nutrients for the soul. Thus the title *The Mythic Artery*.

Nancy's music inspires. It is full of depth and sorrow, joy, compassion, tears, giggles and smiles, tenderness, horror, despair, hope. It is the range of human experience and feeling. Nancy is my friend.

Of herself Nancy says: "I am a music therapist in Canada who has worked in private practice for over 20 years with children and adults who are dealing with physical, cognitive, emotional, and/or spiritual challenges. I am the co-founder and instructor of the Capilano College Music Therapy Program in Vancouver. I also have been a performer for the past 25 years. One of my relaxation tapes is being used extensively in palliative care in several countries."

Something sacred there is about listening
when the whole of our Being is tuned
to resonate with all that enters our field of experience.

Such listening requires an openness,
an interest in contact, in discovery;

a faith, however momentary, that there is a place for
  "everything under the sun."

It is NOT half-listening,
as if we already know what is likely to happen in the next moment.
      It IS a sense of not ever knowing, completely,
      what is here, now, either within or around us

      a willingness to be profoundly surprised.

It is NOT listening from the perspectives of either survival or hope,
tuned only to intimations of threat or promise,
all else deemed irrelevant;
nor is it listening to judge whether something is worth hearing.

      It IS a sense that all sounds and silence, all movement and
          stillness,
      are eloquent expressions of the very nature of
          every aspect of Reality,
      each equally significant in itself, as is, as a part of the Whole,
      regardless of any distress or pleasure we may feel in its presence—

      an alert curiosity and ready acknowledgement towards all
          that we perceive.

It is NOT listening from a feeling of already being overwhelmed,
too tangled in a sticky web of responsibilities,
too tugged off-balance by our responsiveness,
to want to respond to anything more;
nor is it listening in a state of numbness,
so guarded against the residue of old pains
that we dare not allow ourselves to resonate freely ever again.

      It IS a sense of our inviolate core;
      a sense of the consummate importance of honoring the integrity
      of each part of every interaction, ourselves included;
      and a sense of our capacity to survive and be expanded by
      tremendous surges of sensation, however excruciating
          or ecstatic—

      and a still center which is open to touch.

And finally,
it is NOT listening in resignation,

having long ago given up a dream of being part of a mutually
      responsive world
in which we give and receive attention, understanding, welcome,
      and accommodation.
            It IS an act of commitment to expressing that dream,
            to doing one's best to bring it into being,
            to embodying in the moment all that the dream requires of
                  each one of us.
And therein lies its sacredness.

Part III

PLAYING

9

Floors of Music

Joanne Crandall

Prelude to Joanne Crandall

In the early 1980s, when I first moved to California from Vancouver, British Columbia, I taught courses in music therapy at Santa Barbara City College, through the extension division. These courses attracted a wide range of folks. Some were health professionals eager to incorporate music into their work in nursing or mental health. Some were educators, hoping to learn ways of integrating music into the classroom. Some were seekers eager to expand their creativity and consciousness through sound. And a few were performers. Joanne Crandall was one.

Joanne attended such a course and several months later I received a phone call from her asking me if I would be willing to engage in some private dialogs. Would I answer some of her questions?

Joanne was curious about one of the concepts I had presented in class—music as a field.

As a jazz musician and longtime student of esoteric spiritual traditions, Joanne had become acutely aware of the power of music in jazz clubs. She noticed that the atmosphere created by her music had an influence on mood, energy, social relating, and events. She was eager to explore and understand this phenomenon.

Over several months we met on a regular basis for dialogs. Joanne asked questions—often provocative and probing. Then she would transcribe our dialogs and study them. She also gave me copies.

When I perused her documents, I was struck by the quality of information Joanne was able to draw out of me. She always elicited a spontaneous reply unmediated by academic principles and connected to direct experience and an inner knowing. I was always inspired by her natural curiosity, openness, and desire to know and understand. I was also impressed with Joanne's self-motivated course of study. It was an inner journey, inspired through her commitment to the process of developing a conscious approach to her work and a desire to serve her "audience" in ever-enlightening ways.

Joanne and I developed a friendship during the two years I lived in Ojai, my retreat. In addition to our dialogs in my home, I sometimes attended her Sunday afternoon "soirees"—gatherings of friends who, once a month, shared a meal, music, poetry, and prose.

Eventually, Joanne also came to Phoenecia to join the Music Therapy Retreat Group and I was able to introduce her to a broader community of music therapists. There we marveled at fireflies in the night, meditated, improvised, and engaged in still more dialog within a larger community.

Joanne is a mother of six children and a grandmother many times. She is totally committed to her work in the Ligia Dantes Self-Study Program and also plays jazz. She has recorded several albums which offer "music as a field" of influence for meditation, play, and inspiration.

Joanne's book, *Self-Transformation through Music*, is a valuable tool for people interested in the beautiful relationship between inner and outer development through the aesthetic experience.

Of herself she says: "I have been playing the piano since I was four, and was the accompanist for Ballet West Dance Company for ten years. I now direct workshops on the use of music for inner awareness. I currently perform near my home in Ojai and work with the Ligia Dantes Foundation, an organization dedicated to awareness, responsibility, and the exploration of human consciousness."

> The musician is emptiness
> The listener is humanity
> Space is silence
>
> Music is energy, holding awareness of these truths.

For several months I enjoyed a very different environment in which to play music. A new department store had just opened in a city nearby and they were looking for pianists to perform at the beautiful Steinway grand, placed in a most conspicuous spot in the middle of the store. I have performed in what I had thought were all possible milieus—churches, restaurants, hospitals, concerts, dance companies, saloons—through the years, and this new one intrigued me. For several years I have been exploring the concept of energy fields, sound fields, and their relationship to my work as a musician and as an inquirer into my own nature. This seemed like a wonderful new frontier for those explorations and inquiries. It is one thing to experience the power of music while playing in a cathedral, or in a bar—but in a department store?

I discover, my first day on the job, what a broad spectrum of humanity my music will be reaching. The store is expensive, and I thought it would be filled with moneyed people, buying and buying and buying. While there are many obviously wealthy people, there are people of all classes, ranging in economic status from extremely affluent to homeless poor, and in ages from newborn infants to elderly persons of eighty or ninety. There are young couples preoccupied with their first child, weary parents of several children, happy people, sick people (many in wheelchairs, one on a hospital gurney—the aisles are very wide, accommodating many who could not navigate in most stores). Who are all these individuals?

Paul, a man of 70 or so, comes to the piano everyday. His hands shake, his speech quavers, he seems a little disoriented. But when I begin playing his three favorite songs—"You Can't Take That Away From Me," "My Shining Hour," and "You Make Me Feel So Young"— he becomes a young man, singing along in a lovely tenor voice with perfect pitch and rhythm, remembering all the words. He walks away— "See you tomorrow!"

A homeless man who comes in once or twice a week strolls by as I am playing "On The Street Where You Live," grins and says, "Hey man, you're playing my song!"

A middle-aged woman comes over to the piano one day just as I have finished playing "My Foolish Heart." With tears in her eyes, she tells me this was her husband's favorite song. He passed away a few months ago, and she is grieving. I play other songs for her that also bring tears. I ask her if she would like me to play something to bring a smile, and she says, "There are smiles in my tears. The music is holding the sadness."

A gaggle of teenagers come sauntering along. "Oh no," I worry, "they hate this kind of music. They want their rock and punk and rap. Well, keep playing and hope they just walk on by." The handsome young man who seems to be the leader of the gang comes over and says, "All right! Great! Thanks for the live sounds."

It is Christmas time and the store is filled with children. Several come running to the piano as I play "Rudolph the Red-nosed Reindeer." Laughing and dancing and singing along, they are the music, and Christmas, and joy. I play a lot of carols, something I never feel comfortable doing in a bar, and the Christmas spirit envelops me. A man says to me, "I was shopping for my mother, out of a sense of duty, hating this whole Christmas shopping scene. Those carols take me back to my childhood and an experience of my mother that I'd lost somehow. Christmas is music, isn't it?"

It is late afternoon in mid-February. Many people are gathered around a television set in the men's department. I join them as they watch the missiles heading for Baghdad. The air in the store feels heavy, oppressive. I walk back to the piano, sit in silence for a few moments, then play John Lennon's "Imagine."

Today a young girl, smiling and cheerful, says, "I can hear you everywhere in the store. I feel like I'm walking on floors of music."

What happens in that sound/energy field? What happens when we are walking on floors of music? The moment of discovery occurs and we talk or write about it later, and there seems to be a loss. But the insight that is beyond words, beyond recollection, remains with us, illuminating our relationships, informing our actions, enlarging our experience of being human.

The sound/energy field is profound, powerful, mysterious. What seems to be needed in exploring this field is, first of all, a silence— within the musician—that is open to everything, *everything*. That silence carries no judgment, no expectation, no memory—only the present moment.

There needs to be an awareness of the sanctity of the space, any space, in which we find ourselves. The sacredness can only be responded to with reverence and compassion and a great sense of responsibility for everything that occurs in that setting.

From our silence, from our compassion, we begin to discover the utter humanity of the listener. Our oneness is manifest—the listener becomes the musician. The other is ourself.

The energy we call music is the energy of life itself. With beauty and clarity and great power, it reflects and illuminates the immense experience of being human and being humanity on this planet.

May all our days be spent walking on the floors of music.

10

The Almost Unappreciated, Nearly Ignored Power of Sound—and Its Abuse

Christopher Tree

Prelude to Christopher Tree

Christopher Tree is the only contributor to this book who I have not met. Yet I feel that I know him and surely he has had a profound effect on me. The great thing is that since I invited him to write something for *Listening, Playing, and Creating*, I have come to know him more personally. Before the initiation of this project we had never even written.

I became familiar with Christopher and his work through Michael Fles and John Marcus, who are also contributors. When I first met Michael in Vancouver, he was fresh from assisting Christopher in the performance of Spontaneous Sound for the elderly, the young, ethnic groups, the handicapped, prisoners, and others. Gongs, drums, flutes, exotic horns, and sounding metals were his "band." Once Michael showed us a film about Christopher playing his set of musical instruments. This was about consciousness. It was about shifting us into celebrating aspects of ourselves which we had denied and which are ancient and essential to our human spirit.

Once when I was doing research in the library I found a story about Christopher Tree in a 1969 edition of *Time Magazine*. The article described a performance in a large New York Church. It said that Christopher was a lithe figure who captivated the audience with his sounds, and that he took his instruments into prisons and worked with prisoners, as well as with developmentally delayed kids.

And this is what we did in the Children's Spontaneous Music Workshops in Vancouver. In a sense, through Michael, we all became familiar with the work of Christopher. Thus hundreds of people in Vancouver were able to experience the benefits of the work he had begun.

Years later, when I was teaching a workshop at New York University, and gongs had become quite popular, a young man began to tell me the story of how his work on the gongs was inspired by an article he had read about a man named Christopher Tree. I listened all ears, so to speak.

Through his recent correspondence, I have come to know Christopher as a man who is gentle and true, with a sense of beauty and connection that ripples like clear streams and shines like delicate stars. I hope to meet him soon. He lives in the west of France.

Of himself Christopher says: "Christopher Tree has lived in Europe the last twenty years. He began playing music with The Light Show, a spontaneous presentation of light, color, sound, and motion in the '50s and early '60s, when he also first worked at music therapy. Since then, he gives spontaneous sound concerts and workshops, most often for children, as well as concerts with children, and continues music therapy."

"It is not our tongue but our very life that sings the new song."

—St. Augustine

A few strong flute sounds abruptly stop two startled, fleeing deer—then still except for their ears, they listen to softer music.

Another time some deer appear from the forest and come close in a small clearing to hear.

Ends the crying of even hungry babies and holds their rapt attention for half an hour, more.

Lulls disturbed ones to sleep.

Brings the unborn to dance in the womb.

And sure—to turn gloom inside-out.

And what else:

Brings dogs to song.

Turtles to seek.

Girls to call.

And many more subtle things.

The big Down's Syndrome boy holds up the little Down's Syndrome boy, and together, their noses pressed against the door window, they watch, anticipating their turns to come in and play music.

The 12-year-old girl who does not speak realizes conversation playing a drum together and with rare delight bestows a kiss on the cheek.

Anyone who has begun to inquire into the power of sound, even unheard sound, is familiar with a wide range of phenomena, ranging from the integrating *mantra* to dispersing, sci-fi, crowd-control intimidators. This power includes the soothing of savage beasts, within and without, or the destruction of formidable walls and shattering of crystal glasses, and more subtly, the influencing of moods. From the most ancient myths and folk tales to the most recent science journals, wonders are recorded.

In spite of these marvelous musical powers, there is, with few exceptions, no doubt about an exaggerated lack of imagination prevailing about them among people involved in music. Nearly unappreciated, almost ignored, the endless fullness of music is scarcely really considered. And when it is, most often it is dealt with systematically.

the study of *exact* musical intervals—that is, the mathematical frequencies (the number of vibrations per second) of sounds in rigidly defined series (or scales), tends to become a substitute for the direct experience of tones charged with psychoactive energy and used for sacro-magical purposes. (Dane Rudhyar, *The Magic of Tone and the Art of Music*)

Here, the focus is on spontaneous musical sound. If Novalis was correct in saying that the most poetic will be closer to the truth, the spontaneous approach will prove the most efficacious in several fields of musical endeavor.

That spontaneity in the essence of the creative act appears the most obvious in music where it is very possible, on the first spontaneous attempt at singing or playing an instrument (particularly percussive), to have an actual creative musical experience, often on a very dynamic, high-spirited or on a very calm, almost meditative level. This fact alone indicates its great potential for education and therapy.

What about aesthetics, performance?

If it is so that creativity is essentially spontaneous, then it follows that the more spontaneous the music, the more creatively essential it should be.

In all phenomena it is the spontaneous, the unfinished becoming, that quickens, attracts, makes real. One would be bored from the beginning in trying even to imagine deliberate, methodical love making.

With most of our living so cut off from this spontaneous life essential, it is sought for, mostly unconsciously and vicariously, where some still exists.

Sports (no matter how game-planned and percentage oriented) still necessarily retain more spontaneity than most activities and include the play element and the ever-present possibility of the unexpected upset—which attracts the players and the involvement of immense audiences.

In any creative work, the ideas arrive spontaneously.

But, most ideas are grabbed, worked-out, and presented as finished products, accomplished facts.

In spontaneous presentations we do not have the facts, but ideally live knowing, in the playing.

Particularly the child, the retarded, the mental patient, delight to find it is play as serious as anything else, but lighter, familiar.

Playing music together can be the best or even the only way to relate intimately, essentially equal.

The very young infant has impeccable musical discretion, seeming only to tire of music played attentively for it if the music loses the focus.

Growing awareness of the world's sounds, animal sound, songs, the particular slices of the musical pie that each culture has chosen to express, with the history of their developments, offer a vastly wider identification with musical consciousness, loosening ties to known specifics. And the musical instruments of these cultures can help enrich and reintegrate music for a new, more irresistable expression.

More often, these specific musics are studied, learned, and played as such or worked in with other specific musical forms, each with the players using only the instruments traditional to their parts.

But without trying to learn, copy, or otherwise invoke the world's traditional music, qualities can appear from our identifications and from qualities inherent in their instruments. Embracing unique realities of the specifics becomes an including of them in the ever-changing progression of the nonspecific.

Tribal consciousness is fast pacing. But most forces of "world music" are anti-cultural, economical movements. And the ethnic fads idolize, commercialize, destroy.

The older music of Western tradition and its instruments are also almost always learned and played as such—the instruments seldom otherwise. Many have been virtually abandoned.

There are those who long to hear and play these and other out-of-fashion, lost instruments. They want to hear more sounds, experience the tones of all instruments, from the new and sophistocated to the most ancient and simple. Beautiful objects too, these simple ones made of clay, bamboo, gourds, animals, sea shells, coconuts, etc. Children delight in and admire them, like playing them and the unusualness of their sounds.

The new instruments being made here and there are often particularly susceptible to a spontaneous approach and again expand musical consciousness. Like the unfamiliar simple instruments, they are not accompanied by what to expect and leave children, beginners, and the handicapped freer to begin. Through them the conditioned musician can be liberated to begin anew.

It is not too imaginative to have thousands of groups the world over with more or less the same few instruments, machines, and electronic devices, playing (?) more or less the same "hits," or lesser thousands with their in-instruments and in-alternative versions, or hundreds of groups playing the instruments appropriate to their varied elite select renditions, etc., etc.

Of course complete spontaneity is only the idea. However, there can be no practice, only playing (except for dealing with physical practicalities), no performance preparation, plan, or discussion, no repetition intended.

It is necessary to realise, as in all endeavor, that there are times when there appears to be little or no progress, a sense of being stuck in the same place. Worst of all is the necessity of accepting (like the athlete) times of failure to rise to the occasion, when with nothing to fall back on, not much happening is obvious. However, awareness of this continual risk makes evident a living music. And devotion to any work strengthens it.

Using what remains of the baby's impeccable musical discretion, coupled with a continual development of the all-important quality of listening, should lead the spontaneous player along, once it is realized that spontaneity need not be chaos, random exorcism, excretion—and can rather be the bright arrow shot way out of unconscious complaint into an altogether more becoming musical play.

Reference

Rudhyar, D. (1982). *The Magic of Tone and the Art of Music*. Boulder and London: Shambhala.

11

Sound Wave Mirror

Michael Fles

Prelude to Michael Fles

I first met Michael on a typical misty day in Port Grey, Vancouver, British Columbia. No less than a miraculous set of circumstances brought us together. In 1971 my husband and I had recently moved to Vancouver from New Orleans, Louisiana. One day, during my first week in Vancouver, I was driving out to the University of British Columbia to begin checking things out, when I picked up a hitchhiker on her way to the racketball courts. In conversation I mentioned that I was a music therapist. She said: "Oh, that's interesting. I just met a man who is doing music at UBC with developmentally and emotionally disabled preschool children. He's putting a grant together to expand this work. Maybe you would be interested." Thus the first meeting at the house in Port Grey. From this meeting I ended up developing four lifelong friends, including the hitchhiker (Shelley Stewart, now a social worker at G.F. Strong in Vancouver).

Michael was a visionary, a man with a dream and a commitment to kids and music. He had worked with Christopher Tree (also a contributor to this collection) and had learned a great deal about world music, particularly music from the Far East. We did put together a grant and a project which we entitled "The Children's Spontaneous Music Workshops," funded as a Demonstration Project by the Canadian Government. In this work we traveled around the city of Vancouver in two teams to serve a total of up to ten clinical sites and two Native American community centers.

As a visionary, a poet, an artist, a dreamer, Michael Fles has inspired me a great deal. It was in the work with Michael and others in our group that I learned about musical improvisation, about community, about commitment and belief in a dream.

We had a grueling schedule and worked our way around the city in two vans, come rain or come shine (usually rain in Vancouver). In addition to our work with children and adults, every week we would spend a whole day in community improvisation and dialogue, exploring the sound and our relationships in it.

This experience was so central to my life that it laid the foundation for a whole new worldview, which I had previously not imagined. Because we had so many moving experiences with our clients and with each other, our community was strong, and for many of us has endured.

In the mid-1970s, Michael moved to Mexico and lived in Chiapas for several years, then on to France, then Israel, then back to the United States in 1990—always exploring the sound, often in a form which he entitled the Light Show, incorporating a mixed media production of sound and colored light. Sometimes these happenings were performed. Often they were interactive with the audience or children in schools.

In describing himself Michael says: "In the last 22 years, I have done sound and light shows and music workshops—mainly with and for children— in New Mexico, France, Israel, and Germany. Now based in Arcata, California, I continue with sound meditation workshops, color, shadow, dance explorations, University studies, and set construction at Pacific Art Center Theater. My dream is to continue light shows in Japan some day. I would also like to point out the professional/biographical/karmic connection between Christopher Tree, John Marcus, Carolyn Kenny, and myself."

. . . for John

"Beauty is the Terror we are only just able to bear."

—Rilke

Over 25 years ago in Los Angeles a friend off-handedly suggested I visit a man "into Far Eastern sounds." In the narrow room I was invited to sit next to a medium-sized Paiste gong. Slowly Christopher Tree built up the waves of sound, higher and higher like some impossible Japanese sea of stacked-up surf, then, using his body to modulate the overtones, he "glissandoed" them down to a murmur. I was left breathless by the soft strength of a titanic sonic force.

But as the vibrations became more and more powerful, my stomach tensed and cramped: I either had to leave the room quickly or slow myself down and surrender. I chose to surrender, and the energy pulsed through me. Thus began a quarter of a century of exploration into the power of sound.

Later, in working with music as therapy, I let over-active children make the gong sounds as loud as they wanted to—very quickly they would come down to a level of sound that they (and I!) could tolerate. Slowly, over several sessions the gong became a mirror showing them that with their own strokes they could produce rhythmical overtone effects that were surprisingly subtle. These usually restless children modulated their behavior because the softer sounds gave them personal satisfaction and aesthetic pleasure.

What evolved from the workshops and performances was that we could see increased concentration of attention on the part of the participants and audience by the focus and refocus, the dynamic range of sound: from the tiny, barely audible sound of a single small bell swinging rapidly on a string to the deep, almost tidal wave sonorities of the gongs and conch, and more significantly, back again from the large sounds to those just hearable, turning the ear, as it were, inside out.

What can this mean for us personally? Many sound professionals come to therapeutic work for not only scientific/artistic exploration but from a deep inner need. For me the metaphor of gong—symbolic of all the "sound environment" instruments—as mirror is a significant one. You can quickly tell (as with the flute) when you approach the instrument in a disturbed state and watch/listen as the tones even out: for if you give up judging yourself, if you accept awkwardness as a natural part of the process, the gong-tones help you find your own natural rhythm, regain your own voice.

Often, of course, this process, easy to describe, is painful. For what is this resistance but the sorrows and struggles—the unsureness—of day-to-day life, blocking us from the cleansing of the natural sonic experience.

When we become simply an instrument for the sound to pass through, we become free, become, if even only momentarily, part of the cosmic harmony, the music of the spheres.

Again, the gongs, cymbals, chimes, and bells—of course the Tibetan singing bowls!—are a striking metaphor/symbol for this human/cosmic connection because of the infiniteness of their sound; you can hear the overtones go on and on, imagine the vibrations going right into space and back.[1]

Unconsciously this centering, this placing of oneself, goes on also for the disturbed child (the disturbed child in all of us!) when they play these endlessly-sounding instruments. Are they not the microscope lens focusing the sun tone which starts the fire in our heart? Is the sound waking us up to our own being and to our connectedness not only to the earth mother sound of the bass American Indian tom-toms— but to the actual singing of the stars?

Note

1. Carl Sagan in *Cosmos* says that American television programs from the 1950s are potentially receivable by the nearest heavenly bodies that could have intelligent life. What if we were to send Christopher Tree's spontaneous sounds into outer space via radio astronomy? Not only would the aesthetic level be considerably higher, but we would actually be communicating something.

12

Improvisation as a Liminal Experience: Jazz and Music Therapy as Modern "Rites de Passage"

Even Ruud

Prelude to Even Ruud

In our first encounter, Even and I disagreed. It was during the meeting of a study group at the 1982 Symposium of Music in the Life of Man: Toward a Theory of Music Therapy at NYU. We were strangers then. In the study group, Even made a provocative comment. I do not even remember what he said. I reacted. "How can you say that?" I said, "I disagree." After the meeting, I felt guilty. I considered the fact that Even was a visitor to our country, and here I was challenging him, even before we had formally met. So that night at the social gathering which had been planned for our symposium members, I apologized. Amends were made.

Since then, it seems to me that Even and I have rarely disagreed. In fact, we have found many more similarities than differences in our work and in our lives. Even established the first music therapy training program in Norway and Nancy McMaster and I established the first training program in Canada with the same basic philosophy and structure, even though we certainly had not met at the time.

We both focused our dissertations on phenomenology and music therapy, the first two such documents to emerge from the literature with this approach. Both of us are dedicated interdisciplinarians. Our ideas about social and political contexts are very much the same. We are the same age. The list goes on and on.

No longer do we marvel at synchronous ideas and events in our lives. This is just the way it is.

Even has been the most important person in my circle of colleagues and friends when it comes to developing our ideas about theory in music therapy. Our ideas are similar, yet at the same time different. We share an intellectual and cultural context. This is even more striking because we come from two different cultures. We have not had a great quantity of time together, yet somehow we are akin, and this kinship allows a special kind of communication, a rich ground in which both knowledge and friendship can grow.

One year, at Phonecia, Even wrote the foreword to my book, *The Field of Play*. This was a very special time for me because his approach to the task was one of deep respect and admiration. It was also an acknowledgment of our shared work.

Even though we have had some fine correspondence, I think our times together at Phoenecia have meant the most to me. Our encounter in New York in 1982 was dramatic because it contained a rare and meaningful sense of recognition. How often does one discover another who is truly like-minded? But even more significant for me are the times we spent together in Phoenecia as members of the Music Therapy Retreat Community. Here the sense of recognition moved to a grounded discovery of who we are as human beings, as music therapists, as citizens of a global community. We spent many hours on the porch of the dining hall at Phoenecia with our group discussing contemporary issues from our different countries and how our work in music therapy might relate to these issues. We all wanted to make a difference when it came to suffering. We all had a passion for our work. We loved music.

Even's perspective was one which was thoroughly admired and respected by me. His words were truly music to my ears because I no longer felt alone—kinship does something like this, you know.

In his country, Even has a reputation for being an important leader not only in the field of music therapy, but in other fields such as music education, popular music, cultural studies, and most significantly interdisciplinary studies. This bodes well for music therapy and creates important avenues for exchange of knowledge across fields. As an educator and researcher, he is dedicated to social change and has fashioned a life around what he calls "being useful." Humility is another one of his gifts. Humor, too.

Of himself Even says: "I am professor in musicology, Department of Music and Theater, University of Oslo. I am currently head of the department, also adjunct professor in music therapy at Ostlandets Musikkonservatorium. My doctorate is from the University of Oslo and my masters in music therapy from Florida State University. My main research interests are music therapy, music education, music and mass media, and music and cultural studies."

To improvise means to create or arrange something "here and now," to put something together on the way, out of available resources.[1] In music, "improvising" is defined as "the art of spontaneously creating music (ex tempore) while playing, rather than preforming a composition already written."[2] Further attempts to define the concept draw on formulations like "to test, fool around, to nose around with a plan."[3] In everyday life (and particularly during vacation) we meet improvisation at the edge of "the serious life," as a time where we prepare ourselves or where we find ourselves in the meantime. Thus, the *journey* is often a place for improvisation, or situations where we come to meet new persons.

Improvisation contains an element of prepared aimlessness. Improvisations may even be well prepared in the sense that certain elements have been selected before the improvisation starts without the order and extent of the elements having been decided. Themes may have been considered thoroughly without necessarily having to be performed. The jazz musician has acquired an arsenal of musical formulas, scales and motives, or rules which determine how such materials may be performed or recreated. A certain jazz style presupposes knowledge of musical codes and materials. To succeed in improvisation means to play with or against those tendencies attached to the musical conventions.[4] In music therapy, the stylistic conventions may be fewer. However, in therapy there are conventions deciding which group processes, associations, or extra-musical themes belong to the therapeutic context.

Improvisation may also be understood to create a situation where change, transformation, and process come into focus. In this sense, improvisation not only means to get from one place to another, but from one state to another. In this sense, improvisation means to change a *relation* to other human beings, phenomena, situations —maybe the very relation to oneself. In this sense, improvisation is a transitional ritual, a way of changing position, frames, status, or state of consciousness.

The purpose of this article is to demonstrate how improvisation as an important element in music therapy may be meaningfully studied from anthropological theory. Thus I will be able to demonstrate a common aspect of all forms of improvisation in music therapy, regardless of the therapeutic ideology within which the treatment takes place. Drawing on an extended contextual understanding of the musical improvisation, as is usual in anthropological studies, I hope generally to understand the role (or power) of music in improvised music therapy. By illustrating the text with examples from the life of jazz, I will try to show that improvisation in our culture has meanings which go beyond pure aesthetic or artistic aspects of the music. Thus the article may be read as a form of cultural analysis of the role of music in everyday rituals serving to change or maintain aspects of contemporary culture.

Improvisation as Play

The German music therapist Frank Grootaers[5] writes that in music therapy it is exactly those marginal situations in life, which he calls

"Zwischenwelten" (worlds between), which become the focus of attention. It is the spontaneous idea, the unforeseen connection of seemingly meaningless thoughts which come into attention. It is the accidental plucking of sound sources which interests us more than logical rules, compositional precision, or artistic virtuosity. Although music therapists do not renounce musical quality, what concerns us here is the spontaneous common product which stems from the interaction between a client and a therapist.[6] It is the poetic or aesthetic aspects of the musical communication, however, which give them power to transform the improvisation into a therapeutic tool.

Improvisations have many similarities with play. Play is a kind of action characterized by a certain way of *organizing* activities, rather than a particular set of activities. This means that play may occur as we carry out tasks that are generally characterized as work. By changing the rules, we have created new frames of a new referential perspective of the situation. This level of communication, called meta-communication,[7] places a cognitive boundary around certain behaviors and says that they are "play" or that they are "ordinary life." The markers serve to say that "everything from now until we end this activity is set apart from everyday life."

Anthropologists Emily Schultz and Robert Lavenda[8] write that play also allows us to see that the perspective of ordinary life is only one way to make sense of experience. Play allows us to recognize that any particular referential perspective is relative. It exists when there are two sets of goals and rules, one operating here and now and one that applies outside the given reality. Play makes us aware of alternatives, it creates a room where alternate possibilities of actions are possible—a situation basic to the therapeutic improvisation.

This creates what is referred to as the paradox of play: it is supposed to be divorced from reality, yet it is also supposed to be ripe with real-life consequences. It is an activity of "as-if" at the same time as the possibilities made apparent through the play may have real consequences if the activity is taken out of the play frames. Another anthropologist, Handelman,[9] underlines how play is reflexive, it teaches us how events can be understood in other ways when taken out of their context. Anything can be understood differently, the play informs us. The play is not telling us about the way things should be, but rather about the way things might be. And it is of course important to the therapeutic process that the improvisation create a frame which allows for a variety of fantasies from different spheres of life to appear in combinations which would have been intolerable outside the play frame. A musical improvisation, then, is play with musical tendencies and possibilities as a frame within which to explore fantasies and alternative forms of action.

We might add that there is a difference in style between improvisations in music therapy and jazz. Improvisations in music therapy may have fewer musical rules and conventions to follow, the musical frames may be established by the participants while playing. This means that such improvisations may be free of the extramusical connotations often attached to a certain music style. In music therapy, improvisations are total, similar to avant garde or free jazz. At the same time, the resulting musical material may be free to appear as metaphors of the different types of themes which are central to the participants in the therapeutic improvisation. By letting the improvisation be handled within the cognitive boundaries defined in our culture as "therapy," there will be themes which may be significant within the therapeutic context. It is this therapeutic reality, which deals with existential themes, conflicts, or dramatic life circumstances, the musical improvisation—as play—will seek to transform.

Rites of Passage

The term "rites of passage" comes from the Belgian anthropologist Arnold Van Gennep, who at the beginning of our century noticed that certain kinds of rituals around the world had similar structures. These were rituals associated with the movement or passage from one position in the social structure to another, including births, initiations, confirmations, weddings, funerals, and the like. Van Gennep found that all these rituals began with a period of separation from the old position and from normal time. During this period, the ritual passenger had to leave behind the symbols and practices of his or her previous position. The second stage in such rituals involves a period of transition, in which the ritual passenger is neither in the old life nor yet in the new one. This is a situation marked by rolelessness, ambiguity, and perceived danger. The final stage is that of reaggregation, in which the ritual process is reintroduced into society, but in his or her new position.

The anthropologist Victor Turner has greatly increased our understanding of the period of transition. Turner referred to this period as the liminal period, from the Latin *limen*, "threshold." It is characteristic of being on the threshold that one is "betwixt and between," neither here nor there, neither in nor out.[10] The symbolism accompanying the rite of passage often expresses this ambiguous state. As I will comment upon later, people in the liminal state tend to develop an intense comradeship in which their nonliminal distinctions disappear or become irrelevant.

Turner called this modality of social relationship *communitas*, that is, an unstructured or minimal community of equal individuals.

Our task is to show how improvisations in music may be understood as a part of a larger rite of passage, that is, as an experience of liminility. It should be noted that rituals in general, or more specific rites of passage, will appear in many contexts and on many levels both within the world of jazz and music therapy. We may for instance find rituals initiating young jazz musicians into the professional jazz community. Or we may study the training of the music therapist as a long "rite de passage." Within the training program itself we may find situations which may be studied as rites of passage: For instance, Norwegian music therapy students go every semester on a tour to the countryside (separation) where during a weekend they go through a grinding-down process inflicting upon themselves ambiguity and emotional danger (liminality) under the guidance of a Gestalt therapist before they conclude and gather for homecoming (reaggregation).

In the following I will, however, focus on the musical improvisation. One may ask what makes the musical improvisation possible as a symbol of liminality, as a tool to enact a liminal situation, to prepare a transition from one state to another?

Liminality

We noticed how liminal states or processes were characterized by ambiguity and the dissolution of conventional meanings and fixed points in one's life. Essential to the experience is the feeling of being "out of time"—"a moment in and out of time," as Turner writes.[11] The German music therapist Frank Grootaers is close to a description of such liminal processes when he characterizes improvisation as a possibility to experience "the rules of the soul": By nosing around in old matters we may discover new meanings as well as *lose* ourselves in the thoughts. This because in improvisation, many things happen at the same time, Grootaers explains.

"The same" may have many meanings at the same time; meaning transforms, they have to be reinterpreted. The unambiguous becomes repressed by the ambiguous, which again comes into focus. What may have appeared as united or connected will suddenly appear as constructed and accidental. What was previously associated with rest suddenly appears as uneasiness, Grootaers writes.[12] His description creates associations toward Freud's concept of primary processes, forms of thoughts where dimensions of time and categories of space have yet not been developed, and where past and future are not anchored in reality, thoughts are informed by images, or marked by opposition and simultaneity.

For the music therapist Fritz Hegi, improvisation is a way to experiment with the content of life. The improvisation is a field of experimentation[13] where we may learn to transcend previous borders of freedom. It is a space of experience where processes of listening are expanded to the extent that there is nothing "wrong," or without value. We find ourselves in a space emptied of experience where something more honest may come out of the hidden, Hegi writes.[14]

"Flow" and "Void"

In the description of the liminal, as it appears directly within musical processes, we will find that two categories of experience are especially important: flow and void. Improvisations are related to what the psychologist Mihaly Csikszentmihalyi calls "flow"—that is, a psychic state where incidences follow each other in a united, organic way without our conscious participation. We feel we are in control of the situation, Csikszentmihalyi writes, yet we are fully absorbed. We forget to make a distinction between ourselves and surroundings, between stimulus and response, between the present and the past. Consciousness and behavior becomes one, life is expanded and full of meaning. Or as the jazz pianist Mose Allison puts it: "That's the challenge every night; trying to work toward that spot where it's all flowing."[15]

The improvisations seem to enchant the surroundings and create a flow of ideas where "everything should or ought to happen." Through this act of liberation or taking meaning back to point zero, we have made possible a space without categories, at a state where something new may grow out of an empty space. The trumpeter Roy Eldridge remembers how he sat down before he entered the bandstand in order to mentally work through what he was going to play:

> But when I got out there I didn't try to make the B-flat or whatever I was thinking of, because I'd go right into a *void* where there was no memory—nothing but me. I knew the chords and I knew the melody, and I never thought about them. I'd just be in this blank space, and the music came out anyway. It wasn't always easy.[16] (italics mine)

The key word is "void," which exactly points toward the space without categories, the place without meaning.[17] The Norwegian translation of the word "void" contains a number of the characteristics of the liminal situation we are looking for: to undo old meaning, to empty old meaning in order to create a new space to be filled with new meanings, to clear the space for something new.

At the same time this may be a frightening experience, the experience of being "betwixt and between" creates an emotional incentive to search for new meanings and new connections. Or, as Thad Jones has said:

> In such moments . . . the music finds itself at the edge of the cliff, between the known and the frighting unknown. You play for your life with your heart in your throat. The musical ideas flow freely and uninhibited directly from the unconscious without any disturbing intervention from the radio. Maybe the ideas come from a place far away. Maybe you are in touch with the creative principle or God. Anyway, you are in touch with your fellow musicians.[18]

Somewhat hesitating, Jones suggests that the liminal empty space may be filled with a metaphysical content. He is, however, quite certain about the quality of the contact he has with his co-musicians. In other words, he has had the experience of having participated in a communitas.

Victor Turner writes that incidences related to the liminal are ambiguous, and that there is often a rich symbolism expressed through the liminal situation. The Norwegian anthropologist Odd Are Berkaak has, from his analysis of rock music as a cultural form, shown how rock texts and music borrow their motives from and symbolize liminal states and phenomena. In this way rock (as well as jazz) may be read as an attempt to create a cultural space which is not invaded by the language or forms of experience prevailing in the "normal society."[19]

In the same way we could argue that improvisations in music therapy attempt to create a similar space—a psychic (re)dressing room—where people may try out alternative ways of expression and action in order to find webs of meaning which are in accordance with their own biographical experiences and expectations.

If we look closer at improvisation, or those descriptions people may give of their experiences, we meet a number of those symbols or metaphors which take part in creating the cognitive boundaries which are necessary to give the improvisation its liminal characteristics. In other words, we may study those strategies of signification we use when we use and give meaning to instruments, musical material, or extramusical themes.

Victor Turner emphasized how so-called subliminal experiences could lead the person into a new position within the culture. This could happen, for instance, by dressing in rags or in other ways to cultivate poverty. Throughout history, symbols of nakedness and disclosure have been used as opposed to something hidden or veiled. This is a polarity which in both western and eastern philosophy symbolize the split between a real and illusory world. Our daily life has been understood as an unreal, illusory world ("veil of Maya") and the true world is thought to be accessible only through transcendence of bodies, space, and time, or it will be available to us only in a future existence after death. With the emergence of the modern, both of these worlds are placed on earth, in space and time, filled with human beings. The false world is seen as a historical past, a world we have lost, while the true world is in the physical and social world that exists for us here and now. At this point a new symbolism emerges, Marshall Berman writes. As an example he chooses clothes as symbols for the civilized: "Clothes become an emblem of the old, illusory mode of life; nakedness comes to signify the newly discovered and experienced truth; and the act of taking off one's clothes becomes an act of spiritual liberation, of becoming real." Berman makes an example out of Shakespeare's King Lear: after Lear has lost both his political power and his human dignity, he throws away his clothes, a gesture which appears to be his first step toward full humanity, because, for the first time, he recognizes a connection between himself and another human being (I-Thou). This recognition enables him to grow in sensitivity and insight: "Shakespeare is telling us that the dreadful naked reality of the 'unaccommodated man' is the point from which accommodation must be made, the only ground on which real community can grow," Berman states.[20]

Odd Are Berkaak argues that the liminal is not only to be found in such substructural signification, that is, by activating signs which refer to anti-civilized, spontaneous, unplanned action. We have other strategies to seek our way out of the conventional room and into a "phantastic reality." Berkaak mentions four other such strategies of signification: (1) The pre-liminal, where identification happens in relation to "the primitive," "the natural," the child, or what may be situated outside of the cultural circle. We may also seek this "otherness" in the (2) drug experience, in trance or in transcendental experiences, or in the (3) peak-experience, in sublime, the perfect or harmonious. As a last strategy, Berkaak puts forward the (4) hybrid, the totally meaningless, that which is beyond the categories of language. In all these cases, the intention is to break down conventional categories of meaning. Through a disturbance of the senses, what the surrealists called "depayser," is sought an opening for possibilities to give new meaning to the experience, to place experience into new concepts. And what breaks through, according to this mythology, is a more honest, more authentic "self" which is not corrupted by civilization, convention, or neurosis.

The Original and the Natural

What is often happening in these cultural negotiations is the formulation of signs and symbols which point toward liminal experiences, and which again should create in us a state of "authenticity." We may acknowledge such strategies both from jazz and music therapy, whether it will be in the many myths surrounding musicians and the forms of music, or in the choice of instruments and musical material, that is, in the formation of the total emotional, verbal, and mythical discourse around these music-cultural forms.

Regarding the establishment of the pre-liminal, Berkaak defines this as creating "an original context for the interpretation of ongoing action and identity."[21] Within the artworld of jazz, we may find such strategies when critics and sometimes musicians describe jazz as a "primitive" form of art music. For instance, the French jazz critic Hugues Panassie describes Louis Armstrong in terms that witness the cultivation of the jazz musician as "the noble savage," as a person more in contact with the "real human" than the deformed, civilized European:

> One feels the intensity with which he lives each moment; one feels his innate goodness, his uprightness, his simplicity. Gifted with an extremely lively sensibility, his reactions are immediate and attractive in their finesse, spontaneity and intuition. He approaches people and things with his entire humanity . . . music is such a natural part of him that he no longer feels the need to talk about it, just as one does not talk about the air one breathes.[22]

Armstrong has an inborn goodness and humanity, he seems to be equipped with an extreme sensibility, spontaneity, and intuition. The music is a natural part of him just as his breath. In music therapy, similar pre-liminal strategies can be seen when therapists insist upon the regressive aspect of therapy, the situation when the patient returns to a childish, spontaneous, irresponsible state. In "playing like the child," a context is created where we can act "more natural," "more in accordance with our innermost" and so on. The regression is at the same time liminal by providing a wholly new perspective from which to experience the world. Or, in the world of Lili Friedemann, pioneer in German so-called collective improvisation:

The improvisation has a liberating effect. It is an action where one may act playful and wholly human at the same time. The improvisation may level out the effects of one sided intellectual education.[23]

In order to become fully human, one has to get rid of the intellectual perspective, one has to become a child. The perspective of the playful shall counteract all fragmentation and intellectualization.

The preliminal is established not least by such instruments and the musical material which we find in improvisations. First of all, we will find ethnic instruments or instruments inspired by such instruments and transformed for educational purposes. The Orff-instruments, which are part of a great many music therapists' approach, were inspired by African instruments. Lately, music therapists have grown dependent upon the world of music wholesale catalogues. Following this, the musical improvisations often take after the melodic and rythmic material connected to ethnic music forms.

At least we will find that music therapists metaphorize the musical material itself, so as to make it characterize aspects of nature or body. "Rhytmus ist leben," Fitz Hegi writes[24] before he goes on to describe how the rhythm is attached to body functions, to changes in the seasons and states in nature. In this cosmology, the experience of rhythm is connected directly to health and pathology and is viewed as a disturbance in the "rhythms of life." Hegi sees a connection between disturbances in this rhythmical life and the diseases of the civilization. Diseases such as obesity, heart diseases, disturbances in breath and sleep, flatness of emotion, as well as drug dependency, depression, and suicidal tendencies may be likened to a drumskin which is played against its own vibrations until it has broken. And Hegi finds the therapeutic recommendation of exercises in improvisation with the purpose of bringing back "the rhythm of the body."[25]

The Spontaneous, Immediate and Non-reflexive

With respect to sub- or prestructural categories in music therapy this will show itself by reference to the spontaneous, immediate nature of the improvisation. For instance, one of the first European jazz historians, Hugues Panassie wrote:

In music, primitive man generally has greater talent than civilized man. An excess of culture atrophies inspiration, and men crammed with culture tend too much to play tricks, to place inspiration by lush technique under which one finds music stripped of real vitality.[26]

Within this rhetoric, the culture with its "techniques" and "specialized knowledge" is regarded as a hindrance when it comes to spontaneity and intuition. At the same time civilization has replaced vitality with tricks. The ideal seems to be expression without cultural competence.

When the saxophone player Sonny Criss for the first time had the honor to play with Charlie Parker, he concentrated on mastering the technical challenges within the bop—"I was trying really hard," Sitt remembers—until Parker reprimanded him with the following statement: "Don't think. Quit thinkin'."[27]

Because the improvisation is an oral form of expression, where the written score is not a necessary background for the music, improvisation fits easily into this romantic mythology. "Zugleich sind aber die meisten davon stilistische Merkmale aubereuropaischer Musik, die nicht nach Noten gespielt wird," Lilli Friedemann has written. In other words, the consciousness of the oral aspect of this music has been significant for this pioneer in the field of improvisation.[28]

I remember that from the time we established our training program in music therapy at a music conservatory in Oslo (Ostlandets Musikkonservatorium) how it became a joke among the teachers that we were doing sort of musical kindergarten. In other words, within a serious institution for music education, which cultivated a classical bourgeois education built on values like duty and exercise, music therapy distinguished itself through its anti-elite values: In music therapy it became a deed to develop a form of musical interaction where everybody could participate without any previous training or knowledge. It became central to our ideology of music therapy that everyone could take part in the musical activities regardless of psychological, physical, or social presuppositions. In music therapy, total democracy with respect to musical interaction became a norm. This democracy was regarded by the classically oriented musicians as a threatening vulgarity.

The Transcendent, Peak Experience, Trance

Berkaak defines this type of liminality as super-structural, that is, as a way of aiming at the absolute as an ideal in itself.[29] Within music therapy we may find that certain "peak experiences" are classified as religious experiences. If we step outside of the improvised music therapy for a moment, we find an example of the trancendent experience in receptive music therapy, from Helen Bonny's "guided imagery and music." After having heard Beethoven's Emperor Concerto, one participant observed:

Eventually, I heard the opening strains of the slow movement of Beethoven's Emperor Concerto, welcomed them, and experienced an aesthetically pleasing sense of *flowing* with the music. Caught up in its relentless, yet gentle, motion, I was carried higher and higher towards some ethereal, pure white mountain top, bathed in golden sunlight.[30] (italics mine)

The space is here sensed as above reality, as something pure and white, filled with the aesthetically pleasing experience of "flow."

Since music therapists within the tradition of improvisation often deal with clients without language, we may have to interpret pictures of facial expression in musical engagement in order to document the peak-experience. We may also see that it is an explicit aim of music therapy to give patients such transcendental experiences.

Music therapists may also refer to what Berkaak calls the extra-structural. This means to dramatize the world outside ordinary rationality and order: the wild, untamed, and intense. All forms of thought are invalid because they represent a reason for action and experience which is outside of the individual and therefore may be felt as "inhibiting," Berkaak suggests.[31] The ideal is trance and transcendence, a state where the experience of "communitas" is realized.[32]

The Norwegian composer and jazz theorist Bjorn Kruse also emphasizes how a concept like "stream of consciousness" often is attached to creative improvisation, and often interpreted as "stream of unconsciousness" in the sense that it is close to a meditative process—a kind of artistic glossolalia.[33] The jazz violinist Stephane Grapelli puts it as follows:

Improvisation—it's like a mystery . . . When I improvise and I'm in good form, I'm like somebody half sleeping. I even forget there are people in front of me. Great improvisers are like priests: they are thinking only of their god.[34]

Roy Eldridge has also witnessed how he "saw the light" when he played with Gene Krupa:

I'd fall to pieces. The first three or four bars of my first solo I'd shake like a leaf, and you could hear it. Then this light would surround me, and it would seem as if there wasn't any band there, and I'd go right through and be all right. It was something I never understood.[35]

Great jazz musicians often went into a trance. Louis Armstrong once told the trombonist Trummy Young: "When I go on the bandstand, I don't know nobody's out there. I don't even know you're playing with me. Play good and it will help me. I don't know you're there. I'm just playing." The jazz historian Goffin sees Armstrong's talent exactly in this quality:

> Louis possesses the great gift which permits him almost automatically to enter into a trance and then to express his sensibility by means of his instrument [. . .] I know of no white musician who is able to forget himself, to create his own atmosphere, and to whip himself into a state of complete *frenzy*.[36]

Reminding ourselves that the word "frenzy" has connotations like "temporary insanity, paroxysm of mania, delirious fury or agitation, wild folly,"[37] we may understand the kind of forces which might be freed through the trance. Here we meet musically beyond the border of madness, it is a journey into insanity, with an aggression almost out of control.

Paul Nordoff once told me that he could forget about the outer world and find himself in the same "inspired state" as he had created and could observe with his clients. It is in remarks like this, for instance, that we could see his spiritual kinship with the mystical tradition, Sufi thought. Clive Robbins also used to end our meetings reading from *The Tales of the Sufi*.

Improvisation may in this mode be likened to the drug experience. In fact, the Swiss jazz musician and music therapist Fritz Hegi equates the force of the drug experience among the drug addicts with the musical intoxication originating during intensive improvisations. The intensity in the musical interaction seems to replace the need for drugs. The improvisation communicates an astonishing feeling of discovering how the need for drugs might be satisfied through a spontaneous musical expression, Hegi writes.[38]

It was experiences like this which lead Hegi to a redefinition of his work. He took free improvisation from a purely musical context into a therapeutical one (and became one of the leading music therapists in Switzerland).

According to Berkaak, we may also add such themes as energy, animals, nature, or even death to the category of extra-structural liminal references. Many of these themes are central to music therapists. For instance, we may often find that the client takes the role of an animal when we improvise.[39]

We may find that nature often establishes an associative point of departure for improvisation or that death becomes an important theme for therapy.[40]

Communitas

As a replacement for "aesthetic refinement," improvisations in music therapy seek to build a community (communitas) through temporary leveling of all social roles. During the improvisation all traditional role expectations toward the therapist are set to point zero. Instead, music therapists try to reach spontaneous and immediate "free collective improvisations" where complementary and symmetrical forms of social interaction originate spontaneously out of the musical interaction. Improvisation becomes a "common work" where emotion is the main standard for the credibility of the experience. In this way music therapy shares with the romantic mythology its skepticism against the language and the intellectual control of reality. Musical improvisation is thought of as more honest than language. Music may express what is feared or hidden by the language and intellect.

Victor Turner coined this liminal experience of closeness and mutuality between people as "communitas": "These individuals are not segmentalized into roles and statuses, but confront each other rather in the manner of Martin Buber's *I and Thou* ," Turner writes.[41] Typical of this experience is the direct, immediate, and total confrontation between identities. Buber also emphasizes the immediacy of the situation, the mere presentness, the lack of aims, means, and anticipations as necessary before a "meeting" can take place.[42]

With respect to improvisation it is especially Turner's spontaneous or existential communitas which are relevant—the spirit of community before it is written onto rules and social systems. The reference to Buber seems to fit well within humanistic ideology of music therapy which has placed the subject-subject relation as a norm for therapeutic relations—exactly as it is experienced within improvisation.

Trying to relate what is specific to the musical aspect of the improvisation to the liminal aspects of the I-Thou, we may again focus upon the aspect of "flow" —the timeless— which seems to constitute the core of spontaneous communitas. Or in Turner's words:

in passing from structure to structure many rituals pass through communitas. Communitas is almost always thought of or portrayed by actors as a timeless condition, an eternal now, as "a moment in and out of time," or as a state to which the structural view of time is not applicable.[43]

In this "eternal now" the other subject appears as a Thou. Buber also defines this appearance as an aspect outside of time, as an incidence beyond cause and effect. In trying to fix a Thou in time it becomes an It. In reading Buber, we will again meet the notion about the "meanwhile," the time between, experienced as "flow" and uncategorized as "void"; the empty space, a point not captured by any system of coordination.[44]

This moment is known and commented upon both by jazz critics and music therapists. Commenting upon the statement by Thad Jones referred to earlier, the Norwegian musicologist Kjell Oversand has applied terms as if he had been describing one of Turner's communitas experiences.

> What counts here is the aesthetics of the presence. You have to give yourself totally, without reservations. Attitudes like egoism, possessive feelings and the spirit of competition have to give way to generosity, closeness, and communion. You develop a presence close to telepathic intuition. It is not enough that you believe this or that is going to happen. By beholding behind the closed eyes of your co-musicians, and in sensing the nerve-impulses and the movements of the muscles in their bodies, you will attain a security in relation to what is going to happen. In such moments improvisation is like the language which spontaneously originates between lovers, and what is usually called erotics.[45]

In this description, the experience of communitas is taken into the realm of the erotic. Sensibility has gone under the skin and the feeling of communion has attained the status of telepathic dimension.

Also with music therapy, Buber has been called upon as a witness of truth in the refutation of behavior therapy and its ambition to transform all life into a possible reinforcement program. By supposing that the Thou may only exist in a mutual, unconditional relation, all attempts to inscribe the therapeutic relation in an object-world are invalidated. In letting the unpredictable improvisation establish the frame for interaction, we have created a counter-position in relation to the positivist ideal of prediction and control of human relations.[46] If the essential aspect of therapy is seen as changing the relation to one's self, we may find that the liminal aspects of improvisation keeps this channel of communication open.

Transformation

Thus improvisation makes change possible—with or without therapeutic consequences. In jazz, music is often described as peak moments where the improvisation implies to live through a drama which leads to the acknowledgement of wholeness, meaning, self-awareness, and so on. A good illustration might be the rock musician David Crosby's (from Crosby, Stills, Nash, and Young) ultimate meeting with John Coltrane "live" at a toilet in a jazz club in Chicago. In his biography, Crosby informs us that he was full of drugs before he was taken to this club "on the South Side [. . .] to a club called McKey's, which was at 163rd and Cottage Grove, which I can say is very far down. Very far. We were absolutely. I swear to you on my word of honor, the only three white people in there."[47]

Thus both outer and inner circumstances should have been present in order to create a ritual journey, which actually happens. After Coltrane and McCoy Tyner have given their turns, Crosby is literally driven out of the room by the intensity of Elvin Jones' drums. The intensity becomes too strong, and he has to flee into the toilet to handle the situation:

> I was leaning my head against the cool vomit green tile and drawing deep breaths, trying to calm down, when the door went *wham!* and in walks John Coltrane, still playing at top intensity and volume, totally into it. He blew me out so bad I slid down the wall. The guy was still playing his solo. He hadn't stopped. I don't think he ever knew I was in that room. He never saw that little ofay kid in the corner, you know, but he totally turned my mind to Jell-O at that point and that was my John Coltrane experience.[48]

The experience is beyond any attempt of categorization, beyond even the liminal. Crosby's mental equipment is totally transformed into jelly.

I could add to this story another self-experienced "tales of the Coltrane" from the beginning of the sixties, when Coltrane visited Oslo with the same quartet described by Crosby. We were a group of teenagers who for a while every Saturday night had gathered in front of the record player listening to Coltrane. Thus we had established our own little community—communitas—as a jazz avant-garde outpost in the East side of Oslo. After the concert, one of the consecrated actually was allowed to help Elvin Jones with the drums. Following this incident, he got the habit of talking about "Elvin and I," which by the group was perceived as an improper infiltration into an original and sacred community by one of the mortals. The episode generated an unusual amount of witty comments over a long period of time.

John Coltrane was probably aware of the disparate qualities of his followers, even though he did not have any well-defined intentions about his communication. When Coltrane was asked if he was consciously trying to raise or influence his audience, or if he felt any responsibility toward his followers, he gave expression of a true Rogerian "non-directive" attitude.

> Sure, I feel this, and this is one of the things I am concerned about now. I just don't know how to go about this [. . .] I think it's going to have to be very subtle; you can't ram philosophies down anybody's throat, and the music is enough! That's philosophy. I think the best thing I can do at this time is try to get myself in shape and know myself. If I can do that, then I'll just play, you see, and leave it at that. I believe that I will do it, if I really can get myself and be just as I feel I should be and play it. And I think they'll get, because music goes a long way—it can influence.[49]

Coltrane did not wish to enforce upon anyone a ready made theory. He is not supporting the prevailing categorical ways of thinking, the affinity to Bergson's concept of the *intuitive* understanding is closer to Coltrane's epistemology. He is puzzled by how to influence anyone and chooses the Socratiac "know thyself"—transformation may originate in the listener when the music flows freely from himself at the moment when he finds himself in contact with his self.

We might say that the question about the character and scope of transformation appears in the evaluation of the liminal. We need to discuss what is meant by transformation both in the delineation of the sublime in the relation to the liminal and in therapy, where we have to discuss whether the "ritual" change is endurable and profound, or only temporary. The anthropologists[50] have also raised the question, is the ritual process really involving a transformation, or does it only deal with the transportation from one state to another and back again? The "as if" character of rituals should inform us that, even though dramatic, the peak jazz experience will only leave a more or less lasting change. Or, could we really say that such moments may serve as an incentive toward change in the sense that our basic orientation toward life is transformed in crucial ways?

This question seems important to art therapy. And this discussion, which seems to be more remote in the anthropological theory, is a main theme in the theory of art therapy. Here we also find that the question of reflexivity appears. This because, as the anthropologist Barbara Myerhoff suggests, there will easily emerge an opposition between "flow" and "reflexivity." This means that the ritual presupposes that thought and control must be played down in order for the liminal to appear. At the same time, reflexive attention (not, at least, from the side of the therapist) is perceived necessary to install permanent change and transformation. The discussion between letting oneself be taken by the ritual process and at the same time keeping the distance, that is, to attain what Eliade has described as "archaic techniques of controlled ecstasy"[51] is urgent for the therapist, especially in those forms of improvised group therapy where the therapist carries the responsibility of both leading and fueling the creative group processes at the same time as control and overview over the situation are maintained. It is probably within this practice that music therapy is approaching a point in culture where it might generate problems with the surrounding reality—that is, its so-called scientific credibility, as well as the surgeon general.

However, a therapist with therapeutic self-experience, in addition to knowledge about client history and ways of being, will not let him/herself be led by the method, but will find the balance between structure and anti-structure in the improvisation.[52] We might illustrate this with an example from the Norwegian music therapist Ruth Eckhoff, who, taking departure from psychoanalytical theory of object-relations, has taken improvisation into her work, even with psychotic patients.[53] In other words, people (to stay in the terminology) who live in a permanent liminality, where boundaries between me and not-me are lacking and where the surroundings are felt threatening, seen from the background of a chaotic and unstructured world of experience—confronted with these people, the case is of course not to create another "void" through uninhibited "flow." The task is rather to use structured improvisation to help the client organize his psychic life in the direction of the formal and conventional.

In her article, Myerhoff raises the question of what is meant by "transformation," in other words, what is really transformed—self awareness, state of consciousness, belief, feelings, knowledge, or understanding? If we let the music therapist answer, she will suggest a pattern of transformation experienced at different levels. In her music therapy, Eckhoff takes departure from a theoretical model which contains five levels of *experience-in-depth*. The client may (a) act formal, polite, or play a role, (b) be emotionally involved (here and now), (c) act symbolically or through processes of transference, (d) be controlled by archaic feelings, or (e) experience loss of control with a concomitant acting out. In work with the psychotic, the therapist will move strategically from (e) to (a). The opposite process may be a necessary experience for the neurotic client seeking behavioral or emotional change.

This model informs us about possible different levels in the liminal experience. It also tells us that by changing strategy between structured and free, programmatic, and associative processes, we may create in-depth experiences where the processes of transformation coincide with the need of the client.

From Chaos the Communitas

In Eckhoff's work, improvisation is followed by verbal interaction. In this way, orientation toward reality is explicitly tied to language and everyday life. In other words, reflexivity is taken care of through the language. Our question here is, If the musical improvisation is a *non-verbal* process, can it initiate change or transformational processes?

If we attempt to read a case study from improvised music therapy with persons without language, we will see how our model of interpretation may explain even such processes of change. For instance, we find the following case description of a nine-year-old Down's Syndrome boy given by Paul Nordoff and Clive Robbins. The case is given as an example of the response category of "chaotic-creative beating":

> It is important that this child be musically stimulated—he himself must be allowed to improvise. The therapist does not try to impose musical order for this would inhibit the *inherent* creativeness of the child's ego. The responsive work of the therapist precipitates moments of musical perception which lead the child to relate his beating to the improvisation. At first these *fleeting responses* consist of only one or two musically related beats, but they form the basis for therapeutic work which gradually secures the child's confidence in himself. He feels himself within the music and in beating can exteriorize his experience. He enjoys the musical give-and-take and anticipates the next working session [. . .]. His musical intelligence is realized gradually and the *intimate rapport* consolidates the work. Response 3, Limited Rhythmic Freedom, becomes established. *A musical companionship* arises which makes further therapeutic coactivity possible.[54] (italics mine)

This music therapeutical allegory contains several of the elements we have described within the frame of a rite of passage. The child is free to express himself after a supposed inborn creative ability tied to his ego—"a dynamic source of complex rythmic impulses lived within him."[55] Thus, the musical material is linked to the pre-liminal, to a kind of "real human nature" which is present in spite of "extremely limited possibilities and very little speech." In other words, this is not only a more original expression, it is thus an expression freed from cultural competence which is released.

> In response to the improvisation he would play impulsive rythmic patterns and intricate syncopations. His "music" was *free, playful, and completely unpredictable*, yet it bore a *fragmented rythmic structure* that was related to the improvisation [. . .]. He seemed to be at that stage of inner chaos where creative freedom merges into *imcomprehensibility* and *incoherence*. The drum-beating was not at first consciously self-directed activity for this boy. He was *utterly absorbed* in realizing expression of the rythmic impulses that lived within him. Consciousness of what he was doing developed later in the session as he experienced his beating impulses being answered in the music that surrounded him. When this happened, and the boy and I *really met* in the music, the activity that had been a *playful and unpredictable* game began to take on the form of a musical give and take.[56] (italics mine)

The introductory phase is marked by the unpredictable and fragmented chaos moving at the border of the comprehensible. At the very threshold (*limen*) of the meaningless and disconnected, where we do not hear music, but "music," the boy experienced a form of reflexivity where he recognizes himself through the music which comes to him. The experience of "recognition," where the undefined and chaotic immediate inner life finds an answer in an outer form, that is, the improvisation of Paul Nordoff, leads to order and mutually—"a musical give and take."

The mutuality at the same time has the character of communitas. "When this happened the boy and I *really* met in the music" (italics mine), Nordoff recalls. At the same time he reveals that the improvisation has a mark of Buber's "meeting." The experience is "real" in a way that is distinct from the ordinary reality. The music therapist and pianist have stepped out of the formalized roles, their musical interaction have become a relationship on equal terms, expressed in expressions like "intimate rapport" and "musical companionship." After the improvisation (re-aggregation), general change in the behavior of the boy is also noticed: "Towards the end of the work one of the teachers noticed a change in the boy. In his daily life he seemed generally more awake and purposeful."[57]

We might say that transformation here takes place through a non-verbal process. Reflexivity is created by recognition, when the child notices that his own categories of experience are in accordance with his experience of the music—or vice versa. In the discussion between therapists who differ on the role of verbalization in music therapy (music as, or music in, therapy), this might be an example of how change may happen without the experience being categorized through verbal concepts. It seems relevant again to refer to the works of the French philosopher Henri Bergson and his concept of "intuitive perception." This concept points to the fact that all verbal acknowledgement presupposes the acknowledgement of an immediate character, an intuitive acknowledgement which takes hold of the phenomena, not least music, in its movement, transience, and transformation.

Myerhoff comments upon how the processes of transformation originating in performance rituals never can be forced.[58] Thus, transformation will seldom be an explicit goal for such rituals, although it is expected that the person changes his position, status, etc., after the ritual. Since Martin Buber is lurking behind Turner's conception of communitas, it seems reasonable to draw more out of Buber by referring to his "philosophy of the meeting," which touches on this unconstrained aspect of I-Thou. Buber calls the experience of communitas a meeting. This meeting comes to us in *grace*, he writes,[59] which reminds us that such meetings may not be planned or written in any time-managed organized schedule.

This article is dedicated to all the Phoenicians, who keep the rites of passage alive in music therapy.

Notes

1. *Webster's Dictionary* defines improvisation as "to make, invent, or arrange offhand" (Bruscia, 1978: 5-6). In Latin (de, ex) *improviso*, which means unforeseen.

2. *The Harvard Brief Dictionary of Music*, see Bruscia, 1978.

3. "E hat zu trun mit Ausprobieren, Herumkramen, mit planlosem Aussuchen und Stobern," Grootaers, 1983: 245-246.

4. See Kruse, 1990/91: 9.

5. Grootaers, 1983: 245-246.

6. "Music therapists strive to improvise music of the highest artistic quality and beauty, however, they always accept the client's improvising at

whatever level it is offered whether consisting of musical or sound forms, and regardless of its artistic or aesthetic merit" (Bruscia, op. cit.: 5-6).

7. Bateson, 1973.

8. Schultz and Lavenda, 1990: 158.

9. Schultz and Lavenda, 1990: 156.

10. "During the intervening liminal period, the state of the ritual subject (the 'passenger', or 'liminar') becomes ambiguous, neither here nor there, betwixt and between all fixed points of classification; he passes through a symbolic domain that has few or none of the attributes of his past and coming state" (Turner, 1974: 232).

11. 1969: 96.

12. "Durch ihre regelhafte Ungeplantheit garantiert die Improvisation ein Aufleben der strukturellen Gebundenheit des Seelischen schlechthin. [. . .] Beim Herumkramen in alten Sachen z.B. machen wir glechsam Neuentdeckungen und konnen uns gleichzeitig in Gedanken 'verlieren.'" (ibid.: 246) [. . .] In einer Improvisation geschieht mehereres gleichzeitig. Dasselbe kann meheres zugleichbedeuten; die Bedeutungen selbst sind metamorphosisch wandelbar. Bedeutungen gelangen zu Umdeutungen. Eindeutiges drangt auf Zwielichtigkeit; in ein-und demselben Drangen werden wir Ambitendenzen gewahr. Was jetzt noch als Zusammenhalt erscheint, stellt sich ruchwirkend als Verkleisterung von etwas Anderem heraus; was Jetzt als Ruhe sich ausbreitet, erweist sich bald als Unheimliches" (ibid.: 250).

13. Or as Kenny suggests, a field of play, see Kenny, 1989.

14. "Die Improvisaiton ist ein Experimentierfeld dafur, die bisherigen Grenzen der freiheit uberschreiten zu lernen, ohne jemand anders dabei einzuschranken. Sie ist auch ein Erfahrungsraum, um das Zuhoren so zu erwietern, dab er kein 'falsch,' 'schlecht' oder 'wertlos' mehr gibt, sondern nur noch ein ehrliches, offenes oder ein verstecktes So-sein." Hegi, 1986: 21 15 Leonard, 1987: 75.

16. Ibid.: 73.

17. In The Concise Oxford Dictionary, 'void' is defined in terms of empty, vacant, invalid, not binding, useless, lacking, free form, empty space, render invalid, emit, quit, evacuate (Latin vacuus).

18. Oversand, 1987: 74.

19. See Berkaak, 1990.

20. Berman, 1982: 108.

21. Ibid.: 195.

22. Panassie, 1971: 23-24, quoted after Gioia, 1988: 19.

23. "Die improvisation wirkt befreiend. Ein Tun, bei dem man zugleich spielendes Kind und ganzer Mensch sein darf, kann die Wirkung einseitiger intellektueller Bildung ausgleichen." Freidemann, 1974, Vorwort.

24. 1986: 32.

25. "Es besteht ein Zusammenhang zwischen Storungen im rhythmischen Lebenslauf und modernen Zivilisationskrankheiten. All die menschlichen Schicksale wie beispielsweise Fettleibigkeit, Herzkrankheiten, Atem- und Gefuhlsflachheit, Schlafstorungen, Sucht, Depression und Suizidalitat sind vergleichbar mit einer Trommel, deren Fell so lange ihre eigene Schwingung geschlagen wird, bis dieses reifst" (ibid.: 35).

26. Gioia, 1988: 29-30.

27. Leonard, 1987: 74.

28. Friedemann, 1974: 8.

29. Berkaak, op. cit.: 206.

30. Bonny and Savary, 1973: 125.

31. Op. cit.: 211.

32. Ibid.: 214.

33. 1990/91: 9.

34. Leonard, op. cit.: 74.

35. Ibid.: 72.

36. Goffin, 1944: 167, quoted after Gioia, op. cit.: 30, min uthevelse.

37. *The Concise Oxford Dictionary.*

38. Hegi, op. cit.: 19.

39. See the history about the Bear and the Bird in Ruud, 1990a, b. The British music therapist Mary Priestly wrote in a commentary to this story the following: "Having said that I must admit I am intrigued by the improvisations on the bear and the bird because a patient of mine, who did very well indeed, also did improvisations on these two creatures. We reversed the roles between us. He became altogether more bear and less bird. He chose himself, perhaps they have archetypal significance in this hemisphere and are included in the folklore of the north" (personal correspondence, March 7, 1978).

40. See Kenny, 1982, on the theme of "death" in music therapy.

41. Turner, 1969: 132.

42. See Buber, 1968.

43. Turner, 1974: 238.

44. Buber, 1968: 31.

45. Oversand, op. cit.

46. This is one of my main points in my book *Music Therapy and Its Relationship to Current Treatment Theories*; see Ruud, 1980: 40.

47. Crosby and Gottlieb, 1988: 64.

48. Ibid.: 65-66.

49. Kofsky, 1970: 241.

50. See Myerhoff, 1990.

51. For a discussion of the relation between music therapy and shamanism, see Moreno, 1988.

52. "Wisdom is always to find the appropriate relationship between structure and communitas under the given circumstances of time and place, to accept each modality when it is paramount without rejecting each other, and not to cling to one when its present impetus is spent" Turner (1969: 139).

53. Eckhoff, Ruth. Lecture at the Nordic Conference on Improvisation in Music Therapy, Sandane, May 2-4, 1991.

54. Nordoff and Robbins, 1971: 72.

55. Ibid.: 28.

56. Ibid.: 28-29.

57. Ibid.: 29.

58. Myerhoff, 1990: 246.

59. See also Bollnow, 1969.

References

Bateson, Gregory (1973). Theory of Play and Phantasy. *In Steps to an Ecology of Mind*, Paladin.

Berkaak, Odd Are (1990). Erfaringer fra riskosonen—*Opplevelse, utforming og traderings-monster i rock and roll*. Avhandling for den filosofiske doktorgrad, institutt for Sosialantropologi, UiO.

Berman, Marshall (1982). *All that is solid melts into air. The experience of modernity.* Simon and Schuster, New York.

Bollnow, Otto Friedrich (1969). *Eksistensfilosofi og pedagogikk.* Fabritius of Sonners Forlag, Oslo.

Bonny, Helen, and Louis Savary (1973). *Music and your mind. Listening with a New Consciousness.* Harper and Row, London.

Bruscia, Kenneth E. (1978). *Improvisational Models of Music Therapy.* Charles C. Thomas Publishers. Springfield, Illinois.

Buber, Martin (1968). *Jeg og Du.* Cappelens upopulaere skrifter, Cappelen Oslo.

Crosby, David, and Carl Gottlieb (1988). *Long time gone.* Mandarin, London.

Friedemann, Lilli (1974). *Gemeinsame Improvisation auf Instrumenten.* Barenreiter-Verlag, Kassel.

Gioia, Ted (1988). *The Imperfect Art. Reflections on Jazz and Modern Culture.* Oxford University Press, New York.

Goffin, Robert (1944). *Jazz: From the Congo to the Metropolitan.* Doubleday, New York., quoted after Gioia, 1988.

Grootaers, Frank (1983). Improvisation. In H.-H. Decker-Voigt (ed.), *Handbuch Musiktherapie.* Eres Edition, Lilienthal/Breman.

Hegi, Fritz (1986). *Improvisation und Musiktherapie. Moglichkeiten und Wirkungen von freier Musik.* Junfermann-Verlag, Paderborn.

Kenny, Carolyn (1982). *The Mythic Artery. The Magic of Music Therapy.* Ridgeway Publishing Company. Atascadero, California.

Kenny, Carolyn (1989). *The Field of Play: A Guide for the Theory and Practice of Music Therapy.* Ridgeview Publishing Company.

Kofsky, Frank (1970). *Black Nationalism and the Revolution in Music.* Pathfinder Press, New York.

Kruse, Bjorn (1990/91). Improvisasjon—en kreativ prosess. *Opptakt.* Informasjonsblad for Norges musikkhogskole, nr. 2, 5. argang, s. 8-11.

Leonard, Neil (1987). *Jazz. Myth and Religion.* Oxford University Press, Oxford.

Moreno, Josef (1988). The Music Therapist: Creative Arts Therapist and Contemporary Shamen. *The Arts in Psychotherapy*, vol. 5, pp. 271-280.

Myerhoff, Barbara (1990). "The transformation of consciousness in ritual performance: Some thoughts and questions. I. R. Schechner and W. Appel (eds.) *By Means of Performance. Intercultural Studies of Theatre and Ritual.* Cambridge University Press, Cambridge.

Nordoff, Paul, and Clive Robbins (1971). *Therapy in Music for Handicapped Children*. Victor Gollancz Ltd., London.

Oversand, Kjell (1987). Improvisasjon og tilstedevaerelsens estetikk. In Ledang (ed.), *Musikklidenskapelig*. Solum forlag.

Panassie, Hugues (1971). *Louis Armstrong*, Scribner, New York, quoted after Gioia, 1988.

Ruud, Even (1980). *Music Therapy and Its Relationship to Current Treatment Theories*. Magnamusic Baton, St. Louis.

Ruud, Even (1990a). *Musikk som kommunikasjon og samhandling*. Solum, Oslo.

Ruud, Even (1990b). A Phenomenological Approach to Improvisation in Music Therapy. A Research method. 6th World Congress of Music Therapy, Rio de Janeiro, July 16, 1990.

Schultz, Emily A., and Robert H. Lavenda (1990). *Cultural Anthropology. A Perspective on the Human Condition*. West Publishing Company, St. Paul, Minnesota.

Turner, Victor (1969). *The Ritual Process. Structure and Anti-Structure*. Cornell University Press, Ithaca and London. Sixth printing, 1989.

Turner, Victor (1974). *Dramas, Fields, and Metaphors. Symbolic Action in Human Society*. Cornell University Press, Ithaca and London. Sixth printing, 1990.

13

Sound and Meaning

David Burrows

Prelude to David Burrows

David and I first met at Phoenecia. He was not a music therapist, but rather a musicologist and philosopher. A quiet man, an observer, David did not often speak in those early days of dialog in the "barn" up in the woods. But he did dance. And, to me, his dance bespoke his early years growing up in Hawaii. Although in his present life he appeared to be a pensive and understated East coast intellectual, something about those moist woods and our improvisations seemed to uncover the Native influence. And it was a delight.

Every year in Phoenecia, in the quiet of the setting and under the inspiration of our sound, David seemed to blossom and come alive in ways which city life does not permit. At other times we would meet at various cafes around New York University or peruse museums and have exhilarating conversations about music and the meaning of things.

One year David and Barbara Hesser even made a trip out to the Wild West to visit me in California and we all went to The Deer Lodge in Ojai and rubbed shoulders with the Hell's Angels and ate sloppy beef ribs. This encounter had the same quality as our experience in Phoenecia—adventure, discovery, and connection.

David agreed to participate in my doctoral research. His influence was central in my work. He told me that *The Field of Play* sounded like a land, a territory to travel in and get to know. "Couldn't you create a topography to describe this land, a map?" Thus the models for *The Field of Play* were born.

In his scholarship, David lives an interdisciplinary existence. He "plays" in the fields of music, musicology, philosophy, history, linguistics, and more. He weaves many worlds and in reading David's work, even though it is dramatically abstract at times, one feels that rhythm of life—alive and grounded perhaps by his sense of resounding waters crashing on black sands or moist forests waiting for storms. He retains the range and depth of early place and time. In fact, our ongoing "tease" is that I only care about space and David only cares about time. That is absurd, really, because the truth is that "we only care." Categories are places to play.

David teaches music at New York University and in his essay here attempts to reconcile an understanding of the concept "meaning" with ideas he had earlier developed in *Sound, Speech, and Music.*

Consider the possibility that sound has been the main catalyst for the vast expansion of the human field of meaning beyond the dimensions it has for other creatures.[1] I will conclude with some of the considerations I believe support this idea.

But right from the outset "meaning" itself is a problem. It is hard to imagine a point at which all uses of the word intersect:

- know what I mean?
- I mean business
- or anyway I mean well, it's just that . . .
- what is "polyandry" supposed to mean?
- those three have a really meaningful relationship
- and what exactly does music mean to you?
- it don't mean a thing if it ain't got that swing
- and what does it all mean anyway?

On this dubious showing meaning can have to do, among other things, with reference ("what is 'polyandry' supposed to mean?"), it can have to do with depth of satisfaction derived form a pattern of interaction ("those three have a really meaningful relationship"), with an attitude of determination with respect to a future outcome ("I mean business"), or with a larger purpose ("and what does all that mean, anyway?").[2] But in all these cases it has to do with something absent from the immediate sensory surface of experience. In his classic study of musical meaning, Leonard B. Meyer quotes a definition of meaning-fulness taken from a book on logic by Morris R. Cohen: ". . . anything acquires meaning if it is connected with, or indicates, or refers to, something beyond itself, so that its full nature points to and is revealed in that connection" (*Emotion and Meaning in Music*, p. 34).

The roots of meaning lie, I believe, in the body's negotiations involving movement and perception and metabolism on which survival depends.[3] But meaning is directed at things that are not there, things that are reached by means of other things that are there. We start talking about "meaning," rather than "exchanges with the environment," when the negotiations deal with an ideal territory beyond the reach of the body and its senses in the here and now. Building on the animal wisdom that a stick will reach a persimmon that the unaided body cannot, humankind has evolved techniques of mediacy to get at mental persimmons that can be reached by no other means—in fact, with symbols it is often hard to know the persimmon from the stick.

The great thing about persimmons of the mind is that they can be reached from anywhere at any time. In thinking, we are not subject to the constraints of the physical body as it moves, pulled by gravity snug against the earth's crust, through a landscape ruled by far and near, a landscape sparsely furnished with real persimmons and booby-trapped with false persimmons of every description.

The field of meaning is an interindividually collaborative way out of the here and now, a way to avoid being stuck in what the senses say there is. Of necessity, the act of constructing meaning takes place, like any other act, here and now, even though it aspires to connect us with something beyond the present reach of the senses. The field of meaning makes room in the present for what we call the past and the future, including the deep time no one could ever know directly, and the deep space where no one will ever travel. In fact, the elaborated and extended conception of time held by humans is unthinkable apart from the field of meaning, of which it forms an essential part.

Meaning is thus a function of ambition and optimism, that same expansionist tendency that is forever seeing greener grass on the other side of the fence, and the overall success of the field of meaning reinforces the conviction that the good stuff lies further off still, beyond the horizon of the senses. Embarking on the project of meaning rests on the faith, or sometimes the fear, that there is always more than meets the eye. The world itself can seem to be only the sign of a great beyond that emerges as a possible answer to the question: "and what does it all mean, anyway?" (Oddly enough, though, all these beyonds are wholly within, as far as can be known, a matter of neuronal configurations.)

Humankind's most distinctive evolutionary innovation has been its expansion of the field of meaning far out beyond what it is for other living things. The succulent rodent the kitten is chasing is "really" its own tail (and this is a useful reminder that the fields existed before we humans came along). But the making and maintaining and dismantling of meanings is the most characteristic human activity, one we give more energy to than we give to any other.

A radical and paradoxical premise of the field of meaning is that mental entities—concepts, images—that have no standing in the world reported by our senses have nevertheless as much right as physical entities to be considered real. The ultimate test of the premise has to be their impact on the body's survival in the physical world. The persimmons of the mind are inedible, and no amount of talking to ourselves will talk the real ones down off the tree: the impact of concepts finally depends on their usefulness in organizing collective action to bring about favorable changes in the physical world. The field of meaning is the extension of basic interactions among the members of pack or herd or tribe to an ultrareality that our hands will never reach, where our feet will never take us; the basis of meaning is a tacit agreement among the members of some group to act as though certain intangibles (possible persimmons, possible standing on someone's back, possible ladders, possible tree-shaking or tree-climbing) are as much a part of reality as tangibles, visibles, and edibles. The agreement is sustained by the possibility of translating some of meaning back into collaborative action in the here and now. Social consensus is the ground from which meaning grows and without which it will die. Human brains evolved in about equal measure as organs of intersubjectivity and as organs for the representation of the world. The openness of the field of meaning (the constant reconfiguration of its contents in response to evolving circumstance) reveals it as a natural extension of the open systems that it serves: the individual organism and the societal superorganism. The practical consequence of the ability on the part of the members of a community to access one another's memories, plans, programs, and hypotheses through vocal signs for concepts has given Darwinian encouragement to the vast dilation of our capacity for all those things.

Like an unformatted diskette, the field of meaning is unstructured in newborns on its most basic, in this case neuronal, level, and this is what accounts for the freedom different language communities and cultures have to impose widely differing systems of constraints on it, resulting in the world's diversity of cultures and languages. But we are not free to act in the field of meaning without constraints of any kind, because no action of any kind is possible without constraints and resistances: no treks without footing, no chewing without morsels. The euphoria of weightlessness soon turns to panic unless carefully designed compensations are available. In the case of manipulation of symbols, those doing the manipulating must take responsibility for articulating and maintaining the parameters within which the activity takes place, as well as for the actions themselves. In the words of the literary critic Alvin Kernan:

> Meaning, not raw facts, is what humanity seeks, and society is a collection of kits or codes for processing raw facts into meaning. Ordering is one of the simplest and most durable human methods

for finding and making meaning. Take a variety of things and put them in some kind of relationship, a simple sequence, a taxonomy, a hierarchy, or a cause-and-effect pattern, say, and they make sense, apparently for no better reason than the tautological one that order and relationship are felt by human beings to be meaningful.... The periodic table of elements, the Indo-European family of languages, the Ten commandments, the multiplication table, the metric system, the Linnean taxonomy of plants: so extensive are its charts, tables, structures, and classification systems, that culture can be said to be composed of an extensive series of interlocking schemes of order. The ultimate aim of society might well be viewed ... as assembling all these individual systems into a master system of knowledge, a unified field not of physical forces but of culture.[4]

(Note, however, that whenever the "master system of knowledge" is solidified beyond the possibility of renegotiation, the result is a monolithic, authoritarian society.)

It would be hard to think of anything at all that could never be meaningful, that could not be inserted into some structure or other and acquire meaning there: in fact, just thinking of something extracts it from some nexus of meaning in our memories, and is a move (sometimes an abortive one) in the process of constructing new meaning. Yet whenever there is meaning there is at least the potential for meaninglessness: the two are as interdependent as figure and ground. Meaninglessness can be thought of as everything that lies outside the class of everything that would be meaningful in some context.

In fact there is an endemic low-level anxiety about the human condition that derives from the ever-present possibility that the coordinates for symbolic action, dependent after all on the cooperation of many individuals, will slip out of focus and leave us floundering. In dreams, in fantasy, and in madness the bare canvas of the field of meaning sometimes shows through the surface of events and images. Certainly the field of meaning is the home territory of doubt and anomie, which reign there to whatever extent the field lacks the ordered patterning that is a central part of our conception of the meaningful. Meaninglessness can be anguishing, with the anguish of disorientation. Or it can be fun, with the fun of absurdity.

Symptoms of the slippery, labile nature of the field of meaning: irony; much of laughter; most tears. Some of the anxiety rooted in the field of meaning spills over into the physical: we are often to be found clutching and fondling pencils or other worry beads of all sorts, giving chewing gum a good working over, feeling for resistances to compensate in a symbolic way for the nebulousness of the field of meaning. It acts like a vacuum, pulling out of us a flood of arm-waving, scrawling, chattering that reaches desperate and deafening levels at times, all designed to fill in blanks and maintain order. In any active channel of communication silence is more charged than any one signal would be, because it is the potential for a whole range of possible meanings. Because the vacuum is always there, the construction of meaning must go on every waking hour; and while we sleep, dreaming takes up and continues the work.   .

Here is some of what comes to us along with the field of meaning:

- as the great alternative to what the senses tell us is the case, it is what makes it possible for us to conceive nothingness;
- because it has no inherent limits, it is our opening out into grandiosity (as well as down into incoherence);
- because it is outside the surveillance of the senses—because in it things are represented and not presented—it gives us our great opportunity for falsehood, which can only come into being along with the possibility of representing truly;
- there are no certainties here: the field of meaning comprises the field of human possibilities, and, at that, only that share of it that is under human control;
- it assumes the imploded form of "the unconscious."

There is a stratigraphy of meanings. One stratum, not always present (only fitfully so in music, for example) is the indexical, in which the thing that meets the eye (or ear, or . . .) stands for something else, which may very well stand for something else again: the visual squiggle "polyandry" stands for a sound, which stands for a concept, which stands for a complex pattern of behavior. In this case among many others this does not mean much apart from an entire way of life of which it forms a (mostly) smoothly functioning part. And a single sign may function on more than one stratum. In fitting into African American musical style a "blue note," for example, not primarily an indexical sign, will also index that style (and goes on to fit into, and index, African American culture generally).

Ultimately things do not mean much unless they cohere with other things in the field of meaning. So indexical meaning may get us into the field, but meaningfulness depends on the insertion of meaning-bearing units into structures, which in all likelihood form part of other structures . . . and so forth. Constructing meaning involves building and maintaining structures, making connections among their con-stituents, setting up resonances. Social, metaphysical, mathematical structures, all resonating with each other. (Or not, depending.)

Music certainly means well, but does so with a radically different emphasis from that found in the sibling enterprise of speech. As we have just seen, music can participate in the indexical stratum, but it stresses instead the stratum of pattern-making, and can do so in part because of its comparative independence of the indexical, relative to speech. The sound we label "E flat" played or sung by a musician work-ing in the European tradition can make its distinctive contribution because it is not "F," and because of the precise respect in which it is not "F" or "A flat" or any other pitch in the well-tempered tuning system, and further, perhaps, because of its position relative to "F" and "A flat" and other tones within one of the pre-existent schemes called a key. It exemplifies that layer of meaning that has to do with fitting into and confirming, or possibly extending, or possibly attacking patterns and conventions already in existence before the would-be meaningful act takes place.

At the bottom of the stratigraphy of musical meaning is a level of direct responses to such things as loud and soft, high and low, pierc-ing and mellow timbre: this is the level least influenced by cultural con-ditioning, the level permitting the least leeway to individual interpre-tation. It is also the level that acts within the smallest spans of time.

More encompassing timespans may activate such responses as "singing along," either incipiently or overtly, or moving in time to the music. Especially in this last case there is considerable room for differ-ences in interpretation, and once such participation assumes conven-tional forms (such as a conductor's beat, or certain dance steps) then clearly culture is playing a large role. Almost entirely cultural are the judgments we make about key (for conventional European-derived musics) or genre. On several different levels, the operant variables—notably metrical patterns, or modal hierarchies—appear to be cultural stylizations of basic perceptual categories. Any explicit extramusical references make up another level, and the texts of songs play a role here. Freest of all (though not at all free of cultural influence) is any imagery inspired by the music. All this of course unfolding simultane-ously.

Actual music making is not a matter of rehearsing quasi-Platonic forms, or we would spend our musical time running through scales and clapping out duple and triple time. But the surface configurations—the rhythms, the melodic motives and so on that make up musical per-formances (configurations themselves typically conformable, even in composer-intensive repertories, to culturally established practice)—depend in large part for their meaningful effects of closure, intensification, and so forth on their relations to such background reference systems as key form.

Thus each note in a piece is proposed as a point where many schemes intersect. Each note has a position on the loud/soft continuum. If the scheme "key" applies, the note occupies a place within the tonal hierarchy. It falls at a certain place within a phrase; it falls on a certain beat. It has its relevance, both small and indispensable, to form, genre, and style. It is assessed nearly instantaneously with respect to all these systems on all their various levels, and its import—its contribution to the music's meaning—is a synthesis of all these assessments. Naturally, analogous processes of judging fit in relation to norms take place on every level of musical structure, and not just on the level of single notes: the rhythm may fit into a groove, the swing without which it does not mean a thing. And none of the above means a thing unless—the bottom line—engaging in it gives the participant more satisfaction than anything else he or she might be doing at the time.[5]

There is a convergence between this model for the production of musical meaning—each note the answer to a sense of present insufficiency or instability in the form of an act directed at a future resolution that draws on (relatively fixed) schemata and (relatively fluid) experiences accumulated in the present of the past—and the models that have been proposed for semantic meaning: see for example Mark Johnson's discussion of John Searle's conceptions of Network background.[6] Mode and meter together occupy a position in music that corresponds loosely to that taken up by categories like Network and Background in relation to speech. And such models suggest a yet more general underlying model for all of the activities of organisms. Any act at all (biting into a carrot, wiping one's nose) is directed at correcting some immediate aspect of the instability that nowness is unceasingly opening up (itches, hunger pangs), and reaches for future balance by activating equipment and behavioral patterns continued from the past.

Though the field of meaning may, as I have claimed, take over where the senses leave off, we still need our senses to read the signs that get us there. I am suggesting that sound takes us further in that direction than any of the other senses.

Sound is the most sociable of the senses. Sound produced by any member of a bevy or a swarm or pack can be picked up by any of its other present members and resonate them all as a unity; meaning, which depends on the submission of individuals to a code specific to their group, could well have arisen out of stylizations of social buzzing and hooting.

Vocal sound depends entirely on the signaler's own highly portable equipment, requiring nothing in the way of ambient energy, as vision does. It works as well at night as during the day, and is indifferent to weather. It consumes negligible amounts of energy. All these considerations make it a good first choice in communicative emergencies, and an easy option under any circumstances.

As sensation, sound is as much a part of the here and now as any other sensory information—but iconic reporting of the *spatial* here and now, telling us exactly what there is out there and how it is distributed, is not its strong point. Thus, lightly attached to the spatial state of affairs, sounds more readily form new attachments to virtual entities—images, concepts—that may or may not be anchored in spatial reality. The word "persimmon" does not connect us in thought to a class of bulbous, tree-grown entities in nature, but persimmons in the flesh cannot come anywhere close to matching the transformational and combinatorial possibilities of the persimmons of the mind. The human field of meaning presumably acquired its expanded past, future, and elsewhere as a result of our exploitation of this sonic freedom in detachment from spatial reality. (Paradoxically, on the level of sound production this opening out is achieved by means of a two-layered *constriction* of the vocal mechanism, at the larynx and at the supra-laryngeal level involving teeth, tongue, lips, and hard palate.) It was the power to act together in the now, according to shared conjectures based on absent possibilities, that gave the creatures so empowered their adaptive advantage over all the others.

Any of the senses can now take us to the field in which meaning has effect, but my guess is that sound took us there first. Sound is the cradle of meaning.

Notes

1. In this chapter I attempt to reconcile an understanding of the concept "meaning" with ideas I developed earlier in *Sound, Speech, and Music* (Amherst: University of Massachusetts Press, 1990) Thanks to Carolyn Kenny for inviting me to sound off one more time, and thanks to Donna Buchanan, Nancy Weiss Hanrahan, Linda Laurent, Maryann McCabe, Ingrid Monson, Kay Kaufman Shelemay, Elizabeth Tolbert, and the students in G71.2137, "Historiography," in the spring of 1993 (Stephen Coburn, David Cox, Amy Daken, Jeannie Im, and Thomas Osuga) for meaningful conversation.

2. Sixteen meanings for "meaning" were listed by C. K. Ogden and I. A. Richards in their *The Meaning of Meaning* (San Diego, New York, and London, 1989 [1923]); see in particular chapter ix, "The Meaning of Meaning." Ogden and Richards's meanings XIV, XV, and XVI have to do with "reference" as used above. My other examples do not seem to have a place in their scheme.

3. In several studies Mark Johnson and George Lakoff discuss verbal meaning in relation to categories derived from a system of body schemas, "kinesthetic image schemas," such as the "center-periphery" schema and the "source-path-goal" schema. See for example Lakoff's *Women, Fire, and Dangerous Things* (Chicago, 1987), especially chapter 17, "Cognitive Semantics."

4. *The Death of Literature* (New Haven and London, 1990), p. 195.

5. The most active exploration of musical meaning is currently taking place in the field of semiotics. A clear and sensible survey of musical semiotics is Raymond Monelle, *Linguistics and Semiotics in Music* (Chur, 1992).

6. Mark Johnson, *The Body in the Mind* (Chicago and London, 1987), p. 178.

14

Close Encounters of the Musical Kind

Paul Lauzon

Prelude to Paul Lauzon

In the early 1980s we had a Canadian Association for Music Therapy Conference in Toronto. I met Paul for the first time there. He was a Canadian singer/songwriter who had come to the conference to check out music therapy.

Paul was an excellent performer and for me, he embodied the ancient play-ful spirit of the troubadour. He was a storyteller in his songs and shared his experiences in life through his beautiful lyrics, his resonant voice, his facility on the guitar. Several of us were excited about the possibility of Paul bringing his many talents into the field of music therapy. I was excited about Paul's talents too.

Yet Paul had a deeper and more sobering quality than the bard, which through the years came to characterize our love of the work and the apprecia-tion of musical moments. And this quality was the one which made me feel blessed to have him in our field.

Paul had been a longtime student of mysticism. He rarely mentioned this, but when he did, one could easily know that Paul himself knew the mys-tical experience and that in certain quiet moments, he could communicate his understanding, wisdom, and depth to those who shared time with him.

This became apparent to me many years after Paul had completed his music therapy training and had been a practicing music therapist for several years. It was during his first visit to Phoenecia for the Music Therapy Retreat. Why does it still surprise me that when we are surrounded by and held by Nature, so completely, without the worldly distractions, outer layers, those necessary, yet intrusive survival skills, become transparent and fade away to reveal something of greater depth?

As was our custom in Phoenecia, the ten to fifteen members would often split off into dyads or triads to walk or talk. Paul invited me to join him for such a stroll to discuss some of the theoretical work I had developed.

We walked by the still pond and noticed some busted-up old canoes. We sat on the bridge and reveled in the beauty of the forest. We talked about our work and our worlds, then absorbed the silence together. There is a radiant meditative exchange which happens at Phoenecia in which silence and music and words interplay.

These moments with Paul are the ones which will remain primary in my mind, no matter how often the outer layers intervene. In those moments we felt so blessed to be music therapists—and to share our love of the work, our ideas about the work. The entire experience had a sacred quality which brings meaning.

Later in Phoenecia, Paul was out on the lawn teaching us how to juggle oranges—the gypsy bard.

Since those days, Paul has served a term as president of the Canadian Association for Music Therapy and has completed his master's degree in music therapy as well.

Often he struggles, as many do, over the dilemmas of our professional identities—to be a performer, to be a therapist, to be in the forest or on an island in the Bay of Fundy to find the Sound.

Of himself Paul says: "I write and sing songs. I play several stringed instruments, including the Celtic harp. I love to canoe. I hope to be a dolphin in my next life."

ONCE UPON A TIME there was a SINGER who went to perform in a school for special children. During his performance he told the African tale of "Rabbit and His House." To do this he sang songs and wore different animal masks. When he put on the WOLF mask, the children began to scream and to cry and to be afraid. The WOLF protested that he was really a very friendly wolf, and he began to sing a funny song. This would not do. The children were genuinely afraid. The singer quickly removed the mask and finished the tale on a happy note.

This experience shocked the singer! Something very profound was happening. Was there really no critical mind barrier between the children and the mask? They seemed at one with the story, at one with the song.

It so happened that the singer had recently returned from England with a book concerning this very type of thing. It was a book about music therapy with children. This intrigued the school administrator and she suggested the singer might like to come and try some of these ideas with one of the children. And so it was that the singer met Billy.

Billy

Billy is thirteen years old and is diagnosed as autistic. They say he hasn't vocalized in three years. This is my fourth session with him, and

I don't seem to be getting anywhere. I'm trying to follow the book, but nothing seems to interest him. I've got the drum and the cymbal set up, and all he wants to do is twirl the drumstick. He won't even look at me. I don't see that there's much more that I can do. I'll keep playing the guitar. Maybe this would work if I was using a piano, like they do in the book. That must be it. I should be using a piano.

What's this? Billy's looking right at me. He's pointing at the guitar. Okay, if it's guitar you want, it's guitar you get. I strum a G chord. (Reader beware! This simple act, prosaically stated, *I strum a G chord*, is about to enact a revolution, both in Billy and in me. Read on!)

I strum a G chord—Billy leaps up from his chair, shouting. I strum a G chord—Billy leaps again, shouting. This pattern continues and expands and now he is leaping and shouting and hitting the drum and scratching the cymbal and making all manner of vocal sounds and I am frantically trying to follow him and to lead him and to stay in the boat as we rock down the river. This musical fever continues for a long, long time (actually 20 minutes). His teacher comes to fetch him.

I cannot move. I am burned by the force of music. I must find a way to do this again. But what can I do next week? Where do we go from ecstasy? What if in my eagerness to do good, I do something harmful? I don't know what I'm doing. I have to get some training.

Three years later, as a newly graduated music therapist, I am privileged to work with Jennifer.

Jennifer

She spent the first six years of her life in one room, with no companion but a radio. How could this happen to one so vulnerable? Jennifer was blind at birth, possibly the result of a genetic defect. From six to sixteen, she was shuffled from one institution to another. They first called her "autistic," now it's just "schizophrenic"—another label, like paint that just won't dry. Her face is twisted somehow, like a portrait drawn in sand, then washed over by the seventh wave. This gives her a poignant pigtailed beauty.

When she first came for our music therapy sessions she was a bit of a "wild animal," hitting or scratching when upset. This has stopped now, there is much too much to keep us occupied. We have work to do. I am reminded of Heidegger's statement concerning great art: "The artist remains inconsequential as compared with the work, almost like a passageway that destroys itself in the creative process for the work to emerge."

From the moment she came to music therapy, Jennifer has been vocalizing in strange, unusual sounds which poured out of her. The staff calls it her "silly talk." Could I please find a way to curb this, they say, to make her sounds more appropriate? I say that these sounds are the very material we need to work with. Perhaps if we can bring some order into the verbal chaos she expresses, then we can begin to help her.

Six weeks have passed. I am gradually being initiated into Jennifer's secret language. But today something glorious is happening! The words begin to take shape, like an eraser is releasing a portrait from a charcoal-covered page. Jennifer begins by telling me about her favorite places: riding in Mack's truck, sitting beneath a holly tree in the courtyard. She continues, spinning old and new words in a sweet melody, punctuated by the chords I am playing on the piano. Suddenly, we are Here, in that place I sometimes dream of, the place where all is music, and music makes the world. Jennifer continues. I am with her. We go farther, deeper into a sonic ecstasy.

I am sitting at the piano with a blind girl, entranced as I share in her genius. She has found a song, with healing words, and a melody that takes us traveling. She is singing out my name. *We* are changing.

Time passes and I am developing a full private practice. I have been doing music therapy at the local hospital, and working in a studio with special children. One day, as I am leaving, a mother appears with a tiny girl, and asks if there's something that can be done with Tina.

Tina

I am listening. Today, Tina sits upon the floor and turns within her own world. I am listening. She moves to a melody I play. Where this melody begins and ends is a vibrational world somewhere between us. I am listening. She speaks from a silence, still as rain, and fashioned by her. I am listening. Her voice echoes off the windows where the shafts of sunlight come pouring into the room. They touch her face. I am listening.

She is only four years old, yet pushes the world away. She needs to mould her own close and active circle of light and sound. I am listening. They ask me: When will she talk? When will she be walking? What are your goals? I need something other than words to articulate the waiting with no answers, this stuttering hope. There are many seizures—the flailing of arms and legs, a tortured look, the eyes of a cornered animal. I am listening.

Last night, I talked to a friend and colleague about Tina, long distance words across endless miles of telephone line. The night has taken those words and given them back to me. I am listening. This silent stare, so imponderable! I need to find a way to reach her, to hear her hearing me hearing her. I try once again, remembering something I read once: If one is forever cautious, can one remain a human being? I turn around. Something has changed, unfolding across a pale and tiny face atop a twisted body, eyes tightly closed. Slowly, imperceptibly at first morning of the world, across that face a gift freely given, she smiles. I begin to hear the rumble of laughter. I am listening.

I could never get back to Billy because his family moved away. But there is one who reminds me of Billy—another boy, waiting and watching, barely responding to the name of Darren.

Darren

For eight weeks now, he has been circling the room. He stays close to the wall and keeps going around and around. He seems interested in nothing we are doing here. Darren is fourteen years old, and determined to keep the world at a distance. Oh, there are behaviors which say "autistic"—a flicking of fingers, refusal to make eye contact, sudden bursts of laughter, strange words. I've begun to think that autism is nothing if not a refusal to be born, "I didn't want to come here in the first place, so don't bug me. Leave me alone!" "Only thing is, you are here, Darren, and for the next little while, I'm here with you."

Without really thinking about it, I begin changing today's session plan. In the past few weeks, I have been trying to get in Darren's way, to make him notice something: a song, a movement, a picture, an instrument—something to get him interested, involved. Today, I was going to try the big drum. Instead, I place a chair in the middle of the room. I take out a set of bongo drums. I sit in the chair and begin a simple rhythm, a gentle beat. I begin to talk in a singsong fashion about what's been happening, that Darren has been coming every week for music, and I'm wondering what he thinks of all this. I continue the narrative, singing about Darren's response, or lack thereof, and about how I really don't know where to go from here. I change the rhythm and the dynamics of the drumming to go with these rambling thoughts. I keep talking and drumming. Darren is still circling the room. Now a change—Darren's circle is getting smaller. He's moving away from the wall and closer to the center, closer to the chair. It seems like forever, but is no more that ten minutes. Now, Darren is directly behind me. I can feel his breathing. I keep drumming, now I stand, turn around and direct Darren into the chair. I keep drumming. Now I place the bongos into Darren's lap. He cradles them. Suddenly, he lets out a yelp, and begins hitting the drum with an energy that sets me back. I am speechless. The journey has begun.

And the journey continues. There is one who becomes like a daughter to me. I am not the only one to notice that there is a sublime and special magic about Laura.

Laura

She's the kind of child who lights up a room. This is not uncommon with a Rett's Syndrome girl. But Laura is surrounded by a circle of joy that is unique to her. When her mother first brought her to our music sessions, Laura was three years old. In the past four years I have seen her climb more than one Himalayan peak of courage. Like many special children, even the smallest tasks can be monumental: turning the head, holding a spoon, sitting up. The prognosis for walking unassisted or for learning to speak is not positive—they say this just won't happen. In spite of these predictions, in spite of extreme and frequent pain, in spite of a developing curvature of the spine, in spite of frequent illness brought on by allergies and a weakened immune system— in spite of countless problems, not least of which are the everyday problems which all humans share—still, Laura is able to laugh her sparkling laugh, and to generate a total sense of affirmation within those around her, from the depths of her generous heart.

She loves the music we make. Today she sits on a mat and I surround her with instruments: a large gong, two drums, a small harp, bells, a cymbal, reed horns. Every time she turns to face a new direction, she is met by a sound, she is confronted by an aural resonance to her movement. Now she begins to undulate her echoing response to the living sounds surrounding her. Within this rippling wave circle she turns her head. She reaches out with a mallet that she manages to hang on to. I take up the movement and enter into her world of rhythmic song. I am sitting beside her now, within the circle, feathering chords upon the guitar. She leans into the sound hole of the guitar, and utters a word—her name. But she can't talk! Maybe I didn't hear what I heard? To tell the truth, I heard it, yet I wasn't prepared; once again lightning strikes a corner of the sky I had forgotten. That's why I am here, expectant of the encounter. And Laura? I have seen changes: new strength, expanded vocalizations, muscular control, more prolonged laughter, exploration with the instruments, a growing confidence in communication.

I speak gratitude for the opportunities of service. It was Heidegger who said that "Teaching is a giving, an offering; but what is offered in teaching is not the learnable, for the student is merely instructed to take for himself what he already has." My teacher is a wise little girl, just seven years old.

I have done my job best when I have worked myself out of a job. With that in mind, I will cease describing and allow Carl to tell us all about Carl.

Carl

I'm ready for music. I'm ready to play.

The car ride was long. Now school's far away.

It's raining today.

I'm ready for singing. Paul plays piano, and I play piano.

I'm not scared of you.

Okay, let's start now, let's go!

Hmmm . . . one, two, three . . . let it be, let it be, like a bee, like a bee, like a big old bumblebee.

See, mama comes to see every time.

Darlings Island is home to me, home to me, and I love the beaches.

I'm so tall now! Hey, short guy! Don't step on my toes. Spinning, spinning.

What's this music? hello, we're going to say hello. My arms go up to beat the drum and down to beat the drum and right and left again, again. It's funny, isn't it?

Ah, the big gold gong in the corner! Later, for later. Right now, sit down please. Do as I ask you to do. Eat your toast. Don't throw your towel on the floor.

Play the cymbal. The cymbal is simple, is simple the cymbal. Now play the cymbal and the drum.

Zero, zero, come in please! Number 222, come in please! I'm the one who beats the drum, and you're the Music Man. Move my chair, move my chair, now I'm the Music Man. Play the low notes, play the low, low notes, and you're all right, you're out of sight, and I'm the Music Man.

And it's so sad to miss the bus and bang your head and cut your finger and lose your dog. Did the coyotes get her? No! She just kept running and running. And it's so sad. The numbers just won't dance together, I'm sorry!

And it's so sad to miss your friend. Are you my friend? Are you my friend forever?

Low notes, low notes and high, high notes and low notes. Mary had a little duck, the duck ran up a tree, as happy as could be! Low notes and high notes and fingers moving faster, faster fingers running up and down and jumping horses, jumping goats and playing checkers with Paul on the black and white notes. I'm flying, see I'm flying! And Darlings Island is home to me, home to me.

Now Mister Music, strum the guitar.

My heart shall mend, I have come again, to my anchor, my island.

You make that song and I make a song for you. I make it walking on the beach. Merrily merrily merrily merrily, life is but a pickle.

I'm so tall now. I'm not scared of you. Momma always come to see. We have to say goodbye now. Goodbye now!

Like a bee, like a bee, like a big old bumblebee.

I'm ready for music.

Let's play, let's play!

It's been fourteen years since the singer walked into that school for special children. How quickly time flies! If his story is a song, the first verse has been written. The refrain is being composed as we speak. He is instrumental in composing himself. The words need not rhyme. He expects a second, a third verse. The bridge will be more difficult, but not impossible. That is one thing the singer has learned—there are walls, yes, but no barriers.

15

The Sound Image: Music Therapy in the Treatment of the Abused Child

Connie Isenberg-Grzeda

Prelude to Connie Isenberg-Grzeda

Connie and I first met in the mid-1970s when we worked for the Canadian Association for Music Therapy. The work we all did during that time was important in my life and many of the friendships I began then are enduring. I resonate with the Canadian mentality, the sense of social conscience and social responsibility, the feeling for nature, the pioneering spirit, even younger than our own. Those formative years in the association were an opportunity to develop relationships and work together in very meaningful ways, to set the tone for the development of music therapy in Canada.

Many years later, after I had been in California for eight years, I decided that I needed to return to Canadian music therapy. It would be like going home. I saw a notice for a faculty position at the University of Quebec in Montreal, a French-speaking university, and saw that Connie was now in charge of this program. I wrote and phoned and applied and received the position, thus came to experience my dream, and my first winter in Quebec. I took a six-month position as a visiting professor. UQAM offered me an opportunity to teach two music therapy courses and to have release time to write my book, *The Field of Play: A Guide for the Theory and Practice of Music Therapy.*

In these months, Connie and I developed a friendship. It was rich in intellectual stimulation. She had an amazing mind and we were able to brainstorm about everything. We imagined graduate training. We deconstructed and rebuilt music therapy courses. Connie was a wonderful consultant for my book, with excellent skills in critical thinking. She knew just how to build me up enough to feel support, but to gently suggest this or that change here or there for clarity and focus.

Leaving my children in Santa Barbara with their father was tough. Even though it was only for six months, it did not seem natural. But I had been on the verge of one of those identity crises in which Santa Barbara seemed unable to support the music therapist in me enough to make it all work.

Montreal was an unfamiliar place. Although I had been there for conferences and knew a handful of music therapists, there was not enough familiarity to assuage the cultural and meteorological shock. A Quebecois poet and songwriter has written: "My country is Winter." I believe it. I had never experienced this kind of weather before. I found it strange and invigorating, beautiful to behold.

Yet there was no doubt about the fact that I was lonely. Although I had studied French for six years, I was by no means fluent. Connie offered to attend all of my classes, and to translate when necessary.

I returned for shorter visits several times to teach at UQAM. I am extremely grateful for these experiences. Connie and I continued to develop our friendship and our work.

I count my experiences in Quebec as some of the most valuable in my work life. The professional friendships I made, learning the language, experiencing the land, have influenced me in ways which are difficult to describe. I am deeply touched by the spirit of the Quebecois, which I came to know through my music therapy students. Connie is greatly responsible for opening up this world to me. This is a source of inspiration and always will be.

Connie is a full-time music therapy professor at the Universite du Quebec A Montreal where she was central in initiating the first Bachelor's level music therapy training in Canada. She is one of the charter members of the Canadian Association for Music Therapy and has remained actively involved in this association and also the National Association for Music Therapy in various capacities over the last two decades. Her extensive clinical experience has been fueled by a commitment to a belief in music psychotherapy, leading her to pursue training in Guided Imagery and Music, marriage and family therapy, and psycho-dynamically-oriented psychotherapy.

How does one project one's voice into an external world that is perceived as potentially threatening, dangerous, inconsistent? How does one allow voices from the outside into one's internal world if these voices are perceived as potential attacks, as threats to one's integrity and cohesiveness? These are among the questions that arise as we allow ourselves, as therapists, to enter the inner world of the abused child.

In recent years, the subject of child abuse has been eliciting an ever-increasing amount of attention from both the professional community and the general population. The attendant concern for the rights, safety, and protection of children is manifested in greater vigilance, and consequently, an earlier detection of and response to abusive situations. The translated writings of Alice Miller (1983a,b, 1984, 1990) have served to encourage the North American professional community to broaden its concept of abuse and listen to children's stories with a new level of respect. These stories are now heard as accurate depictions of life experiences rather than as fiction or fantasy. Social service and legal agencies rally to the support of abused children in an attempt to improve their lot in life through treatment in the form of therapeutic intervention and placement. Removal from the home, although extreme, can be viewed as preferable to remaining in a nonchanging abusive environment.

The characteristics of abused children, as described in the literature (Hansen, 1982), include: submissiveness, fearfulness, shyness, lack of facial and verbal expressiveness, aggressiveness, destructiveness, negativism, unpredictability, inability to trust people, poor self-concept, poor impulse control, extreme sensitivity to criticism, low tolerance level, and delayed physical, academic, and social development. Since this portrait has been described a posteriori, that is, consequent to the detection of abuse, we do not know if these traits constitute sufficient grounds for a diagnosis of abuse or "battered child syndrome" and if they delimit this condition by excluding other potential diagnoses.

In many cases, referral for treatment is made on the basis of identified needs other than those known to be the sequelae of abuse. Is it essential for the early stages of treatment of the child that the experience of abuse be documented and not merely suspected or is it sufficient for the information to gradually emerge throughout the course of therapy? Therapists who structure their therapeutic interventions by pre-establishing treatment plans designed to respond to the specific needs of abuse victims (e.g., Powell and Faherty, 1990) must know at the onset that the children they treat are victims of abuse. Attempts have been made within the creative arts therapies to identify specific abuse markers in the artwork of children (Wohl and Kaufman, 1985; Manning, 1987) and adolescents (Sidun and Rosenthal, 1987), thereby permitting for early detection of abuse.

As a music therapist, while noting the importance of pre-established treatment plans and "musical abuse markers," I am, at this time, less interested in those aspects of treatment than I am in the manner in which the life experiences of abused children have impact upon their use of and response to the therapist-music matrix inherent to the music therapeutic setting. Conversely, I am interested in the impact of this matrix in the clinical sequelae of the abuse. Are there common elements that can be discerned in the manner in which the therapeutic process unfolds for children who have been abused?

A look at three brief case study vignettes might contribute to our understanding of the phenomenon of abuse as it affects the establishment of the relationship with the music therapist. Although there was suspicion of abuse in all three cases, the referals for treatment were made on the basis of a variety of behavior disorders, including conduct disorder and oppositional defiant disorder (DSM-III-R). The children's family histories will be presented first, followed by a brief description of their involvement in music therapy.

Betty's Family History

Betty was ten years old at the time of her admission to an inpatient psychiatric unit for emotionally disturbed school-aged children. She had been living with her maternal grandparents prior to admission and continued to spend weekends and holidays with them throughout most of the period of her hospitalization.

Betty's family history was characterized by instability and repeated change. Betty's father disappeared shortly after her birth leaving her mother to care for Betty on her own. When Betty was approximately 15 months old her mother left her with her maternal grandparents. The grandparents managed for a while, but with the passage of time the increasing limitations in their ability to care satisfactorily for a young child led to their insistence that a social service agency place Betty, then age three, with a foster family.

Problems within the foster home soon surfaced, a suspicion of abuse was raised, and Betty was removed from that home. She returned to her grandparents until a second foster placement could be found. This second foster home, although an improvement over the first, also proved to be a placement of relatively short duration. The foster parents had extreme difficulty coping with Betty's behavioral response to the birth of their natural child. These difficulties proved to be intractable and resulted in Betty's return to her grandparent's home, where she remained until age five. At that time, her natural mother decided to take her back. She had remarried in the interim and borne two more children (a boy and a girl), both of whom lived with her. Betty remained with her mother and stepfather for approximately one and a half years and once again suspicion of abuse surfaced. Betty was removed from the home and returned to her grandparents.

At this time, her natural father, who had lived in another city since shortly after her birth, returned and gained custody of Betty despite the original abandonment. Betty lived with her father for approximately two months. This very difficult and stressful period came to a precipitous end when Betty developed enuresis and encopresis, thus providing her father with a justification for abandoning her once again. Needless to say, this heralded a return to her maternal grandparents.

Over the following year and a half, Betty's grandparents repeatedly asked that a placement be found. Three more foster homes were attempted, without any success. In the last of these homes, Betty was found engaged in sexual play with a foster sibling and this behavior precipitated a referral for treatment.

Betty was presented as a pretty, sociable, and personable girl, small for her age. She was somewhat clingy and superficial in her relations with women, seductive and teasing with men. She often lied and stole small objects.

Jane's Family History

Jane was eight years old at the time of her admission to the above-mentioned in-patient psychiatric unit for emotionally disturbed children. Her family history was characterized by instability and a chaotic family structure. She, too, was living with her maternal grandparents at the time of hospitalization. The family was known to be involved in crime and the continual movement of family members into and out of the grandparents' home made it difficult to keep track of family members. Many of her aunts and uncles (her mother's siblings) were still living with her grandparents. Her natural father had no involvement in her life. Her mother and her mother's boyfriend were in prison for armed robbery.

Although the grandparents were very concerned about Jane's welfare, they did delegate much of her direct supervision and care to their own children, that is, to her aunts and uncles. The grandparents also often took Jane to their family business where she was surrounded solely by adults. There was suspicion of abuse by one of Jane's uncles.

Jane was presented as a "tough," independent, and defiant child. The style of her initial contacts with adults and peers was pugnacious rather than amicable and yet her internal appeal rendered her an endearing child. Jane was impulsive, truant, stole regularly, and had some slight language delays.

Linda's Family History

Linda was ten years old when her parents sought help at the outpatient psychiatric clinic at which I first met her. The initial interviews revealed a history of overstimulation with an attendant insufficiency of appropriate limits, a portrait reminiscent of Leonard Shengold's

(1989) "too-muchness" (p. 1). Linda's oppositional behavior and her intractable enuresis and encopresis were the primary presenting symptoms. Her oppositional behavior was described as extreme, most often leading to major tantrums and physical aggressiveness directed toward her parents and her eight-year-old sister, Mary. Mother's emotional distance and Father's emotional over-involvement were immediately apparent, as were the limitations in their parenting skills. Although strongly suspected, evidence of abuse was lacking. Physical violence between the parents was acknowledged.

Linda's parents repeatedly sought assistance for Linda's toileting and behavioral difficulties from the time she was three years old, but to no avail. Interventions in the form of home-based toileting programs, family therapy, individual therapy, and medication all failed to produce change.

Linda's family was a middle-class professional family. At the time of treatment, however, Linda's father was unemployed, adding an additional stressor to an already highly stressed family system. After nine months of family therapy on an outpatient basis, Linda was admitted to the psychiatric unit of a pediatric hospital. It was hoped that the hospitalization would provide some symptom relief for Linda and would also enable her parents to work on the intra- and inter-personal conflicts that had prevented them from acquiring some of the behavior management and parenting skills that could allow them to provide their children with a more adequate environment. It was upon admission that Linda began individual and group therapy sessions.

Linda was presented as a friendly, intelligent child whose tendency to cling was offset by her rapid retreat from contact. An apparent "openness" proved less revelatory than concealing. One had a sense that Linda's secretiveness was deeply linked to her psychic, if not physical, survival.

Betty's Music Therapy Process

Betty was in treatment with the music therapist for almost three years. She was very enthusiastic about her music therapy sessions, stating initially that she loved music and that she wanted to play for the therapist. During the initial sessions, Betty spent much of her time making "pretty" music. She directed the therapist's involvement as well as her own and seemed to derive much pleasure from this opportunity to be in a position of control. The contrast between Betty's simple, light-hearted, and gay music and her life circumstances and behavioral patterns was quite striking. During this stage, Betty played existing children's songs and age-appropriate songs from the radio. She was, in actuality, quite musical.

In the second stage of her therapy, Betty began to play percussive nonmelodic music, unaccompanied by sung lyrics. Initally, these rhythmic improvisations were very controlled and she insisted that the therapist repeat particular rhythmic patterns. Although Betty demonstrated a relative rhythmic freedom across sessions, she tended to repeat the same basic pattern within a given session.

In the third stage, lyrics returned, but this time, rather than singing existing songs, Betty began to compose her own. At first her lyrics seemed to describe her wishes, for example, fantasies of being reunited with her mother or fantasies of living with the therapist. Over time, Betty demonstrated a diminishing need to control the therapist's musical interventions.

Betty's song lyrics then shifted to expressions of anger directed toward her parents for having mistreated and abandoned her and this led to her beginning to express her underlying sadness.

Betty never fully replaced acting-out with musical "playing-out," but she did acquire much more impulse control and a far greater capacity to directly express her feelings verbally. This occurred first within the context of the music therapy sessions and eventually generalized to other settings. Betty had no other form of psychotherapy during her hospitalization. Music therapy remained the treatment of choice during the follow-up period.

Reintegration with Betty's grandparent was successfully negotiated post-hospitalization. Concomitantly, she was able to adjust to the looser structures of a classroom within a community-based school.

Jane's Music Therapy Process

Jane was involved in a therapeutic process with the music therapist over a period of two and a half years. The six initial months of intervention were in the form of individual music therapy sessions and then Jane was integrated into a play therapy group co-led by the music therapist and a psychiatrist for the remainder of the treatment period. This shift was made in response to Jane's non-changing, somewhat superficial, albeit active, verbal involvement in the individual sessions with a concomitant refusal to engage in either active or receptive music experiences, instrumental, vocal, movement, or listening based. It was only within the context of that group situation that Jane did become musically involved, as she, on her own initiative, integrated music by bringing cassette tapes with her on a weekly basis. These musical selections became increasingly reflective of Jane's situation and feelings and were used within the therapeutic context as vehicles for expression of greater trust. Her tolerance for empathic response did increase in parallel fashion to a limited extent.

Although her social skills did improve somewhat, she never did become able to manifestly process her life experience as related to her significant others as relived within the context of a corrective emotional experience.

Jane was discharged at age 11, and, subsequent to several unsuccessful attempts at post-hospitalization reintegration with her family during which time she was repeatedly picked up by the police for prostitution and drug use, Jane was sent to a residential treatment center for delinquent adolescents.

Linda's Music Therapy Process

Linda was seen in both groups and individual music therapy sessions for a period of three months. Although Linda spoke very little to the therapist during the initial sessions, she demonstrated considerable interest in music and in the exploration of the instruments played during the first two sessions. She brought her own ukelele from home but did not use it during the first two sessions. She did not engage the therapist either verbally or musically.

Linda began by using the drum. She played with tremendous force, musically discouraging the therapist's active attempts at accompaniment, rendering the therapist's involvement a form of parallel play. Linda's playing style resulted in her sometimes seeming to hurt herself physically through the sheer force of the physical impact of the mallet against the skin of the drum.

Linda then began to play her ukelele, sharing favorite songs with the therapist. Her instrumental skills were not matched by her vocal skills. Linda was unable to stay within the tonality and her vocal renderings of familiar songs did not result in recognizable melodies. When the therapist sang, Linda did not join with the therapist's singing, although she continued to sing. Once again, the engagement was more parallel than interactive.

Whereas initially Linda needed to control both the structure and the content of the sessions, with the passage of time she began to be able to engage in activities that were structured for her by the therapist. Musically, she moved progressively from rhythm, to rhythmic accompaniment, to melody, to melodic exploration. Her difficulty with wind and "blowing" instruments and the lack of control over the melodic component of her use of voice abated somewhat with the passage of time. Linda became able to reproduce a song and render the melody recognizable.

Linda's reintegration to her family will require several intermediate steps if it is ever to be successful. She has moved from hospital to a group home setting.

Discussion

Having looked at these three cases, the first thing that strikes me is that the children all managed to use music to some extent for interactive and expressive purposes, although not always within the context of music therapy sessions. They all began the interactive musical process by establishing control over the manner in which the therapist interacted with them musically. This control allowed them to identify and to communicate the degree of distance/closeness that they could tolerably maintain with the therapist. If we take the liberty of expanding the definition of music to encompass the more global concept of sound, then we may say that these children were all intent upon controlling the sounds that impinged upon them from without, at the same time as they controlled and mastered the sounds which emanated from within.

What is the root of the importance of these sounds in the lives of these children? It is my contention, and probably that of most music therapists, that the musical/sound aspects of the early environment play a central role in infant development and result in the establishment of "sound images" which may endure, albeit unconsciously, and may continue to exert an influence in later stages of development. Lidz refers to the first 15 months of human life as those which witness the most impressive physical and developmental transformations, yet they remain unremembered. What happens during this period ". . . lies beyond the individual's recall, buried in the oblivion of wordlessness. At most, some vague feeling, some amorphous recollection that eludes conscious memory may upon occasion flit in and out of an adult's awareness, perplexing or troubling as might a fragment of a dream" (p. 123). Let us now turn our attention to the role of music/sound in the normal developmental process so as to facilitate our conceptualization of the variations which may ensue in the case of abused children.

In utero, the fetus is enveloped by the sounds of the enclosed environment. The intra-uterine sound environment, although beyond conscious recall, may leave a wordless and amorphous memory trace which serves as a template for all future rhythmic response and provides us with a lifelong sound and rhythmic symbolic image of security, thereby providing for continuity between intra- and extra-uterine life. Rolando Benenzon (1981), the founder of the music therapy training program at Salvador University in Buenos Aires in Argentina, states that the ". . . basis of the rhythm/man relationship must be looked for in the sound contact of the intrauterine fetus and music is the evocation of the mother" (p. 20).

Upon his birth, the neonate is actively able to emit his own sounds. This initial vocal contact with the external environment generally takes the form of a cry. It is the cry that ushers in biological, non-parastic life, and it is the cry that establishes the most basic interactive pattern. The baby cries in reaction to his/her own internal sensations, and the "good enough mother," to use Winnicott's term (1960), responds to her child's call and sets out to meet his/her needs. In so doing, without any forethought or deliberation, she creates a sound response to the baby which precedes the actual physical contact which occurs when she lifts the infant out of the crib in order to respond to his basic needs. What is this sound response? It may vary from one mother to another, but for each mother a somewhat predictable pattern of bodily movement sounds and vocalizations emerges. For example, one may hear the sounds of a bottle being prepared, followed by rapid but relaxed footsteps accompanied by a verbal message (for example, "Don't worry; I'm coming"), which may be supplanted by a reassuring vocalization or song as the mother draws nearer to the child (for example, "sh, oh, tut"). Just as the infant's cry takes on a meaning and serves as a form of communication, the mother's sound response takes on its own meaning, in that it helps to situate the mother and child in space in relation to each other, and as a result of its predictablity, it begins to represent the mother's imminent gratification of the infant's needs. This anticipatory aspect lends the sound image its own comforting qualities. To quote Benenzon (1981):

> If the environment is satisfactory many of the sounds acquire early symbolic associations of pleasurable events. The mother's voice is associated with the oral gratification of the child, the rocking of the mother with the sleepy satisfaction after food. (p. 29)

The consistent and appropriate response to the baby's cries results in the baby's growing belief in the importance of his own inner sensations and his confidence that he is able to use his sound system to communicate his needs and to elicit a response from his environment which will be comforting and need-satisfying. In other words, through this process, the child is able to develop a sense of trust in himself and in others.

Erik Erikson, in his description of the manner in which basic trust is established, emphasizes the essential quality of the relationship between the mother and the infant whereby the mother's sensitivity to the infant's needs enables her to provide the external consistency, continuity, and predictability which, once apprehended sensorially by the infant, allows for the discovery of, the exploration of, and the organization of the infant's world and the consequent establishment of ". . . a rudimentary sense of ego identity" (1963, p. 247). It is within the musical/sound sphere of experience that much of this interaction occurs.

Once the child's basic needs have been met, the mother and child will often continue to engage in a form of mutual and reciprocal vocalizations which is characterized by synchrony, that is, by a rhythmic and intonational connection which leads to an enmeshment or intertwining of responses, a "sounding" together as one.

How does this situation differ for the abused child? She, too, uses her cries to communicate her needs and she, too, is responded to. Parental response, however, is neither consistent and predictable, nor based on sensitivity to the needs of the child. The lack of consistent response renders the environment confusing and frightening, and the frequent negative sensory responses represent danger. The sound image described earlier in relation to the non-abusive environment is replaced by one which is inconsistent, discontinuous, unpredictable, threatening, harsh, and painful. Kohut and Levarie (1978) tell us that "Specific noises may come to evoke specific fears, and sensitivity to them may give clues regarding the point of regressive fixation" (p. 140). They go on to say that some people may ". . . hear in the specific inflections of a male voice the voice of an angry father and react to it with anxiety or aggressive defense" (p. 140).

The emotional content of speech depends more upon the music of language, that is, the intonational, inflectional, and prosodic elements of speech than upon the content, itself. Paul Moses (1954) talks about how the early environment sets up the child's vocal patterns which persist into later life.

Just as a dog obeys his master without understanding the articulatory part of the words but catches the melody and the dynamic accents, the child in this wordless period senses the moods of his parents and reacts to soothing words and to irritating approaches. The child recreates the sounds heard. He will emit a sound when frightened which will, from then on, represent "fright" to him. (p. 21)

It is this inconsistent and contradictory emotional content which may be too difficult for the abused child to tolerate. Consequently, the child may actually blunt his senses. Ray Helfer (Helfer and Kempe, 1988) states that ". . . those reared to mute their senses have learned, very early in childhood, that their lives are less confused and hurt less when people do not look them in the eye, listen to what they say, touch them, or get too close" (p. 38). The screams, the sighs, the groans and the cries are too much to bear.

These children do not learn to trust their internal messages or their capacity to appropriately externalize these messages, nor do they trust their environment to respond to them in a consistent and positive fashion. They feel that they have no control.

The lack of development of basic trust makes it difficult for abused children to achieve musical synchrony with the therapist. The rhythmic enmeshment may be too threatening in that it symbolizes the loss of their tenuous sense of self. Within sessions, the child is able to control the extent to which there will be a rhythmic connection with the therapist. When the chid is able to relinquish this control to the therapist, it may well indicate the emergence of a basic sense of trust.

The music therapist working with abused children attempts to provide them with a contained and secure environment, reminiscent of the womb, in which the child is able to begin to explore his inner self and his sound images. The basic tools of the music therapist, that is, instruments and the voice, allow the child to pace himself as he moves from silence to sound. Whereas instruments allow for the distancing of affect, an objectification, and the possibility of a transitional space, the voice, by virtue of its internal locus, provides for a much more immediate, and hence, much more threatening expression of effective content.

The child moves from silence to sound. He explores his personal sound images and his ability to use his sounds expressively and interactively through instruments and through the voice. It is only then that the child begins to use sounds to communicate his trauma directly. This communication may take the form of songs written by the child, in which the lyrics reflect the content of the trauma.

It is apparent to the music therapist that the manner in which the child engages in the musical relationship reflects his overall interactive style. As the child becomes more committed to the musical interaction, his musical involvement facilitates and perhaps even liberates further self-expression. Music is a symbolic, evocative, but non-referential modality, unlike art or the spoken word. Music may thus serve as a catalyst for expression in these other modalities, as well.

References

Benenzon, R. (1981). *Music Therapy Manual* (W. Grabia, Trans.). Springfield, Illinois: Charles C. Thomas.

Erikson, Erik H. (1963). *Childhood and Society* (2d ed.). New York: W.W. Norton & Co.

Hansen, J. (Ed.) (1982). *Clinical Approaches to Family Violence.* Rockville, Maryland: Aspen Systems.

Helfer, Ray, and Ruth Kempe (1988). *The Battered Child.* (4th ed.) Chicago: U. Chicago Press.

Kohut, Heinz, and Siegmund Levarie (1978). On the Enjoyment of Listening to Music. In Paul H. Ornstein (ed.), *The Search for the Self: Selected Writing of Heinz Kohut: 1950-1978,* vol. 1, N.Y.: International Universities Press, Chap. 3, 135-158.

Lidz, T. (1983). *The Person* (revised ed.). New York: Basic Books.

Manning, Trudy Martin (1987). Aggression Depicted in Abused Children's Drawings. *The Arts in Psychotherapy* 14, pp. 15-24.

Miller, Alice (1983a). *Drama of the Gifted Child.* N.Y.: Basic Books.

Miller, Alice (1983b). *For Your Own Good.* N.Y.: Farrar, Straus, Giroux.

Miller, Alice (1984). *Thou Shalt Not Be Aware.* N.Y.: Farrar, Straus, Girouz.

Miller, Alice (1990). *Banished Knowledge.* N.Y.: Doubleday.

Moses, Paul J. (1954). *The Voice of Neurosis.* New York: Grune & Stratton.

Powell, Lesle, and Sandra Faherty (1990). Treating Sexually Abused Latency Age Girls. *The Arts in Psychotherapy* 17, pp. 35-47.

Shengold, Leonard (1989). *Soul Murder.* New York: Fawcett Columbine.

Sidun, Nancy, and Ronald Rosenthal (1987). Graphic Indicators of Sexual Abuse in Draw-a-Person Tests of Psychiatrically Hospitalized Adolescents. *The Arts in Psychotherapy* 14, pp. 25-33.

Winnicott, D. W. (1960). Ego Distortion in Terms of True and False Self, pp. 140-152 in Winnicott, D. W. (1965). *The Maturational Processes and the Facilitating Environment.* London: The Hogarth Press.

Wohl, Agnes, and B. Kaufman (1985). *Silent Screams and Hidden Cries.* New York: Brunner/Mazel.

16

Singing Practices and States of Consciousness

Penelope Nichols-Rothe

Prelude to Penelope Nichols-Rothe

Penelope is a recent friend. We have come to know each other through our affiliation with Antioch University. Penelope called me a couple of years ago, when she first returned from her studies at Harvard. She said that she had been referred to me through a mutual friend, Shierry Nicholson, a faculty member at Antioch University in Yellow Springs, Ohio. Penelope had once been a student at Antioch and had studied with Shierry and developed a friendship with her.

Penelope and I met for lunch and immediately realized that we shared many common interests. We were both singers. We were both meditators. We were academics and cultural contemporaries. And most significantly, we were both extremely interested in the relationship between consciousness and music. We had several wonderful dialogs about this connection. These were rich and deep, those rare talks in which one loses time.

Penelope was able to teach some courses in the Liberal Studies program here at Antioch Santa Barbara and has since moved on to New York to pursue new interests. Our encounter was brief and intense and I had the great privilege of being present when Penelope began to explore ways of integrating her experience with performance with her recently acquired learning at Harvard with her interest in personal development through teaching voice. Her contribution here has that fresh sense of discovery which accompanies new work and the sense of substance which characterizes an integration of that which has come before.

It is no surprise that Penelope's new home is just a few miles from Phoenecia. I know that I will see her again.

Penelope is a Grammy-nominated singer, songwriter, and artist who says she has "jumped ship and gone into Music Education Research." She has a doctorate from the Harvard Graduate School of Education and teaches courses in music and psychology.

In the past few years I have been exploring farther and farther into the borderline area between psychology and singing practice. With my students, I have been taking treks into a world where the imaginary used to work on vocal self-expression and early childhood memories seem to meet. My experience as an artist, singer, and teacher do not fit neatly into one theoretical category, although many theories give insight into what my students and I have been experiencing as singing practice and performance.

I would like to take you with me as I look at two recent singing practice experiences. Theoretically, I would like to examine these experiences from a Cognitive and Transpersonal perspective. I hope to gain some insight into the nature and function of musical memory, how musical memory can seem to trigger whole states of consciousness, and raise some new questions about the teacher/student dialogue in singing.[1]

What I am bringing to the telling of this story is a lifetime of experience as a singer, composer, and teacher. The way that I see these experiences is informed by my own life experience and my training in observational research techniques, as well as by my study of Cognitive and Transpersonal psychological theories.

The Wisdom of the Body

The process of learning to sing brings with it many questions for both the student and the teacher which do not fit under the heading of technical skill development. In both of the interactions which I will describe, the focus of the exercises was to expand the students' ability to express feeling with their voices. My own experience as a singer and a teacher makes me think that when you make any sounds with your body, you are paying attention to a part of yourself which does not normally get heard. As a result, the students and I were working with exploring the range of ways we could make sounds with our bodies, including ways of singing. What we experienced, as I will describe, raised some very interesting questions: for instance, why does the exploration of ways of singing and sound making seem to trigger a lot of memories from early childhood? Part of the quality of these memories felt like a reawakening of old learning pathways—how are these learning pathways triggered by the experience?

Even now, in reviewing the experiences to write about it, I can still feel the vividness of the perception, as if the child in me is reawakened by revisiting that place. The experiences seem to exist in a space outside of linear time. From a transpersonal perspective, I have to ask myself whether we as a culture use the concept of time to our advantage when we see it as being primarily a linear progression of events, as opposed to a more holistic view, in which time is experienced as many events happening simultaneously or as a specific state of consciousness. In this view, our perception of time is framed by memory, not information inherent in the sound making, but the entire field of an experience from childhood. In other words, the music gives you the feeling that you are really "there."

The Secret Garden

My story begins in my studio, where I am working with a student on expanding her range of vocal expression. We had been experimenting with a number of "toning"[2] exercises throughout the lessons. It occurred to me as a natural progression from toning to ask my student to follow me on a vocal journey. We had been starting some exercises with a short period of meditation. We did this for a few minutes to stabilize and deepen our breathing and focus our attention. I have found that meditation preceding the exercises seems to create a borderline between mundane ways of thinking and a new "open territory" in which to explore.

After a while, I began humming a random legato melody. My student tried to follow me exactly at first, but then she got the idea and started on her own random melody. The melodic line dived and swooped like an airplane, so my voice became like an airplane engine.

During this part of the experience, I had an eerie feeling that my brother was with me and that we were in our room in our beds and he was playing "war" with his toy airplanes after the light had been turned out and we were supposed to be asleep. I think I was four and he was five when we used to play airplane.

Shortly, my student was also sounding like an airplane engine. My voice turned into a cry and a falling sound. My student cried too, but in a "little girl" voice (this was the same voice that she normally sang in). When I heard her little girl voice, my voice grew into a large growling beast expressing curiosity at the sound of the little girl voice. Then she started to spit and yowl like a cat. I yowled back and then howled like a wolf. We howled together for a little while and that turned into a deep head tone with a lot of vibrato, like a "Theramin," the instrument from the old science fiction movies.

We continued on like this for a while longer. I just let my voice wander in as random a fashion as possible making all kinds of growls, chirps, animal and bird sounds and singing spirals, circles, like drawing with your finger in the air. She followed me and created her own sounds. When we finished, we both talked about experiencing a reawakening of childhood memories. For me, a feeling of wholeness accompanied my explorations and a state of mind that I can only describe as filled with a fresh mystery and wonder that I have not felt since my earliest memories. As if I had opened a gate into a "secret garden" with walls of ivy and vines of jasmine surrounding a mysterious pool where an old-fashioned mirrored Victorian globe sits on a pedestal promising mystical visions to those who care to look. This image actually corresponds to a neighbor's garden I used to visit when I was about five years old. My student experienced the vocal play existing in a time "before I had to sound nice." She told me that these experiences transformed her understanding of who she is as a singer and as an artist, and what she could do with her voice.

How did this experience relate to the reawakening of old learning pathways? When was the last time you or any adult you know engaged in vocal play of this sort? Most likely, from the ages of two or three months old to the ages of three or four years old when "spontaneous song making" gives way to learning the songs of the dominant culture. Research in the development of musical competence, as reported by Howard Gardner,[3] suggests that infants and small children engage in "sound play" much like what we were doing and that this play exhibits creative and generative properties useful in the development of musical intelligence. In the vocal play that we did, there was definitely a sense of rediscovering a lost world and that the actual melodic contour that we were making up was functioning as a map or pathway to enter that world.

This was the first part of my story, and in and of itself it raises many questions related to my experience as a singer and teacher. Looking at our interaction as one of "reflective practice," my role as "exemplar" served to get us into the realm of consciousness which we were exploring together, but beyond that, I found myself as much an explorer as my student as we went on.

Pathways to Childhood

Jeanne Bamberger has done a lot of work with the nursery rhyme "Twinkle, Twinkle Little Star" in the field of melody recognition and music cognition. She calls nursery rhymes like Twinkle the "Simples" of our culture, meaning "the simple tunes and rhythms so common to the music of our culture that in constructing a hearing we actively seek them out, constructing them anew as features which we expect to find as giving music its coherence."[4] It came into my mind to do the same thing with "Twinkle, Twinkle Little Star" that we had just done with free form sounds. I wanted to see what effect removing the expectation of a "constructed hearing" would have on our perception of the meaning of the experience. So, we took the words of the song only and played with them and with the melody; it sounded like this:

As we continued to explore in this way, a most interesting experience began to unfold. The images the words conveyed began to take on a feeling of mystery and luminosity. I began to see these old questions in new light:

TWINKLE, TWINKLE LITTLE STAR . . .

I saw a single star blazing in a clear evening sky . . .

HOW I WONDER! . . . HOW? . . . I WONDER?

I had to stop and ask: "Who is it who wonders?" (with such a fresh feeling of innocence and curiosity). My student said, "I feel like I'm hearing this for the first time!" I felt the same way. I realized then that this feeling was the way I felt the very first time I heard "Twinkle, Twinkle Little Star." My insight of the moment was that de-constructing the melody of the nursery rhyme liberated the images of the song and allowed me to re-experience the feelings I had as a child hearing it glistening in my imagination for the very first time, before repetition of the melody had cemented it into habit, pushed down into the background of my memory.

We had been working on this for two and a half hours at that point and we needed to stop. Before we ended the lesson, we recorded what we had done with "Twinkle" in its new form. Since this was our last session, I was not able to continue to work with my student in this way. But the experience left me feeling like an explorer who comes upon a hidden world just as she is forced by circumstances to turn back.

From a transpersonal point of view, I have to ask myself, what time frame did I experience? Or, what time frames did I simultaneously experience? Obviously, around two and a half hours passed on the clock. My experience was that time did not seem to pass at all while it was happening, I would have thought about twenty minutes had passed. And in terms of the freshness and vividness of the "Twinkle" experience, I have to ask, is my infant-to-four-year-old self coexistent with my adult self, for this experience to be so readily accessible, given the right "pathway"? How does this passage of time relate to the phenomena of change, if all of these states of consciousness can exist simultaneously?

Jean Gebser gives a potential framework for understanding this experience in his theory of five structures of consciousness which can be seen as existing simultaneously, integrated into our experience of what we call reality. His "Magic Structure," in which time does not seem to exist and an "uncanny awareness of one another's rhythm and location, moving as one rather than as a collection of individuals,"[5] seems to be one way to describe some of the elements of our vocal play and Twinkle experiences.

The questions that I started with at the beginning of my story are related to each other through my student's experiences and my own. The meanings and perspectives overlap and lose their theoretical boundaries when compared to actual experiences. This may imply that we do not have definitive answers for how vocal play, as I have described it here, accesses these deeper levels of consciousness. I certainly come up with more questions, in looking at these kinds of experiences, than I have answers. In conclusion, I would like to propose some possible connections and areas of further exploration for those interested, including myself.

Singing and States of Consciousness

Why did each of my students recall memories and experiences from childhood as giving meaning to the experiences that they were having singing as adults? My hunch is that singing creates a cognitive pathway. Threads of understanding and experience may be stored in the mind in some way that is accessed, in this case, through singing. Further, I have the feeling that this is only the tip of the iceberg. The term "Cognitive pathway" does not seem to fully convey the nature of the experience. In the case of the Twinkle experience, the liberation of the images from the melody, as I mentioned earlier, seems to be the key to unlocking whatever "secret garden" of early childhood may be available.

A review of research in melodic information processing suggests that the contour of a melody is very important to melodic recognition in long-term memory.[6] Could the act of singing and, in particular, singing in the ways that I have described, be connected to the reawakening of these contours? That would imply that kinesthetic factors, the actual singing of the contours and saying of the words, were implicit in reawakening these experiences and memories, not just the process of audiation (remembering the melodies in one's imagination). The powerful and immediate quality of the "Twinkle" experience goes far beyond simply remembering the melodic contour of the song. That is why I have said that terms like "cognitive pathways" and "melodic contour," which have specific meanings in the domain of the research that they came out of, do not fully convey the scope of the experiences that the exercises described here invoke. But somehow, a feeling that some kind of memory pathway had been triggered from a cognitive perspective persists.

Looking at these experiences from a transpersonal or holistic perspective is enlightening because this field of research is concerned with looking at phenomena through a larger lens than earlier psychological paradigms. From this larger, holistic perspective, the conflicting language of melodic recognition, contour, and triggering of cognitive pathways versus the feeling of "being there" in a "secret garden" in some other state than normal linear time, can be resolved and reframed.

As I mentioned before, one perspective from this Transpersonal field is from Gebser's "Magic Structure of Consciousness." Ornstein describes our normal state of consciousness as a "somewhat arbitrary personal construction." He points out that another mode of consciousness exists in other cultures that are "arational, predominately spatial rather than temporal, and receptive as opposed to active." Tart describes, in his research about altered states of consciousness, a specific state he calls "discrete altered states of consciousness": "A radical alteration in the overall patterning of consciousness, . . . Like that sometimes achieved through meditative techniques."[7]

In terms of new questions for a teacher/student dialogue in singing practice, two elements in these experiences really struck me. One was that the concept of reflective practice—to do an exercise or have an experience and then reflect on the experience together, and then to move to the next experience out of that reflective insight—is the kind of creative process which I have come to treasure in being a teacher, a safe place is created for both the student and me to explore and practice and even make mistakes which could turn into new avenues of inquiry. Both of these perspectives strike me as being a productive setting for learning about singing and the nature of vocal sounds and melodic memory.

These ways of looking at the experiences I have described in my story go much further in giving me a sense that someone has experienced going to the same states of consciousness where my students and I have gone. I have the feeling that riches exist there for the intrepid explorer, a wellspring, perhaps, for reviving the mind and spirit as well as a deeper understanding of the nature and purpose for singing.

Notes

1. See *Artistry, The Work of Artists*, V. A. Howard, Hackett Pub., Indianapolis, Cambridge, 1982 and discussions of the concept of "Reflection-in-Action" in Revisiting Children's Drawings of Simple Rhythms: A Function for Reflection-in-Action, in Bamberger, J., *U-Shaped Behavioral Growth*. Academic Press, Inc., 1982.

2. I am defining "toning" as working with tonal qualities such as humming one pitch and changing the texture of the sounds made with the voice, as opposed to "vocal Play" which I define as following one's imagination using one's voice, making all kinds of sounds with the voice or body which give "voice" to the imagination. The distinction is that in the first case, the students attention is on the sounds the body can make. In the second case, one's body creates sounds which follow the wanderings of the imagination.

3. Gardner, H., *Frames of Mind*. Basic Books, NY: 1983, pp. 108-109.

4. Bamberger, J., *The Mind Behind the Musical Ear*. Harvard University Press, Cambridge, MA: 1990.

5. Behnke, E., *Toward Integral Consciousness for an Integral World*. Gebser Studies: vol. 1. Felton, CA: 1987.

6. Dowling, J, Melodic Information Processing and Its Development. In Deutsch, D. (ed.), *The Psychology of Music*. Academic Press, Inc., 1982, pp. 426-427.

7. Ornstein, R. E., *Psychology of Consciousness*. W. H. Freeman & Co., San Francisco, 1972. Tart, C. T., *Transpersonal Psychologies*. Psychological Processes, Inc., El Cerrito, CA, 1983.

Part IV

CREATING

17

Meetings with the Unsounded Voice

Peter O'Loughlin

Prelude to Peter O'Loughlin

In the mid-1970s the Canadian Association for Music Therapy held its annual conference in Montreal. A young man introduced himself to me and said that he was considering coming out to Vancouver and taking our music therapy training program at Capilano College. This was Peter.

Peter had been taking some coursework in music therapy in Montreal and became serious about furthering his education in the field and subsequently moved to Vancouver to begin his studies. He brought his many talents into our West Coast community along with his bright spirit, his creativity, and his wonderful aesthetic sensibilities.

Although Peter was a fine musician, some of my fondest memories of him are as a dancer. For years, he had followed the tradition of Sufism and, on many occasions, he led us in the Dances of Universal Peace.

Several years after graduating, Peter assumed my former position at the University of British Columbia Dayhouse, a therapeutic community which offered an integrated approach to psychotherapy, and which had a long-standing commitment to music therapy as one of the treatment modes.

Peter, who was once my student, over the years has become my colleague and friend. We share an intense connection in our relationship to aesthetics and spirituality. We have witnessed and participated in each other's changes over many years now.

Peter is full of passion and fire and commitment to his aspiration of finding the best way to participate in the process of healing. He inspires many people on his way. I am one.

Of himself Peter says: "Working on this essay has helped to remind me of how intimately my whole life is carried along by Sound. It is the fulcrum on which I find my balance. As a social worker, music therapist, and choir director, it is the world of Sound which frames the purpose of my life, and any contributions I am able to make through my music or words is in homage to what Sound has given me."

The drum is moved on slowly, one by one, around the circle. There is pain in this circle: women and men gathering in their struggles to heal personal wounds, traumas, degradations, and disappointments, risking disclosure and vulnerability in an unchartered passage toward wholeness and self-acceptance. The drum moves on. I wait for the in-breath of this next person and the sound which will be its gift from within.

The power of the human voice is unmistakable. We enter the world with our own cry, after nine months of absorbing the impressions of our mother's voice in the womb. Our contact with the world is constantly carried out in the medium of the voice, be it speaking, singing, shouting, crying, laughing, groaning, or any other variation of vocal expression. We have visual memories of those we meet, but whereas our recollection of a person's face often becomes vague, their voice continues to be recalled vividly in our aural memory. In meeting an individual, we make assumptions about him based on many social cues such as size, gender, dress, and physical mannerisms. But all of these assumptions can be wiped out with one word if his voice does not fit our presumptions about him. Even if that person is easily stereotyped by his initial presentation, such as a large and gruff looking man who appears to belong in a football uniform, his voice (for example if it is gentle and concerned) leaves the stronger and more lasting impression.

Her eyes communicate fear. In fact, there is a glimpse of terror before she casts her glance downward toward where her hands rest, without strength, on the drum. By giving the instructions to "take a breath in and let a sound out," I realize that I have asked these group members to take a leap of therapeutic faith of heroic measure not apparent in the simple structure given. For this woman, as for several others in the group, it is an immense test of their trust of the others as well as of themselves.

While the power of the vocal expression is readily apparent, the power of the unsounded voice holds its own profound influence on the individual and those around him or her. These are the sounds which are held back in silence, in secrecy, in respect, in silent rage, in love. The effect of the unsounded voice can be healing and refreshing when it is kept in silence out of an awareness that such silence is timely and healthy. But more often, particularly in therapy, we experience the unsounded voice as the suppression which comes as a result of oppression. It is the conscious and unconscious obstruction of feelings whose natural impulse is to move outward through the vocal cords, but which remain blocked by ingrained family and social rules and taboos. There is no healing in this type of silence, only shame and confusion about the memories and emotions lurking beneath the voice.

After hesitating in silence, she takes her inhalation. But it sticks, locked physically by her throat, emotionally by a history as yet unrevealed. There is only a small sound which can escape this tightness, partly a gag and partly a whimper. The rest of the breath is expelled in anxious frustration, and she shakes her head in a manner between anger and sadness.

Sounded and unsounded voices interact. In healthy communication one listens while another is speaking; the silence between the notes of music define and shape the notes that we hear. In the case of the voice which is limited because it is blocked by fear, there is an interaction with the history of other voices which were expressed. It is the often painful influence of our aural memory. As we develop, we may hear screaming in our home, violence, threats, rules about speaking about feelings or family secrets, in addition to the social dictums about acceptable role behavior, all of which can add up to the commandment of "Thou shalt not be heard."

I ask her to try again, reassuring her that there are many sounds which we all keep hidden inside, that there are no "right" or "wrong" vocalizations. But she responds in a barely audible tone "I can't . . . I can't." We all know what these words really mean: "Something inside of me doesn't allow me to let that sound out." The sadness which wells up in her eyes is held fast from escaping the body in the same way as the voice's expression is repressed.

There is a split in the individual whose voice has been suppressed in this way. Simultaneously, she or he desires to unleash the sound while feeling obliged to maintain loyalty to the family or social "programming" which quieted that voice in the first place. Such a split can provide fertile ground for therapeutic intervention, but it can also be a pitfall for an overzealous practitioner. The therapist and group need to practice sensitivity to this split, offering safety and pacing which respect the group member's defenses. Both sounded and unsounded voices have power to be either generative or destructive, and ego strength and boundaries should be assessed before embarking on vocal "openings" in therapy.

She is gripping the sides of the drum as if holding onto a precipice. I invite her to place her hands palms down on the surface of the drum, a strong skin-covered barrel used for support and external focus. As she begins to move her hands in circular motions on the drumhead, her breath returns to a more natural cadence, joining the smooth sound of the instrument. "Breath in, small sound out. Begin with anything—a sigh, a hum . . . any sound will be right . . ." She allows herself to emit a sigh, brief and soft, and then another which is longer and fuller, an "ah" which begins to open and drifts into an "oh" by the end of the breath's span. The door to the unsounded voice is beginning to open and fear gives way to freedom.

Metaphorically, as well as at the physical level of vibration, movement is life and lack of movement is death. The individual who caps the well containing the primary feelings of pain, rage, and shame, as well as joy and love, practices a kind of death in which lifeforce arising is always swallowed back down into the bruised stillness. This inertia can often be thawed through appropriate applications of movement, such as the hand moving on the drumhead, use of touch by the therapist (with permission) on the person's heart center or solar plexus, and joining the person's voice momentarily in an initial gentle sigh or hum. Once there is movement, the flow of release becomes self-sufficient; control or manipulation by either the individual or the therapist is at this point counterproductive to the natural birthing process of what has been hidden.

When the sound comes, it seems to arrive from another dimension. Certainly, we have not heard this woman express any sound beyond her normally muted speech. As a therapist who has midwifed many such openings, I am calm in anticipation of the voice's full expression. But nothing prepares me for what emerges beside me, a groan which grows with repetition into something more like thunder, a startling sound which is no longer human nor identifiable in human terms, but rather is the pitch of life itself swelling from a source larger than this one being's body. In unison it is the bellow of a lion and the howl of the wind, a cry of death and a call of the newly living.

We know that later we will hear the stories of trauma and abuse which led to this outpouring of unlimited feeling. But right now the sound is the story, complete and wholly authentic in its resonance. Each of us in the room is encompassed by its force in a way which gathers all our stories and unexpressed longing into its reverberations. There is no one person making this sound.

The primitive discharge of the fullest sounds begins to quiet into a flow of more familiar feelings: first anger, then the gentle aftermath of tears which announce both grief and joy. As the vocalizations begin to soften into breath alone, I ask her "Is there more?" In wisdom and fresh self-acceptance, she answers, "Yes, there is, but that's enough for now."

I am deeply grateful for the opportunity to be present at such moments, when trust in self and others has provided the terrain for encounters with the nature of sound. It has reinforced for myself over and over the belief that the power of the voice is not exceeded by any other, whether it be the soothing tones of a lullaby, the words of a friend, the inspiration of oratory . . . or a profound cry from within after the words "Breath in, sound out."

18

Modes of Consciousness in Guided Imagery and Music (GIM): A Therapist's Experience of the Guiding Process

Kenneth E. Bruscia

Prelude to Kenneth Bruscia

When I first moved to California in 1980 I was asked by the National Association for Music Therapy Western Region to present some work for their conference in Long Beach. I knew very few people there at the time, being fresh from Canada and not really a part of the Southern California professional music therapy fabric.

However, from time to time, one merely recognizes someone. It does not have to be a person one has met or has even heard about. This is how I came to know Ken Bruscia. In fact I never even really met him then. I just recognized him. The sense of recognition said only: "This is someone you will know, someone who you will have a connection with."

In 1982, I found out what that connection was or could be. It could be said that Ken and I are contemporaries in age. We share a work, a culture, a time. But as our "works" have developed, it seems that the uniqueness of our connection has to do with our passion for theory. Yet we are alike and different in our approach. Ken attended the *1982 NYU Symposium on Music in the Life of Man: Toward a Theory of Music Therapy*. His paper was a deep reflection, a self-hermenueutic, entitled, "Music in the Life of One Man." Although Ken and I have had merely brief encounters over the years, this paper was one which stayed with me, and which I read over and over again. I thought that it took courage for Ken to reveal himself in this way. And I was also in the middle of questioning my approach, looking for a source, a beginning to my theoretical work, which could have integrity and which would accurately portray the depth of my connection to the work. Since then, Ken and I have led parallel lives. Though we have not been part of the same dialog experiences, such as the ones in Phoenecia, we do occasionally connect and it always reassures me that he is there, doing what he is doing to expand our work, reflecting deeply on his own experience of the work, and writing and speaking about it.

Sometimes I have described Ken as the ethnographer for music therapy. He has collected and published a great deal of material documenting and interpreting other people's work. In this way, he is the classic academic. In an age when some music therapists insist on classical "indigenous theory," with a limited engagement in tradition, Ken documents that which has come before. Gradually, he has begun to articulate his own ideas on the topic, which are informed by a breadth and depth of studying our "tradition" and our contemporary music therapy practitioners.

Ken has also been a diplomat for our field, spreading the good news of music therapy with his intellectual acuity and charisma, throughout the world.

He did pioneering work with Barbara Hesser in shaping the American Association for Music Therapy and inaugurated both undergraduate and graduate degree programs in the late 1970s at Temple University. He has his own publishing company in music therapy (Barcelona Press).

There will always be something new for Ken. And this is the stuff of inspiration. He is one, as you will soon discover, who explores the territory of the relationship between one's own development and the development of a life's work.

Ken is a professor of music therapy at Temple University. He has worked as a certified music therapist with a wide range of clientele and is now in private practice specializing in Guided Imagery in Music. He has served as president of the American Association for Music Therapy and the National Coalition of Arts Therapies. His publications include several books and articles about music therapy.

Introduction

"Being There"

This is a self-inquiry that began by questioning what it means to "be there" for another person, and particularly within the context of a therapist-client relationship. The question arose as I was writing a case study on my work in music psychotherapy (Bruscia, 1991), and realized how much I concerned myself with "being there" for the client.

Interestingly, this phrase is used in everyday language—quite frequently and unambiguously—to describe an apparently everyday occurrence; it is not mere jargon created by therapists to define a specific clinical phenomenon. Thus, there seems to be a general consensus that these two words are sufficient and appropriate for describing an experience that is commonly understood, and which in my opinion, seems to be a rather complex and subtle one. Nevertheless, I cannot help but wonder why these two particular words have been selected out of the host of other possibilities.

It seems significant that we describe the experience as a way of "being" rather than a mode of "doing" or "having." Moreover, this way of being seems to be spatial rather than temporal. Even more curiously, the location in space is "there" rather than "here." When I say that you are "there" for me—where did I go that I am no longer "here"? Where did you leave to go "there" with me, and where are we both now that we are together?

Upon analyzing my case study in light of these questions, I was struck by how much I was continually moving and being moved through different experiential spaces. As I tried to explain these "moves" as attempts to "be there" for the client, I realized that "being there" involved moving many different places, both toward and away from him and myself. Sometimes I moved closer to him, to be "there" beside him, but just as often I moved away from him—to be "here" with me or be "there" without him or "there" opposite to him. Sometimes I even moved away from both of us, so that I could see us being "here" or "there" and "together" or "apart." Nevertheless, I still suspect that all of these moves were efforts to "be there" for him— albeit in many different ways.

Another question that arose in my self-reflection is exactly "what" was I moving to "be there" for him? Certainly, I was not moving "me" in my entirety, and though my body was intimately involved, I cannot say that it was the main part being moved; besides, it is impossible for anyone to physically be in the same space as another person. This suggests that there was another dimension of me moving—a dimension that does not have the same spatial limitations as my body—a dimension that allows me to be in space without occupying and being limited by it.

For purposes of this paper, I have dubbed this dimension of myself "conscious," and defined it as a state of awareness maintained by any psychological activity, including both covert and overt processes (e.g., sensation, affect, behavior, thought, etc.).

Some Notions on Consciousness

The idea of moving my consciousness through space without occupying it is both challenging and freeing. I can be there without having to leave here, and I can be here without having to leave there. Or if I so wish, I can stay there without being here, or stay here without being there. Thus, I can be transported to another space without moving there in the literal sense of leaving where I was before. Hence I can be in more than one space at a time, and the process of transporting myself can be described as one of expansion rather than migration. Conversely, I can be in one space at a time, and the process of staying there can be described as one of centering.

As my consciousness expands and centers, I also have the option of varying its intensity. That is, I can be "less here than there" or "less there than here," thus shifting the "weight" of my consciousness, just as I shift the weight of my body from one side or part to another.

Every time I expand, center, or shift my consciousness, I enter a different mode of consciousness. The process is similar to modulating in music or changing modes. In music, modulation takes place when melodic and harmonic structures expand, center, and shift with respect to their modality (scale) and tonality (resting tone). Continuing in this analogy, music is like consciousness in that it can be in one mode fully, in transition to another mode, in several modes at once, or not in a mode at all.

Guided Imagery and Music

Guided Imagery and Music (GIM) provides rich opportunities for both client and therapist to experience different modes of consciousness. In fact, changes in consciousness are essential to this method. Originally conceived by Helen Bonny (1978), GIM is an individual form of therapy, healing, or self-actualization which involves imagining to music in an altered state of consciousness while dialoguing with a guide. When used in psychotherapy, GIM is an uncovering technique which accesses unconscious material, facilitates cathartic release, and leads to deep insights into the inner psyche. Central to its effectiveness is a client-therapist relationship which provides the safety and trust needed for the client to investigate deep inner regions of the psyche. In addition, in-depth training is needed to use the technique.

Each session begins with an exploration of issues, concerns, or objectives pertinent to the client at the time. This may be accomplished through verbal discussion or nonverbal techniques (e.g., mandala drawing, expressive movement, musical improvisation, clay work, etc.). Based on themes or images that emerge through these preliminary explorations, the therapist guides the client through a relaxation induction, and then focuses the client on a starting image in preparation for listening to the music. The music may be one of several taped programs specially designed for use in GIM. Each program contains works from the classical music literature, which have been carefully selected and sequenced for specific therapeutic uses. In the music-imaging process, the client may have body sensations, visions, feelings, memories, fantasies, or any variety of internal experiences, all of which are regarded as images. A dialogue is maintained throughout the imaging, with the client describing his/her experiences as they occur, and the therapist probing, supporting, reflecting, and amplifying them. The therapist writes a transcript of the dialogue for later reference. When the imaging and music come to a close, the therapist helps the client to return to a normal state of consciousness. A verbal discussion follows, focusing on the client's reactions to the imagery and aspects of the experience that are therapeutically significant. Nonverbal techniques cited above may also be used to process the imagery.

Purpose of This Chapter

Now that basic notions about consciousness and GIM have been put forward, I can more clearly state the purpose of this chapter. It is to examine how a therapist expands, centers, and shifts his consciousness while guiding several sessions, and examples of each construct will be given through analysis of a transcript of one GIM session. Thus, the chapter can be described as phenomenological in its focus on experience, and introspective in its method of inquiry.

For the sake of clarity, parts of the theory will be presented alternately with excerpts from the session transcript. I have used gender-specific language throughout the chapter because I am describing my work with another male, and because the theory is built around my work with males.

Theory

Worlds of Consciousness

When guiding an imagery experience, I continually expand, center, and shift my consciousness in relation to three experiential spaces: the client's world, my own personal world, and my world as a therapist.

When I move into the client's world, I attempt to become aware of and—to the extent possible—experience what the client is experiencing, in the way in which he is experiencing it. I begin by observing and attending where the client is or how he is in that place, and then attempt to put myself in that same position with the same attitude or response to it. For example, if I observed that his breathing speeds up, I speed mine up to the same pace and then empathize with the experience of breathing faster. Or if he begins to cry, I may allow myself to cry with him, as he is crying, and for whatever reason he is crying.

When I move into my personal world, I focus my awareness on myself and allow myself to experience—as fully as appropriate—whatever I am experiencing, and in whatever way I am experiencing it. For example, if my neck is getting tight, I allow my attention to go there so I can feel it and perhaps discover what I need to do to relieve it. Or, during a session, my attention may momentarily shift to events of the day, or I may have flashbacks of my own life.

When I move into the therapist's world, I experience myself and client as a dyadic unit, with each of us falling within boundaries of a client-therapist relationship, and each of us fulfilling certain roles and responsibilities. I experience the client as a person seeking my help, and I experience myself as a therapist who uses his professional expertise and personal commitment to provide that help. I experience our relationship centered around a contract which commits us to a common goal (therapeutic change, healing, actualization of the client), with complementary roles of helper and helped, and boundaries dictated by personal and professional codes of ethics. When I become aware of myself in this world, my experience is mediated by who I am as a therapist with this client; similarly, my experience of the client is mediated by who he is as a client with me as a therapist. Thus, my own body sensations, feelings, and thoughts are experienced in terms of how they relate to the client, the client's experience, my role as a therapist, our shared objective, and the boundaries of the client-therapist relationship; similarly, the client's body sensations, feelings, and thoughts are experienced in terms of how they relate to me as therapist, our objective, and the boundaries of our relationship.

Levels of Experiencing

My experiences within each of these worlds can focus on many different things, and I can experience them with varying degrees of immediacy or elaboration. I have found four such levels of experiencing, which correspond roughly to the four "functions" identified by Carl Jung (1933) (viz., sensing, feeling, thinking, and intuiting).

At the most immediate or "sensory" level, I can experience things spontaneously through my body, physically apprehending what is there directly through my sense, and with no elaboration of or reflection upon the experience other than simple description of the sensory information. For example, I see the client's body tension, I feel a knot in my stomach, I see his face reddening, I feel my hand on his shoulder, I hear the music getting louder, I see the vivid yellows in his painting. Of primary concern are sensorimotor realities, physical facts or objective representations of subjective experiences.

At the next level, I experience things effectively, and identify the feelings and emotions aroused by whatever is taking place. I do this by allowing my psyche to make associations with or effective representations of what is happening, thus enabling memories, emotions, or unverbalizable feelings to surface and perhaps trigger further reactions. Through these associations, representations, and the subsequent reaction, it is possible for me to discriminate one experience from another within the affective domain. Thus the knot in my stomach feels like frustration (not fear), similar to what happens when I am disappointed; his body tension seems to be fear (not anger), similar to how one braces for trauma. This level goes beyond pure description of the experience because it involves elaboration of it with regard to how one values or appraises the experience (e.g., whether it is painful or pleasurable, good or bad, threatening or safe) and because it leads to some kind of effective classification of it (e.g., sorrow, joy, peace, anger, etc.).

At the third level, I experience the world reflectively, attempting to make meaning out of my sensory and affective experiences. Here I go beyond pure sensory description and simple affective elaboration, and begin to analyze the experience within the cognitive domain. This requires stepping out of the experience to observe myself experiencing it, thinking about the nature of the experience, and then searching for ways to explain it so that it can have meaning. The main objective is insight. Thus, the knot in my stomach is something that happens when I get frustrated with others—I hold back my feelings about them by tying knots in my stomach, and this gives me the pain I need to punish myself for getting into such a knot in the first place. Or, his body is tightening to brace himself against something he fears I will say to him, and this is a sign of transference in therapy.

Finally, I experience at the intuitive level. I do this when I go beyond sensory data, feelings, and thoughts, and create my own model of the world or my experiences of it. Like the previous level, I reflect upon my experience, but when I intuit, I have spontaneous "inner" knowing of something which is not based merely on "outer" events in the same logical fashion—nevertheless, there is an organic completeness to the meaning I have created. When I intuit, I go beyond what is given, and what we know of the nature of things, and gain insights about the universe which are unverifiable or even unfathomable. It is a way of spontaneously integrating all three levels of experiences.

To summarize: the sensory level involves spontaneous description of immediate physical experience with no elaboration of it; the affective level involves spontaneous elaboration of immediate physical experience within the affective domain; the reflective level involves self-observation and elaboration of sensory and effective experiences within the cognitive domain; and the intuitive level involves spontaneous integration of sensory, affective, and reflective experiences.

Jung asserts that these four functions describe the completeness of human experience: "Sensation establishes what is actually given, thinking enables us to recognize its meaning, feelings tells us its value, and finally intuition points to the possibilities of the whence and whither that lie within the immediate facts. In this way we can orientate ourselves with respect to the immediate world as completely as when we locate a place geographically by latitude and longitude" (1933, p. 107).

Session: Part One

What follows is the opening section of a GIM session that I guided with Tom, a young man with the AIDS virus. This was the tenth session in a series aimed at helping him to deal with buried feelings regarding the disease. I selected this particular session because of the intensity and complexity of his images, the important role played by music, and the myriad challenges that it posed to both of us.

The left column gives the running dialogue that took place in the imaging portion of the session. All of the statements are quotes from my written transcript of the session. In the right column are recollections and reconstructions of my experiences and reactions, which I have classified according to the theoretical constructs presented. Although the transcript contains rather detailed information, it was impossible to recall my reactions from moment to moment in the kind of detail presented below; thus some of the reactions are hindsight, elaborations of what I do remember. In all cases, what I have stated as my reactions are authentic in the sense that they are typical of the way I work.

Transcripts can be read in two ways: straight down the left column (which provides a chronological sequence of the client's imagery along with my interventions), or back and forth from left to right columns (which shows how moves in my consciousness affected my experiences and interventions). Abbreviations are as follow:

C = Client's World   1 = Sensory
P = Personal World   2 = Affective
T = Therapist's World   3 = Reflective
                          4 = Intuitive

The session began with Tom drawing a mandala that had concentric circles of bright colors enclosing a center of green. In my relaxation induction, I suggested that he was resting on the grass of a meadow, on a sunny day, surrounded by flowers. The taped program I used was entitled "Creativity III" designed by Linda Keiser. The tape begins with Wagner's "Seigfried Idyll," a 17-minute fantasy based on four recurring motifs from the opera. The melodies overlap and extend endlessly, with the support of rich orchestral textures. The mood is continuously tranquil and tender, but the form of the piece tantalizes the listener. The music holds the listener to it, not allowing even the slightest swerve of focus, sometimes even teasing the listener with its endlessness.

Dialogue	Modes of Consciousness
Tom: The flowers are azaleas—bright magenta—the grass is very green and lush. I see myself kneeling on the ground, digging into the earth with my hands.	
	T1: His breathing is regular; his face is calm. *T4:* He may use this scene to dig up his past. *T3:* The music offers the right support for this. Let him explore without any influence.
Ken: mm—hmm.	
Tom: I feel bones down there. They seem to be cracked into several pieces. I found a skull. It's broken in two. The edges are real jagged.	
	C2: I can feel him getting nervous about what he's digging up. *P2:* I don't want this skeleton to be him. *T1:* His body is tensing.
Ken: How are you feeling?	
Tom: Confused. Why am I digging up such bones in such a beautiful place?	
	T1: He has a mischievous look on his face. *P2:* I really

enjoy his sense of humor. *T4:* I think he is going to blame me (or my selection of the music) for his images (as he has done previously). *T3:* Give him options so that he can take responsibility for what is happening.

Ken: Is there something you'd rather be doing in the meadow?

Tom: (Smiling) No . . . now that I've started this, I'm curious about these bones.

C3: Tom knows that my question was an attempt to avoid his accusations. Or he may have the impression that I think he is "chicken." *T3:* Do not get into the transference. He needs to gather more information about the bones.

Ken: How many bones are there?

C1: I can imagine a skeleton forming.

Tom: Enough to make a person . . . I am arranging them on the ground.

Tom: I wonder if the bones are me. But, when I look around, I get flashes of this person being stoned to death.

T3+4: Wasn't Mary Magdalene being stoned for promiscuity when Christ redeemed her? I wonder if Tom is digging up guilt over the past. *P2:* The music is sad. *P4:* This scene is going to bring him great sadness. *P2:* I wish I could spare him this. *C2:* I feel his vulnerability. *T3:* I may be reacting more emotionally than he is, and in different sensory channels. I am in hear-feel and he is in a visual mode. He needs more vivid visual information.

Ken: How does the person look?

Tom: He's covered with blood.

Ken: Can you see his face?

Tom: Yes. It's so strange. He doesn't look like me, but I feel what he feels very deeply.

T3: Tom is keeping his distance by being an observer in this scene. He frequently uses splitting and denial to dissociate from difficult feeling. I should explore whether he is ready to get a little closer to the feelings he has "buried."

Ken: Are you very far from the man?

Tom: Yes, I am watching at a distance, because it is too dangerous to get any closer to the mob.

P1: My back is uncomfortable. I need to sit up straight. *T4:* My back may be empathizing with the man, or with Tom's need to stand up for him.

Ken: How are you feeling?

Tom: I have a splitting headache watching this. The

man wants it to be over. He has no idea why they are stoning him.

T3: There is another connection between Tom and the man. The man's skull is cracked and Tom's head is splitting.

P2: I cannot understand his refusal to step in and help the man—it is not like Tom. *T3:* He may need help or encouragement to do something . . . to take some responsibility.

Ken: Is there anything you can do or say?

Tom: I wish I could tell him to just let go . . . he needs to let go.

Ken: He needs to let go.

Tom: He's getting weaker . . . He's fallen to his knees. He can't stand up anymore. The rocks are hitting him all over.

C1+2: I imagine how the rocks feel hitting the man's body, and how sad and powerless Tom is feeling, as he watches from a distance.

Tom: Some of the people have stopped throwing stones. Their faces have changed from anger to curiosity . . . as if suddenly, they do not know why they did this to him. They're very quiet now.

C2: It is a relief to discover that perhaps these people are not all bad.

Ken: What else do you notice?

Tom: The others are still angry, and are throwing rocks viciously. They're shouting: "Die! Die! You bastard!" They have such blind hatred for the man.

P3+4: I wonder if Tom feels that people have blind hatred for him.

Ken: How do you feel about the man?

Tom: I feel his pain . . . and at the same time I feel the anger and confusion of the people who are stoning him.

Tom: He's lying down on the ground now. Everyone has stopped throwing stones and they are staring at him . . . waiting for him to die . . . as if they want to move on.

T1: Just when the music sounds as if it is ending, it starts again. *T2:* The music will not let the man go.

Ken: How is the man now?

Tom: He's barely hanging on, but his eyes are fixed on all of them.

P2: The scene of Christ's crucifixion comes to mind. Christ had no hate or anger, and forgave those who hated him blindly. *T3:* Tom has identified with Christ figures before.

Ken: Do his eyes say anything?

Tom: I can see that he has no hate or anger for them, just sadness.

> *P2:* The music is so tender. It sounds like the man's eyes caressing the people who have stoned him . . . so understanding and forgiving.

Ken: There's sadness in his eyes.

Tom: Yes. The end is nearing . . . He is starting to let go. (The music ends). Oh my God . . . he's dead. They have killed him.

> *C2:* I feel Tom's sadness for the man.
> *P2:* I feel sad for Tom.
> *T3:* Tom needs to be in touch with his sadness.

It is very difficult to describe what Tom and I were experiencing in those last few moments of the man's death. Both of our voices were cracking; our words fell into the same rhythm and tonality; and our bodies seemed filled with the tension and expectation. The most intimate and powerful aspect of this experience, however, was the music. It seemed to carry us along and into indescribable feelings, almost as if it was composed to support what was happening in Tom's images. And during the long periods of waiting for the man to let go, the music "held" us in suspense, while also presenting the deep sorrow and regret that both of us were feeling but neither of us could express.

Theory

So far the transcript has provided some clear illustrations of the three worlds and four levels of experiencing. What has also become clear, however, is that many aspects of my experience as a therapist are not adequately handled by these constructs. Specifically, there are noticeable differences in my consciousness within the client's world and within the therapist's world. That is, some experiences in his world were more vivid than others, and some were easier to empathize with than others. As a therapist, I was presented with the possibility of entering into a "transference" relationship, which would have substantially changed my experience. Thus, two further constructs are needed, one to deal with the various personal positions within the client's world, and the other to deal with parameters of the client-therapist relationship. These will be discussed in detail below.

I ended the first excerpt of the session with the man's death, not only because that is where the first musical selection ended, but also because this was a turning point in the session. Up to that point, both Tom and I were riveted on his images. What was happening to the man was at the forefront of our consciousness, and provided the main pretext for our interactions. Toward the end, however, the music seemed to assume greater significance in shaping our experiences.

This raises another important theoretical consideration—one that lies at the very core of GIM and one that explains the uniqueness of music psychotherapy in general. In addition to imagery, there are other contexts or media by which I can move my consciousness and focus my experience during a GIM session. When I move from one world to the next, or when I move from one level of experience to another, I travel through a medium. Something takes me from one place to another, keeps me there, or moves me away, as I allow it intentionally or unintentionally, or as I use it to do so. These media of transportation are central to a theory of consciousness for GIM, and are therefore examined below.

Personal Positions within the Client's World

A basic and inescapable fact of being a therapist is that sometimes I can enter the client's world and sometimes I cannot. There is a limit to my ability and willingness to stretch my own personal boundaries and structures to experience what the client is experiencing. Some terrains of his world are so foreign or threatening that they are simply beyond my grasp, as a person and/or therapist. Or, I simply want no part of them, for either personal or professional reasons.

Thus, when I enter the client's world, I have options with regard to how distant our experiences will be. Theoretically speaking, there are five positions I can take within the client's world.

Fusion. I experience the client's experience as identical to my own, with few, if any, provisions or adaptations necessary. Moving toward the client is moving toward myself. Our boundaries and structures are united, as indicated in the abbreviation C=P.

Accommodation. I experience what the client experiences by adapting my boundaries and structures to accommodate his experience. Thus, I experience his experience as he does, which is not exactly the way I do. To move toward the client, I have to move away from (or against) my own self. As abbreviated (C/P), the client's world takes presidence over my personal world.

Assimilation. I experience what the client experiences by assimilating it into existing boundaries and structures already within me. Thus, I experience his experience as similar to my experiences of the same thing. To experience the client, I move toward myself. As abbreviated (P/C), my personal world leads me into the client's world.

Differentiation. I do not experience the client's experience because it is substantially different from mine. Thus I do not experience his experience or his way of experiencing it. Rather than moving toward the client, I move away from him and toward myself. I establish my own boundaries and structures and consciously keep them separate from his. As abbreviated (C=P), our worlds are not alike.

Objectification. I am in the client's experience as an object. I do not experience what the client is being or doing, rather I experience myself as the receiver of his actions. As abbreviated (C→P) or (C→T), the client is acting upon me as a person or therapist.

Parameters of the Client-Therapist Relationship

Following rather traditional notions, the client and I may react to one another within transference/countertransference projections or in an authentic way. In a transference (TT), the client reacts to me as if I were a significant person in his life, most often as a parent. The reaction may be positive or negative, depending upon the kinds of feelings the client has about the significant person and then projects onto me. In a countertransference (XT), I react to the client's projections as if I were the significant person in his life, or I react to the client as if he were a significant person in my own life. In an authentic reaction (AT), the client reacts to me as a subject unfolding to him in the present—not as an object from his own past. Thus, I am who I am and the client is not confusing me with significant others in his life. Similarly, I react to the client per who he is, not as someone else in my own life. Within the present theory, I have authentic reactions as a person and/or therapist. (It should be noted that this is somewhat different from usual conceptions of authenticity as personal self-disclosure of therapist).

Media of Transportation

GIM offers several media for transporting my consciousness. The main ones are altered states of consciousness, music, imagery, physical interaction, and verbal interaction—all of which are continuously available to both client and therapist. Although they overlap considerably, and relate directly to one another, each of these media helps the client and therapist in unique ways and makes its own unique contribution to the psychotherapeutic process.

Altered State of Consciousness (ASC). GIM provides rich opportunities for experiencing different modes of consciousness—for both client and therapist. In fact, changes in consciousness are essential to this form of therapy. The first change takes place during the "relaxation induction" when the therapist helps the client to relax the body and focus the imagination. In effect, the therapist is inviting the client to enter an altered state of consciousness. An ASC occurs whenever a person leaves any part of here-now reality and moves to a different space and time. In GIM, the client's awareness moves away from the therapy room and begins to travel through various realms of the imagination.

It is important to note that during a GIM session, the client is not only the person in an ASC—the therapist himself may go in and out of normal and altered states. The reason is simple. The therapist is experiencing the same things as the client (viz., the induction, the music, and the imagery). During the relaxation induction, the therapist can easily absorb the trance-like effects of his own voice quality, or entrain with the rhythmic lull and repetitiveness of his own words. Then, as the music and imaging begin, the therapist also becomes subject to their "altering" effects, with the music transporting his consciousness increasingly farther away from the here-now axis, and with the client's imagery providing maps and directions to specific worlds and experiences within them. Entering an ASC for brief periods greatly facilitates the therapist's ability to move between worlds and layers of experience. I have found that ASCs serve to loosen my personal boundaries, make perceptual and affective experiences more vivid, free up my thinking, and enhance my intuitive capacities—all of which are tremendously valuable to the guiding process.

Music (MUS). The next major change in consciousness takes place when the music begins. Music has long been recognized as a very powerful facilitator of ASCs, and when used within the GIM setting, it literally "transports" client and therapist through the spaces and time zones of consciousness. It does this by operating directly on the entire person: entraining autonomic functions, stimulating the senses, probing the emotions, presenting ideas, and inspiring the spirit. It is also important to note that these multidimensional effects of music are cumulative. As the music extends in time, the listener goes deeper and deeper—or farther and farther away—and simultaneously, the elements of music become more and more powerful (or subtle) in their effects. When the music first begins, an ascending pitch sequence might stimulate an experience of gradual elevation or a small step to the next level, whereas later the same sequence might suggest a leap into heaven or a rocket trip to Mars.

Besides its effects on inducting altered states, music helps the therapist to move through various modes of consciousness in several other ways. First and foremost, it is a bridge into the client's world. One of the most important aspects of the music in GIM is that it is experienced simultaneously by both client and therapist at all times. It is like being in the same boat. That is, I hear what the client hears as he is hearing it, and in immediate relation to the sensations, feelings, images, and thoughts that the client is experiencing. Thus, it literally synchronizes our experiences so that we are "musically entrained" with one another as we proceed through the imaging experience. The music therefore builds immediate rapport, facilitates deep empathy, leads to a special intimacy between client and therapist, and brings insights into the client's experiences that cannot be gained otherwise.

But just as music serves as a bridge to the client, it can also touch me so deeply that I am plummeted into my own personal world. This is particularly common occurrence in GIM, because part of the therapist's training consists of experiencing all of the GIM tapes as a traveller or client. Thus, associations have often been formed with certain musical selections, and when they are heard, they trigger flashbacks of the therapist's own images and personal struggles. When this happens, the music can put the therapist back in his own boat, by himself, going down his own river. The transcript below gives an example of this happening. Naturally, this return to one's personal world can be used as an asset to the therapeutic process, or it can become an insidious obstacle to it. In this regard the therapist's personal reactions to music are very much like countertransference reactions: negative results occur when they keep the therapist from responding appropriately to the client's needs; positive results occur when they help the therapist to respond more sensitively and effectively. Incidently, I have found that the best way to deal with personal reactions to music is to move or shift my consciousness into the therapist's world.

Imagery (IMA). Meanwhile, as we have already seen, the imagery itself also contributes to an ASC. As the client becomes engaged in imagery, more and more awareness is required, and his consciousness begins to "shift" its intensity from being "more-here" to "more-there." This definition constitutes entering an ASC.

Similarly, as the therapist becomes engaged in the client's imagery, his consciousness begins to shift between altered and normal states. When this occurs, the client's imagery provides an ideal "intermediary object" in GIM. That is, it provides the occasion, container, and medium for multifaceted interactions between client and therapist. Frequently these interactions would not be possible without it. Perhaps the best way to describe them is that they travel through one another's consciousness.

Using an image as an intermediary object helps the client and therapist share the same space in consciousness. My first thought when the client becomes engrossed in a particular imagery scene is to explore where I can be positioned in relation to it. For example, if a client is walking through the forest with a friend, and they are confronted by a dragon, as the guide I stay aware that I can be in several places in relation to this scene: I can remain the guide, and help him deal with the dragon from where I am in the therapy room; I can enter the scene by imagining that I am in the client's shoes; I can imagine that I am his companion and help him to deal with the dragon from that point of view; or I can be the dragon itself—all of which still lie within the domain of the client's world. If I am truly not a part of the image in the client's psyche, I can position myself rather freely within the scene; however, the client may also place me in the image, either directly or symbolically. For example, suppose if after a few questions, I ask the client what the companion is doing, and he answers: "He keeps asking me questions about the dragon." I might suspect that, since I have also been asking questions, I may very well be his companion in the image. On the other hand, if the client describes the dragon in a way that fits me (e.g., he has a grey beard!), then I have some reason to suspect that I am the dragon.

The net effect of participating in the client's imagery is that it allows me to move my consciousness with relative ease, while also giving me easy access to the client's world, and something concrete to hold onto in the process. It is literally the "stuff" through which the client and I can interact.

Physical Interaction (PHY). Another medium of transportation is physical interaction between the client and me. This may include subtler forms such as eye contact and body language, as well as more direct forms such as touching and holding. These bodily communications may take place at any time, during discussions and ordinary states of consciousness and during the music-imaging and altered states.

Verbal Interaction (VRB). Verbal interaction is probably the most traditional medium for transporting one's consciousness. It includes not only the actual words and sentences exchanged, but also the tone of voice, phrasing, and rhythm of speech. As I listen to what the client is saying and how he is saying it, I can move my consciousness into his world; conversely, as I speak, I can invite the client into my world.

Session: Part Two

The excerpt below is a continuation of part one. The analysis has been expanded to include the new constructs (and abbreviations) introduced above. It should be noted, however, that the various kinds of client-therapist reactions are not always evident or relevant, and therefore have been included in the transcript analysis only where pertinent.

Dialogue	Modes of Consciousness
Tom: (silence)	*C=P 1/PHY:* During the silence before the next piece began, Tom sighed but his body did not release its tension. He had a sad expression on his face, and he held his eyes as tightly as if holding back the tears. I felt like my body was responding identically to his.
Ken: (silence)	
Tom: I feel so sad.	*AT 1+2/MUS:* The andante movement of William Schuman's Second Symphony begins with a melancholy melody in the woodwinds, supported by muted but full harmonies in the strings.
Ken: Yes, it's very sad.	

AT 3/MUS: The melody has an ambivalence about it, probably due to the intermingling of major and minor thirds, yet the overall mood is supportive and nurturing. It occurs to me that the main motif has the same descending minor third and melodic contour as the universal "children's tune."

Tom: (starts crying)

AT 1+3/PHY: This is the first time he has allowed himself to cry. Somehow the plight of this man has touched him deeply.

Tom: Other people are starting to cry as well . . . we are trying to console one another.

AT 1+3/PHY/MUS: Given the nurturing music and its association to children, I extend my hand underneath his neck to support him as he cried. (This kind of physical interaction had never been a problem before).

Ken: (cradles Tom's neck)

Tom: (stiffens his body in response to Ken's hands under his neck)

P 2/PHY: His response touches the very core of my being, as if my deepest wounds have been re-opened.

P 2/MUS/ASC: The music suddenly overtakes my emotions, and I feel myself trembling inside.

Tom: They seem so lost and confused, as if they don't understand how they got there.

Ken: They seem lost.

XT3: I have to listen to what Tom is saying, separate from the music.

XT 3/PHY/MUS: An unbelievable and uncanny coincidence has taken place. I have done to Tom exactly what happened to me in my own images, with exactly the same music. XT3/ASC: Someone who cared for me had tried to pick up and cradle me, and I stiffened my whole body as Tom did, as if neither of us have the trust we need to accept such a gesture of love and nurturance. My own guide was cradling my neck just as I was doing to Tom. I realize that I am having a full-blown countertransference reaction. XT 1/ASC: I begin to take deep breaths, and make conscious attempts to relax parts of my body that have tensed. XT 3/IMA: I try to refocus myself on Tom, recognizing that I may be misconstruing his experiences because of my own projections.

Tom: I feel like I have to forgive them all.

Ken: Is that what you would like to do?

AT 3/VRB: I wonder why he said "have to"?

P1+2/MUS: The Schuman is over (I feel relieved) and *AT1+3/MUS:* Elgar's "Sospiri" has begun. It is slow and mournful, and is ideal for supporting where Tom seems to be headed.

P 3: I do not have the intense associations to this piece.

AT 3/IMA: This may be a good opportunity to get him into the scene, so that he can stop being the split-off observer.

Tom: Yes.

Ken: Is it safe for you to step into the scene now and try?

Tom: Yes . . . It's OK now. I feel like I am becoming one of the men who stoned him. I am sitting on the ground with them . . . next to the dead man. Some of us are crying. It feels as if we are really no different from the man.

P/C 2/IMA: This scene feels like a "viewing" or wake. AT 3: The music seems to be grieving for us all. AT 3/IMA: It seems significant that he did not enter the scene as himself, and that he became one of the penitent ones who wants forgiveness.

Ken: No different?

Tom: No . . . we all die with regrets.

P/C 2+3/IMA: I feel like he wants to confess his own regrets before he confronts his own death.

Ken: Does everyone there have regrets?

Tom: No . . . some of the people are still angry and are walking away.

AT 3/IMA: Is he splitting again?

Ken: Do you want to say anything to them?

Tom: Yes: "Wait a minute! Why have you done this to him?" (resumes crying).

C=P 2/IMA: I feel Tom's confusion and sorrow. I feel his identification with the man. P3: Tom is finally standing up for the man and perhaps himself.

Tom: They're telling me: "He was guilty—he was bad."

Ken: But what did he do?

Tom: Nothing . . . he was innocent—he was just different.

P/C 4/VRB: Being gay makes Tom different and innocent. AT3: But in Tom's heart, this innocence makes him guilty, and this difference makes him bad.

Ken: He was innocent . . . just different.

Tom: They have blood all over their faces. They need such forgiveness. God, I feel like everyone here needs it and needs to give it.

AT 3/VRB: He jumped from "they" need forgiveness to "everyone" needs it. Why?

Ken: What else are you aware of?

Tom: I have blood on my hands, too . . . just like them.

P/C 1+2/IMA: I can feel his sense of dirtiness and blame.

P/C 2: I would want to wash my hands . . . *P/C 4:* Out! Out! Damned spot!

Ken: Do you need forgiveness too?

Tom: (crying) More than they do. I need to forgive *myself.*

C/P 2/MUS/IMA: I feel his pain, and I can hear it so deeply in the music. *AT 1/MUS:* The last piece on the tape begins. It is the "Adagietto" for Mahler's 5th Symphony.

Ken: Are you ready to do that?

Tom: Yes, but I am afraid that I will stand out like a dead man—I will be different from the rest.

AT 3/IMA: Why is Tom so afraid of being himself in this place? Why is he so adamant about staying anonymous and unidentified?

Ken: Is there a way that you can find forgiveness without standing out?

Tom: Yes, I can bury this man, and take the memory of his struggle with me . . . When I look at his body, I see no anger . . . I see only the pain of innocence, and the love he gave without condition.

P/C 2+4/IMA: I sense that Tom is burying a part of himself. AT 3/IMA: I wonder if the dirt is absorbing the blood on his hands.

Ken: What else do you see?

Tom: The ground is like nothing happened. The anger and hatred has gone from this meadow. The dead man has helped those of us who remain. We are connected, all of us. We are not afraid now . . . We can now leave this place.

AT 3/IMA: Tom needs to take forgiveness and love away with him.

Ken: Is there anything else you would like to bring from this place?

Tom: I still have his blood on my hands . . . to remind me that I am guilty of not forgiving myself.

AT 3+4/VRB/IMA: The blood he takes with him is his AIDS diagnosis. Having AIDS is like a constant reminder of being stoned to death for being gay or promiscuous. Tom is split between feeling guilty and innocent, and being the one who punishes himself, and the one who forgives.

As Tom returned to the normal consciousness, my head was reeling—almost as if I too had a splitting headache. This was such an incredible session: I came so near to him that I ran into myself, and then I came so near to myself that I almost collided with him. The intrusion of my own images and feelings made it imperative for me to split away from myself, and to "be there" with and for him—as therapist to client.

Theory

The need for a therapist to continually expand, center, and shift his consciousness is poignantly demonstrated in the transcript above. As I look back at this session, and similarly difficult experiences as a guide, I realize that what helps me the most is knowing that I can move my consciousness, and that often timing is a key factor.

So far theory has been primarily concerned with spatial aspects of consciousness—or where a therapist moves with regard to world, position, level, and medium. Another important factor is *how freely* and *when* a therapist moves. Are the moves restricted or free? How are they timed? And from a practical point of view, how are spatial and temporal aspects coordinated?

Freedom of Access

A therapist must have freedom to move his consciousness *wherever* needed or desired. Within understandable limits of personal and professional boundaries, he should have no major problems or limitations in moving—at will—anywhere within the worlds, levels, and media. In the example above, I had to be able to move away from the music, away from my world of images, and center myself squarely on Tom's world—his physical responses, his feelings, and his images.

It seems self-evident that if I am to "be there" for the client, I have to be free to move anywhere his experience leads me, or anywhere that I feel is therapeutically important for me to go on his behalf. I cannot lock myself out of certain places, unless there is a very good reason for doing so. My presence is therefore inextricably tied to my capacity to enter as many different modes of consciousness as necessary.

Consider for a moment the implications of staying in one world. If I stay only in the therapist's world without easy access to the others, I will be limited in my ability to empathize with the client or offer him a truly authentic personal response. If I stay only in the therapist's world without easy access to my own worlds, I will be limited in my ability to help him as a therapist, and I will put at risk the integrity of my own personal space. I will literally lose my personal and professional boundaries. If I stay only in my personal world, I will be limited in my ability to empathize with the client, and my insights and interventions as a therapist will be biased, self-centered, and, in all likelihood, irresponsive to the client's needs.

Similar limitations occur if I have to stay in the same level or medium of experience. I must have free access to move from affective to sensory to intuitive to reflective levels—within the images, music, words, and physical interactions.

Timing

Closely related to free access is timing. A therapist has to move not only *wherever* it so demands, but *whenever*. Put simply, I cannot stay for inordinately long periods in one world, position, level, or medium, nor can I flit from one to another so that I remain nowhere for a sufficient length of time. And in the process, I cannot move too quickly or slowly. Thus, to "be there" for the client, I not only have to stay long enough to be truly present, but I also have to be ready to move on whenever one of us gets stuck, and I have to move at the pace of the client's experience.

From a practical point of view, questions still remain about how a therapist knows when to move where. How does he know whether he is in the right place at the right time? What factors must be considered in directing his consciousness so that it enhances and facilitates the therapeutic process?

Although the theory has not specified exact conditions under which a therapist should direct his consciousness to the various spaces, it has dealt with this issue to the extent possible. The main point of the theory is that in exploring the various modes of consciousness, the therapist learns where, when, and how he should be moving. Thus, it is the very process of expanding, centering, and shifting consciousness that informs the therapist whether he is in the right place at the right time.

In addition to the moving self, there are other ways of knowing how to time oneself. The first cue can be found in the focal experience itself. When I focus on the client's world, for example, I will notice that his experience is unfolding in time, and that it has a quality of speed. In addition, his experience may very well be centered on time and its effects on his world. For example, the client may report his images slowly or quickly, his breathing may accelerate or deccelerate along with his heart rate, and events within the images themselves may occur at various tempos. These are all important cues to knowing whether I am in the right place at the right time, and whether I have time to take samples of other spaces. When the client slowly says, "I am walking down the path, and the horizon is becoming clear very gradually," I know that I do not want to rush ahead of him within the image, and that I may have time to sample my own personal world before he reaches his destination. On the other hand, if he tells me that his heart is beating fast, or that he is spiralling through a tunnel at high speed, I know that I want to stay where he is and move quickly with him; I do not want to take the time to go elsewhere, as I may very well lose him along the way. In short, when he travels to many places quickly, I travel the same way; when he floats through space, I do also.

Of course, the music is also an important indicator of timing. It is the temporal holding environment—par excellence. It sets the tempo, moves the feelings, lays out the ideas; it hurries by or drags along, and has the power to rush or delay everyone in its presence. A general rule of thumb is that if the guide moves his experiences in time with the music, he will nearly always be in the right place at the right time.

Another really effective way of ensuring that my timing is correct is to move my consciousness at regularly timed intervals, so that I am continually taking periodic samples of various worlds, positions, levels, and media. In doing this, I allow myself the moves that are spontaneous (i.e., freely following moment-to-moment flow of events without much self-monitoring) and I alternate this with moving reflectively (i.e., purposely bringing into awareness modes of consciousness that require exploration, or assessing limitations in the present mode).

For me, this "timed sampling" technique is easiest to implement through my own body. This may be peculiar to my style of working, but I find that when I move my body in any way, given the smallest part of slightest shift, my consciousness is usually stimulated to move as well. I therefore make regular changes in my body position, and use this as a cue and schedule for taking different samples of consciousness. I set the pace for these regular body changes according to the tempo of the client's experience and whatever medium is in the foreground. When clients move through GIM slowly and talk haltingly, I change at a slower rate; when they move and talk quickly, I change at a faster rate. Similarly, I pace myself with the tempo of the music and the flow of events in the imagery. Thus, as I entrain by bodily movements to the tempo of the client's ongoing experience, I maintain an awareness of my consciousness in relation to his experience. Generally, I find that using my body in this way provides a reliable indicator of the need to move my consciousness while also keeping me grounded in physical reality and helping me to reestablish my boundaries at any time.

Attention to one's boundaries is a constant concern when a therapist moves through various modes of consciousness. This way of working requires having personal boundaries that are clear and defined, yet open to fusion and permeation. Otherwise, going into and out of the client's world can be quite disconcerting, if not dangerous. Moving into the client's world poses considerable risk for a therapist who lacks sufficient ego-strength, training, and maturity.

Technically speaking, and within the context of this theory, boundaries become most easily threatened (1) when the therapist stays in one world, position, level, or medium for too long of a period; or (2) when the therapist stacks up several levels of experiencing within the same spacing (e.g., combining sensory, affective, and intuitive levels in the client's world).

Concluding Remarks

Gender Orientation

As hinted earlier, this theory may be male in perspective. That is, it may be more relevant to men operating from the masculine side of their psyche, or to women who take a male orientation toward space and consciousness.

It occurred to me that if there are archetypal differences between female and male with regard to space, and if these differences center around tendencies to be container versus contained, and penetrator versus penetrated, then the idea of moving into and out of different worlds may make quite different demands on male and female therapists. Consider for a moment how different the experiences of "in" and "out" are for those who take the role of container versus contained, or penetrator versus penetrated. And going even further, consider how different the spaces would be when these roles are taken to reserve or define space to be shared by one's self and significant other. Containers would reserve space inside; the contained would reserve space outside. Penetrators would cross boundaries from the outside; the penatrated would open boundaries from the inside. Containers are more stationary, whereas penetrators are more mobile.

Another fascinating question is whether male and female therapists are innately different in what they naturally offer to a client once spatial boundaries have been crossed. If I am a container, I will provide support and protection for the client to grow, very much like a bird provides a nest for its young. If I am contained within the same space as the client, I will work to set it free, very much like the bird that teaches its young to fly away from the nest. As a penetrator, I will encourage the client to explore other worlds, and to enter new spaces; as penetrated, I will help the client to be receptive to others who enter his world.

These differences in spatial orientation may explain why my theory feels so different to me than theories of music therapy developed by women. For example, in her work with autistic children, Alvin (1978) establishes "territories" for both the child and herself, and when the time is right, introduces games of "invasion" to ready the child for sharing the same space with her. Although games of invasion may be more male than female, and although the child played the role of invader and invaded, Alvin's goal was to get the child accustomed to sharing space with her, which in turn would allow her to provide a safe and supported container for their interactions. From my point of view, she was creating a therapeutic "nest." As a male therapist, I recognize the value of her approach, though it feels somewhat foreign to me, but more importantly, I can see another goal for the invasion game—to free the child from his need to be contained by such boundaries, or to help him fly away from his own nest.

Similarly, in one of the first spatially oriented theories on the subject, Kenny (1989) describes music therapy as a "field of play" which has its source in the creation of a "musical space." In her definitions, she explains: "A field seems to be a reasonable way to perceive or imagine reality. If we can imagine that boundaries contain a space, we are not bombarded by sensory and psychic stimuli. The concept of the 'field' allows us to focus and appreciate that which is in the field, and the conditions and relationships among the participants contained within this space" (pp. 72-73). "The musical space is a contained space. It is an intimate and private field created in the relationship between the therapist and client. It is a sacred space, a safe space, which becomes identified as 'home base,' a territory which is well known and secure. In early childhood development, it is similar to the space created between mother and child" (p. 79). As a male therapist, the idea of creating a musical space and locating a field of play is quite different from moving my consciousness in and out of various experiential spaces—they both seem to come from different archetypal patterns of helping others.

Pointing out the differences between male and female perspectives in no way implies that male-oriented theories are true or useful only for male therapists and clients, or that female theories are true or useful for females only. Nor is one kind of theory truer or more useful than the other. I am not saying any of this, nor do I mean to suggest anything like this.

The importance of examining and admitting to gender orientation is threefold. First, it helps therapists to acknowledge the unavoidable biases that their gender brings to their theories, research projects, and clinical practices, either unconsciously or unintentionally. This is especially important in professions such as music therapy, and with techniques such as GIM, which have a predominance of one gender (viz., females). Second, it adds to our understanding of the conditions under which male and female clients need male or female therapists. And third, it points to a real need for therapists to be able to function from the opposite gender's point of view. Male therapists must have free access to their female sides, and female therapists must have free access to their male sides.

Therapist Qualifications

It is already clear that, within the context of this theory, therapists need to have highly developed yet flexible gender identities. In Jungian terms, a male therapist needs an adequately developed "anima" and a female therapist needs to have an adequate "animus."

As mentioned earlier, a therapist who works in this way also needs to have clearly defined, yet flexible and permeable boundaries, both as a person and a therapist. At one moment, the therapist may need to maintain clear physical and affective boundaries in his interactions with the client, and at another, he may need to allow these boundaries to dissipate.

Another quality that strikes me as essential is the ability to go beyond "either-or" polarities. The whole idea of expanding one's consciousness is that I do not have to be either here or there, but that I can transcend that distinction. This not only helps me to handle challenges to my boundaries, but also helps me to stay open to the ever-emerging needs of the moment.

Therapy as Art

Therapy has often been described as an "art" which requires creativity on the part of both client and therapist, and active engagement of both parties in a creative process. This is particularily true when an art form such as music is used as a modality of therapy.

In light of the present theory, GIM is the art of exploring consciousness through music. As such, a GIM therapist has to be an artist of consciousness who uses his creativity in the creative process to "be there" for the client with the music as his co-therapist.

Simple Complexities

Human beings are complex organisms. We are not merely objects that can be reduced to one or two dimensions, and then explained in deterministic terms. What makes us unique as a species is our subjectivity—and the ability to experience ourselves as subjects. The challenge of the human condition, then, is to fully grasp the complexity of subjective experience.

Though there are internal and external forces that would have us believe otherwise, life is not simple—nor are the problems that confront us in the process of living, and the solutions that must be found to life's dilemmas. It should therefore come as no surprise that psychotherapy is not simple either—no matter how much we would like to deny its complexities and avoid being overwhelmed by the responsibilities that it imposes on us.

If we are to grasp the uniqueness of each client, and if we are to understand him as a subject who has the freedom to shape his own life, then we must go beyond the laws of objects, and we must begin to approach the unfathomable depths of his psyche. To do so, we as therapists must be prepared to move our consciousness—with courage, humility, and respect—into uncharted regions of the client's world, our own world as a person, and our world together as a client and therapist.

This theory has been an attempt to map out a few roads that can be travelled through these territories. This reader is forewarned: "The map is not the territory" (Grinder and Bandler, 1976, p. 4).

References

Alvin, J. (1978). *Music Therapy for the Autistic Child*. New York: Oxford University Press.

Bonny, H. (1978). *Facilitating GIM Sessions*. Salina, KS: Bonny Foundation.

Bruscia, K. (1991). Embracing Life with AIDS: Psychotherapy through Guided Imagery and Music (GIM). In K. Bruscia (ed.), *Case Studies in Music Therapy*. Phoenixville, PA: Barcelona Publishers.

Grinder, J., and R. Bandler (1976). *The Structure of Magic II*. Palo Alto, CA: Science and Behaviour Books.

Jung, C. (1933). *Modern Man in Search of Soul*. New York: Harcourt.

Kenny, C. (1989). *The Field of Play: A Guide for Theory and Practice of Music Therapy*. Atascadero, CA: Ridgeview Publishing.

19

Death and Rebirth Experiences
in Music and Music Therapy

Benedikte Scheiby

Prelude to Benedikte Scheiby

Only a few years ago, I received a letter from a Danish music therapist asking me if she could come to California to interview me about my work in music therapy. She had received a fellowship from the American Council of Learned Studies to study the approaches of various veteran music therapists throughout the country. She had heard about my work through Ken Aigen, various other members of the New York University Music Therapy Community, and Even Ruud, in Norway.

Benedikte came to my home in Santa Barbara and we had quite an afternoon talking about music therapy. Almost immediately, in Benedikte, I felt a sister. This is hard to explain. We seemed different in every way. We certainly did not look alike: Benedikte, golden shimmering hair with the fairest skin, strong Scandinavian features; I, with my dark hair and olive skin, with a distinctive Native American look. Yet, our connection, as we both discovered, seemed ancient and real.

Perhaps our connection was not an accident after all. Through Even Ruud and other friends from the far North, I had learned that I had a natural affinity with Scandinavian folk. Benedikte, on the other hand, had always had a fascination for the Native American people of North America. I also felt in accord with her European approach to music therapy. It carried a depth and her analysis and interpretation appealed to me.

Since then, Benedikte has married Ken Aigen, moved to New York, and given birth to beautiful Sara. She has attended the Sun Dance Ceremonials of the Sioux Indians in South Dakota and therefore become more familiar with my culture from her direct experience. I invited her to come and teach in our graduate music therapy program here at Antioch University and she, as one of the Antioch University adjunct faculty, offered intensive training in her analytical/transpersonal approach to music therapy.

Our dialog is ongoing and we are continuously discovering ways in which we can learn and grow from each other personally and professionally, as much as a three-thousand-mile gap and busy lifestyles will allow. Our work has shared many themes, as has our lives. And we will continue to discover even more.

Of herself Benedikte says: "Since I received my education as 'Diploma Music Therapist' in 1980, I have tried through my career to integrate teaching, research, clinical practice, and musicianship. I have also developed a music therapy approach that integrates analytical music therapy (Mary Priestly) with a transpersonal approach, which might be reflected in the article. This article is atypical compared to my other written material. Atypical in one way that it is written from the heart! It is my intention to give the readers an experience that comes close to my own *personal experience* rather than performing an academic exercise, with which I am more familiar. Carolyn Kenny has been and is a big inspiration for me in that perspective. For ten years I worked as a professor in a music therapy program in Denmark (Aalborg), and as an adjunct faculty member on a program in Germany (Hamburg). I am currently an adjunct faculty member of the staff of both the Music Therapy Program of New York University and the Art Therapy Program of Pratt Institute. In addition, I maintain a private practice in Brooklyn.

The article was economically made possible with the help of the American Council for Learned Studies, which awarded me a research fellowship."

I am in a big concert hall and I am one of three members of a music collective that is going to perform an improvised concert built on the process of biological birth. The room is completely filled up with people. The room is all dark. We and the audience are sharing two minutes of silence. I get in touch with my own excitement, expectations, nervousness, intensity, and a wave of high-level energy approaching me from the audience. Will we succeed in our intention? We hope to become the vehicle for a physical and emotional re-experience of the four different stages of birth delivery by means of exposing the audience to poetry, improvised music, movement, light, and slides mirroring these stages, and, as a consequence, to facilitate the ability to understand one's life process as a constant flow of death-rebirth experiences.

> It was at the time "before":
>> before the origin
>>> before the form and the contents

> At the time when only "musical winds" existed
>> —before the music

as a blow from the wind in whirls and spirals
"out in" and "into" the universe of nothing

Before these words
    before this "ego"

At the time "before"
    when the sounds were light
and the light were patterns and sensations

At the time before "the difference"
    before "the world," "YOU" and "I"

. . . And the lights streamed out in the sounds
    turned the universe that didn't exist inside and out

I recollect and know
    know that it was at the time
    when time was equal to the space
    before life
    before death

    I am listening to Annelise's recital of her poem, but slowly my attention is going in the direction of the sounds that are backing her up. I hear the synthesized sound of an airy wind increasing and decreasing in volume and the sound of metal windchimes in the background.

    It makes me feel weightless and I drift around in outer space, looking at the twinkling stars, the moon, and the planet formations. The speed that I am drifting is very high. It is dark night. I am an astronaut exploring the universe attached to a safety line.

    Then the sound of the wind leads me to the ocean, where I see big waves surrounding my little body, and the wind is so strong that I am pushed from side to side in the water, where I am compared to the power of the ocean. Sometimes I cannot differentiate between whether or not I am a part of the water.

    Now I hear the wind sound as a breathing rhythm, sometimes faster, sometimes slower, as if I am in my mother's womb listening to her breath.

    The sound of the wind and the subtle metal sounds fade out slowly together with the last word of the poem. Now the sound environment changes to sounds from the whales communicating under very high register, and there is a glissando quality to them like bulging lines up and down. The light in the room has turned bright blue.

The whales appeal to my voice and I feel like groaning and screaming together with them, and I become a baby whale playing around in the crystal-clear water, keeping near to mother. I feel supported and in close touch with the other whales that surround me.

This experience leads to a glimpse of re-experiencing a very happy memory from when I was a child swimming under the water in the ocean during the summer at my grandparents' summer house. I was amazed and excited to see the world underneath the surface of the water. Everything seemed to be of a much bigger size, and the sounds were distorted. I experimented with how long I could hold my breath, and there were moments of anxiety when I realized that the distance to the surface was much longer than I thought. Could I get up and breathe, before it was too late? This was an experiment with life and death in a small scale.

This memory is replaced by an embryo consciousness listening to all the sounds from the womb of my mother. Some of the "whale groans" are so loud that I feel a little bit threatened by them.

I pick up my acoustic amplified cello and start to "communicate" with the whales, sliding up and down the strings with my finger and playing with the echo effect.

I sense the deep connection and specific community with the whales, which again makes me feel my closeness with and my dependency on being in touch with the nature inside and outside of me.

A new and different sound is introduced. A sound from the big wooden block being hit by a soft beater in a steady rhythm in the same tempo as the heartbeat.

I hear my mother's steady heartbeat and it makes me feel very relaxed and calm resting in my inner self. It makes me feel held and secure in the darkness around me. I sense a kind of timelessness that is very relieving. I am in a total symbiosis with my mother's body.

I am now back in the concert hall again and it is time for me to join in the heartbeat by playing the same heartbeat on damped piano strings to reinforce the sound. This is, after a period of time, taken over by a little slow motif that I develop on the piano. It consists of four tones in the middle register repeated in different inversions, backwards, forwards, and in the same pulse as the wooden heartbeat sound.

It gives me something to hold onto, and I am no longer so nervous about how the concert will go. It puts me in a trance-like state of mind. At the same time as I am playing my repetitive motif, I hear the Brazilian *pau de shuba* with its sound of little sea shells sliding up and down the tube.

FIGURE 19.1

Total Symbiosis in the Sound Field

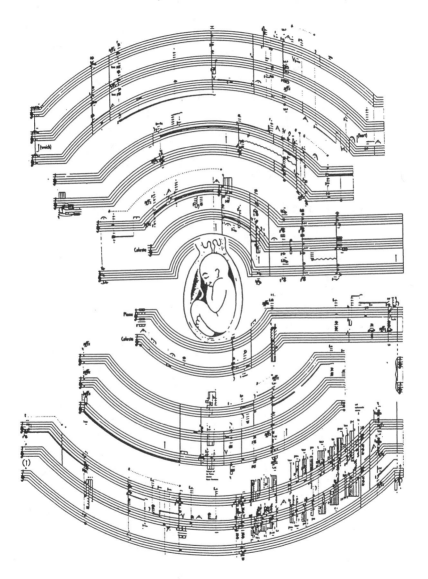

That gives me associations to the breaking waves of the ocean—a very soothing sound for me.

In the background I also hear and see water being poured from one Tibetan gong shell to another. This is taken over by one penetrating tone played on the edge of a crystal glass—a tone that never stops, an endless and timeless tone. Simultaneously, a cymbal is gently struck by brushes supporting the sea shell sounds.

It seems as if it is impossible to move further to the next stage of delivery—this state is too comfortable to be in.

An abrupt squeezing arhythmical sound is introduced from the Brazilian Surdo drum and introduces the transition to the second stage of delivery. It interferes with the rhythm from the wooden block and takes over the sound image while the wood block slowly disappears in the distance. I am now adding a dissonant interval to my little motif on the piano.

My content and happy state of consciousness changes character. Something is not right. The sounds seem to be intruding upon me. The abrupt sound increases in volume together with added dissonances and augmented fourths from the piano and it feels as if I am getting tortured by it. I feel caught in a sound trap that I cannot get away from, and my breathing becomes irregular. There is not enough room for me. And there is no way out. My heart starts beating in a faster rhythm.

On top of the constantly repeated Surdo sound a telephone starts ringing continuously without being answered.

I feel the stress of the telephone not being answered. The sound of the telephone brings me memories of a constantly ringing telephone at work and at home and the feeling of never having any free time for me. A workload of papers and appointments that never ends. Never any finished gestalts. I feel suffocated by the Surdo. It is my throat that makes this squeezing sound.

I also get in touch with a memory of a very painful part of my childhood, where my alcoholic mother tried several times to commit suicide, and when I once found her in her bed half dead because of sleeping pills. Every day seemed to be a continuous threatening nightmare—a time in my life where I felt that my existence constantly was threatened in one way or another. With this memory in mind I move over to my cello.

The memory helps me to play my role in the music, which at the moment is to play squeaking sounds on the strings by pressing the bow very hard to the strings. By means of the electric amplification, there is an echo on the sound.

My cello projects a sound that can be compared with the crying of a baby or a little child who is left alone and very unhappy. The echo of

FIGURE 19.2

Heart Beats Faster in the Sound Field

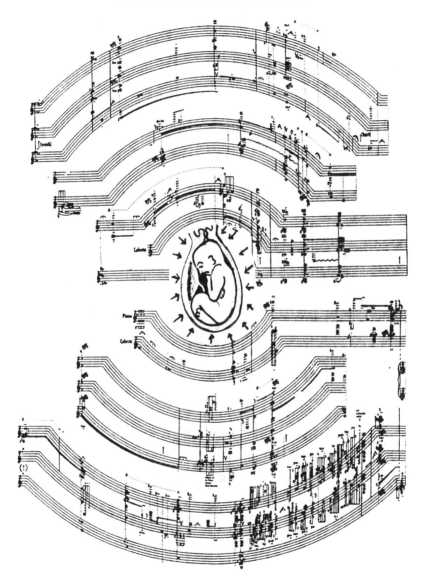

the sound mirrors the physical and emotional emptiness. I get a feeling of temporary relief by playing the cello, because I am able to move into my body and play out the painful memory. I almost get tears in my eyes.

The cello sound is accompanied by a compressed voice that is sighing, groaning, expressing a constant pain.

Now I get flashbacks from recurring nightly dreams about hiding from the Nazis and not being able to get any sound out of my throat.

The next image is a very famous painting representing the Norwegian painter Edvard Munch called "The Scream"—the image of existential anxiety in a human being standing on a bridge between life and death in brilliant colors. I start to feel a little bit of nausea.

The transition to the third stage of delivery is introduced by background noise from a machine factory, a war siren, intense hammering on metal objects, and a ticking metronome in a fast rhythm. I move back to the piano and start to play very loud handfuls of unpredictable clusters, and I am accompanied by my fellow musician, Lene, slamming on the metallophone so that it sounds like pieces of glass exploding and breaking: arythmic and expressing an aggressive quality coming from the deep center of the stomach. The big Chinese gong is sending out growling sounds and also abrupt loud metallic jolts. The light in the room has turned deep red.

I get associations to volcanoes that explode, New Year's Eve fireworks, and I seem to enjoy this stage's wildness and fighter spirit. I like the louder and stronger volume. I get memories from a sudden unexpected snowstorm that I ran into all alone while skiing in Switzerland. Luckily, somebody found me and showed me the way back. My whole body was shaking so I hardly could stand upright on the skis.

Another image of a woman giving birth to a child comes up in my consciousness. It is as if she is fighting for her own life and the child's life at the same time, and there is blood all over. (As a medical student I worked periodically on a ward where women gave birth and sometimes I attended the births.)

My clusters on the piano transform into minor dense clusters and play in a very strict rhythmical pattern with accents that give connotations to the erotic music of Stravinsky's "Sacre du printemps" in the part where the ritual dances are performed. I am backed up by Lene on the metallophone and Annelise on the drum. The "dancing/erotic" music ends up in a fight between the different instruments.

From my inner eye I see native people dancing wildly in formations that look like warrior dances on one hand, and on the other hand like rites of passage and initiations. I am one of the dancers and feel both pain and lust and an enormous amount of energy.

Now my mind is carried back to a childhood experience, where I was fighting with my mother who, in her alcoholic aggressiveness, tried to kill me with a bread knife in the corner of our bathroom. I fought for my life as I am doing right now in the music.

The next image is memories from a re-birthing workshop run by the psychiatrist R. D. Laing, where I physically and psychologically re-experienced my own biological birth process. I am lying in a fetal position underneath eleven people who form a big womb surrounding me and who are breathing together in the same rhythm. I am starting to feel that I can not get enough air, and start to work my way out through the "human birth channel." It is hard work and I start to fight very intensely and energetically. The two strong hands of Laing provide resistance on my head, and finally I push his hands away and glide out of the channel. What I remember most strongly is the fight for my life—a fight that is very familiar in my life.

The instrumental fight culminates when I crash the big Chinese gong accompanied by a very loud birth scream from Annelise—a scream that shakes my whole body. I still hear it from my inner ears. White light is blinding the audience. Annelise plays a happy light melody on the flute, supported by me on the cello. The melody ends up with the well-known "children's tune" motif (Nordoff, P., and C. Robbins [1977]. Creative Music Therapy. New York: John Day) universally sung or chanted by children in ring games or at play in the whole world (figure 19.4):

This core motif is taken over vocally by all of us who sing it in harmonies, rhythms, and tonalities, while we are holding each other's hands and swinging our bodies like little children when they play and sing.

I feel a tremendous relief and relaxation in my body and an overwhelming love for my two fellow musicians. I feel ready to open up to the response from the audience who we have asked to stay and share experiences.

It is very moving to listen to the feedback from the audience. The music seems to have brought out the message and reached the core of the theme. People are very open about their inner journeys. The atmosphere is warm and so different from what I have experienced in more traditional concert settings. I feel that we all are connected in a big warm ocean of emotional and physical waves.

One person tasted blood in his mouth during the third delivery stage. This made her life complicated in the sense that she had diffi-

FIGURE 19.3

Fighting for Life in the Music

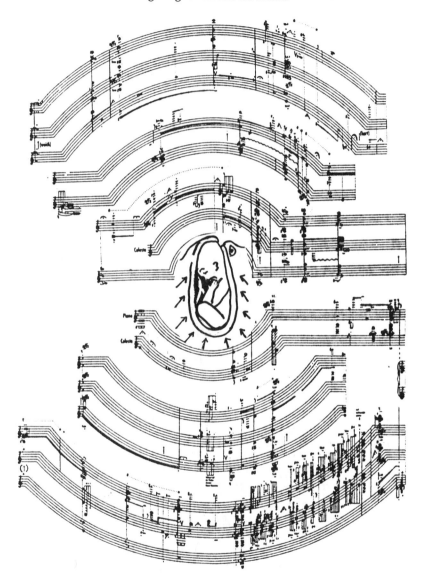

FIGURE 19.4

Children's Tune Motif

culties in taking action. One person felt how unpleasant it had been to be in her mother's womb. She was delivered by Caesarian operation.

I started to feel that our many months of rehearsals, crisis, and hard work had paid off in a very rewarding way. As we worked collectively on the many issues connected with the concert, our group had been through its own personal death/birth process.

One problem, for example, had been to make a graphic score that left enough openness and freedom to allow us to follow our improvisational ideas and musical intuitions. Another problem was that sometimes, due to the inner dynamic of each delivery stage, we got stuck in one or another of the birth stages during the rehearsal. Our nightly dreams were strongly colored by the working process, in that all of us had dreams about situations and symbols which clearly referred to the death/birth processes. Personally, I remembered that I had a dream where I was acting as a midwife for a woman who gave birth to a child in a big church. Annelise had a dream where she saw a strong blue egg with an embryo-like structure in it. She drew the image which was shown as one of the slides during the concert. (See figure 19.6.)

What I did not realize at that time, in the autumn of 1987, was the enormous impact this concert would have on my private and professional life. It set off a radical change in my whole life and gave birth to the best part of my personal mythological fairy tale. I finally allowed myself to meet my life companion—also a devoted music therapist—even though I had to cross the Atlantic Ocean to do it. Two years later I got pregnant. In connection with a music therapy research fellowship, I attended a Sioux Indian Sun Dance Ritual in South Dakota. At that time I was six months pregnant. What I experienced during the purification ceremonies and the Sun Dance rituals was a series of very physical, psychological, and musical death/rebirth rituals. The sweat lodges were so hot and intense that I felt that I was on the edge of my endurance, especially in my condition. The women's singing helped me through. In the actual Sun Dances men and women pierced themselves, danced for hours without breaks to the accompaniment of fierce drumming, whistled from flutes made from

FIGURE 19.5

Getting Born in the Sound

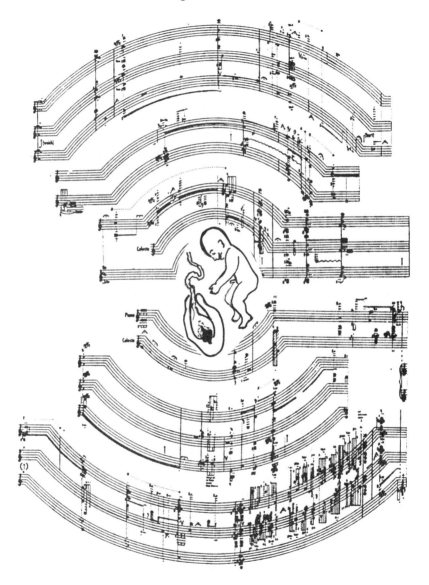

FIGURE 19.6

The Strong Blue Egg

eagle bones, and sang. The dances reminded me of the images that I had seen during the third stage of delivery at the concert—"... native people dancing wildly in formations that look like warrior dances on one hand, and on the other hand like rites of passage and initiations."

Three months later I gave birth to a very special, musical little girl. I perceived the birth as one long ritual. It was a very physical and psychological confirmation of the reality of the existence of the different stages of delivery and of the strength of the bond or navel string that had been formed among the concert group members. Lene, Annelise, the slide projector assistant from the concert (Kaj), and my husband attended the birth, which was rather unconventional. My husband and I were floating in a small pool in the delivery room with accompaniment by the music of whales. Lene and Annelise were supportive with their voices and their bodies and Kaj was filming the events. During the last phase of the birth the music and the images from the concert quickly passed in front of my inner eyes, and it had the same ending— a loud scream from a vital little baby girl.

Realizing the meaningfulness of giving myself a good womb and nourishing surroundings, I also stopped myself from being a workaholic full-time university professor and private practice clinician. I began to give myself more space and time to enjoy my family, a fulfilling present part-time job as a music therapist in private practice, and a position as a university teacher.

During the years of my practice as a clinician I have shared numerous experiences of death/rebirth released by means of improvised music, either made jointly by the client and myself or by me alone accompanying the client's process. The client would either have the full experience during one session or during a series of sessions. I have chosen to describe this particular experience because it occurred recently and stays very clear in my mind. Second, it also struck me how simple musical improvisational tools can provide and release such a deep and important event.

My client is a twenty-five-year-old music therapy student with no former experience of therapy. She wants to work on issues such as loneliness, reaching out, dependence on family, self-esteem, and letting go of her dominant intellect, and she also sees music therapy as a possible teaching experience in her training and development as a music therapist. She says that she prefers to play classical tonal music and that she has a hard time with atonal music. She also says that it is difficult for her to stop thinking while she plays.

The client was born in an oriental culture where the whole society, culture, and life philosophy is in opposition to what one experiences in

New York. The individual is subordinate to the community. One does not show emotions and serves the family for life. Needs are put in row. One obeys the authorities. The woman's role is to give birth to children and serve her husband and family. It is a highly introverted and meditative culture. The concept of music therapy as psychotherapy does not exist.

With this in mind, you can imagine what kind of culture shock this client must experience. Her whole safety net has been torn away drastically.

I realize that I have to work in a very slow tempo and cautiously with this client. The transference issues transparent in the music—which is purely tonal and very structured—are not addressed in the first session. I noticed that she chooses to play the piano in most of the sessions in addition to Tibetan gong bowls, cymbals, and Indian drums. I work on building trust, letting her express herself and building up a musical relationship that is not threatening. I realize that the client is a little bit late for every session, and it gives me the idea that she might feel that she does not deserve all that attention and care. She is extremely polite and submissive. I can see and feel the young girl who exists inside this adult woman.

The titles of the improvisations in the first sessions are as follows:

Session 1: "My inner policeman"
Session 2: "I am reaching out to you"
Session 3: No title, but the client suggested that the overall title for the whole session was: "Searching my self and searching sounds of different instruments"
Session 4: "Responsibility"

In the fifth session she expresses that she wants to use most of the time to speak. I respect that, and try to listen to the music behind the words. She says that a problem for her is that her thoughts interrupt her expression. When fifteen minutes of the session are left I feel that we have "gone nowhere" with the words. She looks tired, and says, "I want to hear your music—I want to listen." I realize that she wants to be in attention, nourishment, support, and holding. This seems to make sense after her work in the fourth session on her feelings of anger in connection with carrying a lot of responsibility for taking care of her family. I decide to offer a musical meditation where I provide the music and she can close her eyes, take the music in, and allow herself to "be." She responds positively. I suggest that we do not talk after the experience and allow it to be processed nonverbally.

I choose my very big ceremonial Indian drum, and tell her that I will play something that might remind her of her heartbeat.

I play a soft "heartbeat" and breathe deeply and loudly. I see the client is relaxing, her breathing is getting deeper, and she looks as if she is enjoying the music. Gradually her fingers start moving. Her fingers explore themselves like those of an infant lying in her cradle. A smile spreads across her face. I sense that it is a very intimate and precious experience that we are sharing together. I am afraid to stop the heartbeat when time is over, and I let the sound die out pianissimo. It seems as if more than fifteen minutes have passed. She slowly opens her eyes and looks tired and satisfied. She slowly gets up from the chair, pays for her session, and we shake hands for goodbye.

The sixth session begins with the client blurting out that she really needs to speak about her experience in the previous session:

> In fact I felt very comfortable and relaxed. I was very relaxed. Especially when you started to play the drum. You said, you will make the heartbeat. It reminded me of something. I imagined that I was in my mother's womb, right? I felt exactly that way. So the drum made me imagine my mother's heartbeat. Yes, that was very comfortable. I heard that—I don't know who said it—that every people wants to return to mother's womb. It is a kind of theory. I agree with it. I wanted to go to something very original.

She also said that she felt that her fingers were making little movements naturally. And that she could not stop yawning when she returned back home. She was very relaxed. I asked how it was to be in her mother's womb. She answered with a big smile on her face: "Yes, it was *very* nice!"

The following words—said with a "sacred" quality after a long pause—still resonate in my ears. They seem to be an essential and poetic expression of the art of "being." Let this little statement be the last phrase sounding in the reader's ears:

> Now I have an idea about what music therapy is.
> It is not a learning process.
> I think every person needs a space
>   for showing and expressing their emotions
>   as they feel,
> But in the society

It is very difficult
   to show their emotions.
Because of morality
   or something.
Even that I am normal and healthy
    I need a space
       for expressing something inside of me.
I have never had such an experience
    to let my feelings go.
Always I keep my feelings inside me.
I think it is not good for myself.
I know sometimes it distracts,
    I mean,
It makes me stressful,
And also in some moments
    it will come out in some other way
      in other directions.
So I need to relieve this stress.
So that's why I need these sessions.
But very difficult to be there—here—
    As I am.
Because if I am here
As I am,
I need to express my feeling
As I feel,
But always on the contrary
    thinking come out in front
      of the feeling.
In everywhere,
    in school
It is difficult
    to be
    As I am!

Note

I owe a great debt of gratitude to the following institutions that supported me economically and made it possible for me to write this article: Aalborg University, Denmark; America Council of Learned Societies, U.S.A.; and Knud Hojgaards Fond, Denmark.

I would also like to thank: "The Group of Intuitive Music," without whom the concert never would have existed; Ken Aigen, my husband, for inspiring me, keeping me to the fire, and spending many hours correcting the grammar and spelling; Carlolyn Kenny, without whom this article would have never been written; and Barbara Hesser, for providing and facilitating the writing process through her GIM session with me.

20

Candomblé: Afro-Brazilian Ritual as Therapy

Joseph J. Moreno

Prelude to Joseph Moreno

When Nancy McMaster and I began our work together at Capilano College in the mid-1970s, we heard about a special course being offered at the University of British Columbia Summer Session. The course was a two-week general music therapy workshop which included experience in the area of musical psychodrama, and would be taught by a music therapist named Joseph Moreno.

I had received my psychodrama training from Bob Fleishman at Loyola University and was currently working at the University of British Columbia Department of Psychiatry Dayhouse, a therapeutic community conceived and directed by Dr. Ferdinand Knobloch, who had trained directly with Jacob Moreno, founder of psychodrama and, as I learned later, Joe Moreno's uncle. Dayhouse was designed with psychodrama as a core approach in an intensive psychotherapeutic setting for patients with personality disorders and neuroses. So, at the time I was in the center of the overlap between music therapy and psychodrama in my own clinical work.

I was very eager to learn about Joe Moreno's approach.

Nancy and I both benefited a great deal from Joe's ideas and I subsequently established a collegial relationship with Joe which has endured throughout the years.

We both seem to be fascinated by some of the same interdisciplinary quests. Years after our link through psychodrama, we discovered another common interest—ethnomusicology. When I was a graduate student at the University of British Columbia conducting interdisciplinary studies in educational psychology, ethnomusicology, and anthropology, I heard from Joe that he had initiated his own study in ethnomusicology. This study program was a combination of intellectual and personal development which led Joe deeply into the phenomenon of shamanism.

Even though we shared common interests, our approaches often differed. This was a great learning for me. Joe and I seemed to be fellow travelers on the same journey, yet often we chose different paths. Even though in our occasional dialogs along the way we would disagree, I knew that the path Joe had chosen for his journey was integral. For this reason, I came to respect and admire him and to be inspired by the unique views he brought to the work. The hallmark of interdisciplinary engagement seems to be differing approaches to the same phenomenon. Joe Moreno has been and still is a person who reminds me of the value of this "collaborative quest."

Of himself, Joe says: "I am the director of the Music Therapy program at Maryville University in St. Louis, Missouri. I have carried out field research into the world traditions of music and healing in Kenya, Brazil, Peru, Fiji, Pakistan, and with Native Americans in the United States. I have presented my work in music and psychodrama and ethnomusicology in 20 countries. I currently serve as chair of the Commission for Information and Exchange of the World Federation of Music Therapy."

In considering the Afro-Brazilian religions of candomblé in relation to therapy, it is important to recognize that all religions can be seen as forms of therapy. Religions provide belief systems that assist their adherents in coping with life problems, and in providing forms of group support. For example, in Hinduism, no matter how poor and miserable the life of an Indian peasant, the individual can better cope through a belief system, based on reincarnation, that suggests that in the next life things will be better and one's present life is only a passing stage of development. In Christianity, as another example, group support is provided through shared participation in religious observances, and guidance is provided through prayer and through direct interaction with ministers and priests. In these, as in most world religions, security is enhanced through shared belief systems.

If we consider religious systems as forms of healing or therapy, then we are really entering the field of ethnomedicine, which has been defined as "the study of beliefs and practices relating to disease which are the products of indigenous cultural development, and not explicitly derived from the cultural framework of modern 'medicine'" (Hughes, 1968). In this context, "disease" is seen as representing both psychological and physiological illness, and the separation of those two domains is increasingly being seen as an artificial one. Just as anxiety and stress can lead to physiological symptoms, so can a positive belief system stimulate the immune system in disease prevention and healing.

Candomblé is an Afro-Brazilian religion, involving spirit possession, rooted in West African Yoruba traditions, and developed by African slaves in Brazil in the nineteenth century. Rather than a duplication of the source traditions in the new world, candomblé became "a sort of cultural synthesis of the West African mythological world" (Béhague, 1984, p. 222). Additionally, because the slaves were pressured into accepting Catholicism, and at least overtly renouncing what was then perceived as their "pagan" beliefs, a form of religious syncretism was developed. Through this system, the various Catholic saints were seen as doubles of the Yoruba orixas, the African spirit deities, initially to disguise their beliefs from the disapproving masters. Today, in Brazil, candomblé and the related Afro-Brazilian syncretist religions such as umbanda have as many as twenty million adherents. Although Brazil is overtly a Catholic country, candomblé and candomblé-derived beliefs and rituals still pervade the entire cultural fabric of the country at all socioeconomic levels. This holds true for those of both African and non-African descent.

Candomblé, like any religious system, provides the comfort of group support, but is particularly oriented to providing practical solutions to ongoing life problems, and this very pragmatic emphasis has certainly contributed to its popularity (M. Gonzalez-Wippler, 1989). Music plays an intrinsic role in candomblé. Béhague (1984, p. 223) has stated that "while music may appear simply as an ornamental, complementary yet essentially reinforcing element of certain religious practices, it has an organic functionality in most traditional cultures. In certain religious rituals, such as the Afro-Bahian candomblé, music and dance become the main vehicle of religious fulfillment, and therefore are fully integrated with the social organization of these religions." Of course, it is as meaningless to try to separate the role of music in candomblé from the total ritual as it is to attempt to create an artificial distinction between psychological and physiological disease: the wholes function as inseparable entities. However, the prominent role of music in candomblé makes it of particular interest from the perspective of music as therapy. Also, since candomblé is derived from African traditions, and since Africa is the presumed source of the evolution of the human species and therefore human culture, when we study African or African-derived music and healing rituals we are really touching upon the most ancient and primal core of these practices.

Initiation and Therapy

For participants in the world of candomblé, initiation is a very serious matter. Most initiates are adults at the time that they make this commitment, so their involvement represents a conscious decision, not simply an accommodation to a religious system into which they have been born. Initiates have generally had a series of consultations with a cult leader before their decision to join a terreiro, the can-domblé cult center. Their reasons for initially consulting a cult leader are typically related to personal problems: not a single precipitating crisis, but rather a response to a pattern of problems in such areas as personal relationships, work, health, and other difficulties (Béhague, 1991). If the cult leader feels that a person is in disharmony with their orixas (the Yoruba spirit deities), and can benefit from initiation, he or she may eventually make this kind of recommendation. Since the initiation and the resultant bonding of the initiate with their orixa and the group is presented as a means of solution to the problems expressed to the cult leader, the initiate's involvement in candomblé is therapeutically focused from the very beginning. From the first tentative consultations with the cult leader from outside (one might compare this to "out-patient" consultation) to the decision to undergo initiation (a commitment to therapist and group) the process is a therapeutic one.

In candomblé, the novice must first undergo an initiation period that is characterized by a minimum period of three weeks of confinement and isolation. During this period, the babalorixa—the pae de santo—or the ialorixa—the mae de santo cult leaders—get to know their new members well: a very important part of their roles is to arrange the right match between the novice and the spirit of the orixa who will possess them, and with whom they will be joined for the rest of their lives. In this early divination (which is directly derived from the traditional West African Ifá divination), the cult leader is challenged with a very important decision: to match the observed personality of the new initiate with an orixa that will enhance and blend well with the individual's personality structure. For this, the cult leaders need to have the kind of intuitive sense of an individual's personality that is the hallmark of any effective therapist, and this early decision is critical. A poor match between initiate and orixa could later lead to severe inner conflict for the initiate, friction within the cult center, and, in the extreme case, the potential withdrawal of the individual from the group. As a result, cult leaders make these decisions only with the greatest care. In comparison, a responsible psychiatrist would not make the final diagnosis of a patient's symptoms before a period of extended observation and testing, realizing that the results of placing a patient within a particular diagnostic category could have a lasting and even permanent impact on the individual's future. In a similar manner, cult leaders weigh their decisions for the correct initiate-orixa match only after the most intense observation and considered deliberation, because they know that this critical relationship will be a permanent one that cannot be severed or changed (Béhague, 1991). The right match is critical both for the ongoing maintenance and stability of the group as well as the reputation of the cult leader. Cult leaders, like psychotherapists, maintain their reputations through the continued effectiveness with those whom they serve. Of course, a cult leader in candomblé would not have arrived at a position of leadership without having already established his or her intuitive skills and counseling abilities over a long period of apprenticeship within the cult center.

The match between the initiate and orixa is interesting in that the match is never selected to correct or downplay any aspects of the individual's personality, but rather to complement, and thereby validate, the initiate's personality type (Béhague, 1991). The traditional characters of the orixas are varied enough to encompass and complement the full range of personality types with orixas like Shango, the god of thunder, being compatible with an extroverted and dynamic personality, while orixas such as Omulku, the spirit of disease (who can both cure as well as bring about illness) can be compatible with a more introverted, compassionate, and caring personality.

In this way, the initiates' very first significant experience in candomblé are validating, and, by implication, suggest that whatever the initiate has been as a human being prior to his/her initiation has been the result of the influence and guidance of their orixas: natural, inevitable, and, in fact, divinely sanctioned behavior. For example, homosexuality can often cause conflict and identity crisis for individuals coming to terms with their own sexuality in relation to the societal norm. Since some of the orixas are bisexual, connecting the individual to the appropriate orixa can provide the means for developing a comfortable self-acceptance. In a similar manner, other behaviors that might otherwise cause guilt or remorse can be more readily accepted in a belief system in which one can ascribe personally unacceptable behavior to the influence of one's orixa, behaviors which cannot be controlled. This kind of belief system can minimize guilt and the anxieties that are associated with that emotion.

This kind of personal validation enhances self-esteem, which is certainly an important goal in most therapeutic procedures. In its totality, the initiation is a therapeutic process in which the cult-leader-as-therapist is symbolically validating the initiate, and this ego support is further enhanced by the group, which lavishes careful attention upon the new members. In general, candomblé cult groups are caring and compassionate toward their members, and, for example, handicapped children are seen as "children of the orixas" (Béhague, 1991) and are fully integrated into the life of the cult center.

The social support provided for initiates in candomblé is all-encompassing, and its significance in providing a kind of group therapy cannot be minimized. In its social structure and function, candomblé can be profitably compared with Alcoholics Anonymous (AA). In AA (which also has a spiritual orientation), recovering alcoholics receive support from a group of peers who are always available. Additionally, AA members have the support of an individual sponsor who is also available to counsel them at any time. In candomblé, initiates of a cult house have an even more pervasive and ongoing support derived from group belonging, sharing, and identification, and their cult leader, like an AA sponsor, is always available to counsel them through any kinds of personal problems or crisis. In this regard, it is interesting to note that while alcoholism is widespread in Bahia, it is relatively uncommon among the initiates of candomblé (Béhague, 1991). As in AA, the members of a cult center, from the cult leader to the initiates, have all confronted and presumably overcome the problems that motivated them to seek the support of candomblé in the first place.

It is also notable that 80 to 90 percent of the initiates are women. Whereas women play a generally secondary role in Bahian Society, in the domain of candomblé they are a major and powerful force. Many women cult leaders have achieved national and international reputations, such as Mae Menininha de Gantois and Olga of Alketu, both famous mae de santos and curandeiras. The cult houses of candomblé provide an important avenue for the empowerment of Afro-Brazilian women.

Throughout the weeks of the initiation period, the new initiates are maintained in an altered state of consciousness, primarily in the state of eré, a mild trance-like state, alternated with brief periods in which the initiates are fully possessed, the santo state. The eré state is a period in which the new initiates have some vague awareness of the former self, but only in a remote way. Cossard (1970, p. 47) suggests that they are involved in a gradual "splitting of the self," distancing themselves from the normal preoccupations of self, the primary ego, and developing their receptivity toward a second and double consciousness—the beginnings of their intimate relationships with the orixas. This process can also be seen as therapeutically valuable. For example, in trying to come to terms with personal problems in Western-European derived psychotherapy, the therapist-client relationship usually focuses entirely upon the inner life of the patient. This may encompass both ongoing personal problems, as well as the patient's past formative experiences that may have lead to the present self-destructive behavioral patterns. Although a focused examination and confrontation of the self can certainly have therapeutic value, there is a widespread and growing recognition of the critical role of the group in a therapeutic process. Group therapy provides opportunities not only for peer support, objectivity, and feedback, it also provides a forum for patients to develop empathy for others, and training in learning to identify outside of themselves.

This moving away from the self to an other-oriented focus is important, and candomblé provides a ritualized means of accomplishing this. This other-oriented identification is not initially directed toward other persons, although that does come later. Rather, the first step away from the primary self is toward a new and internalized consciousness, the "other" being the incorporated spirit of the orixa.

Rouget (1985) describes the candomblé initiates in the eré state as being child-like in their overt behavior, but it also might be suggested that they are internally engaged in a transitional maturation period directed toward a state of becoming truly expanded adults. They are in the process of becoming adults who have moved away from self-focused absorption in the sense that they are moving beyond their former selves to begin to fully and permanently encompass another—the spirit of their orixa. In this initiation period, the adepts are no longer what they were, and not yet what they will be, which clearly parallels the experience of clients in therapy.

Once the new cult members have become candomblé initiates, and have developed a relationship with their orixas, they have fully incorporated this second consciousness. In times of need and crisis, the orixa provides a safe place for withdrawal from the anxieties of the primary consciousness, a psychic retreat which can be reached through the trance state. Once initiated, Béhague (1991) has suggested that between a combination of ritually observed as well as spontaneous occasions, an initiate may enter the deep santo trance state as often as thirty to fifty times a year. These presumably therapeutic trances provide an interesting parallel with clients involved in the experience of European and American psychotherapy, whose usual weekly visits to their therapist may approximate the same amount of annual time spent in exploring their unconscious as candomblé initiates in trance.

Cult leaders are normally involved in ongoing counseling with the initiates in their cult center, a permanent therapeutic relationship during the initial divining is the appropriate adept-orixa relationship during the initiation period. Rather, the cult leaders are regularly consulted by their initiates for a wide range of personal problems and guidance in decision making throughout their lives. Cult leaders also provide consultation for persons outside of the cult center, and for these consultations the diviners receive monetary payment, a direct analogy with the Eurocentric model of the therapist-client arrangement.

Divination and Therapy

The cult leaders structure their divination of the adept-orixa relationships, as well as their general counseling, in the manner of the West-African Ifá divination as practiced by the traditional babalao in Yoruba culture. In Nigeria, the diviner throws palm nuts (cowrie shells are used in Bahia), and their specific configuration patterns refer to correlated versus that are memorized by the diviner. Bascom (1969) suggests that these thousands of verses represent, in effect, the unwritten scriptures of the Yoruba culture. In theory, the configurations and the selection of the corresponding verses should be an entirely objective process, but in practice the diviners probably select verses, or emphasize parts of verses that they feel are appropriate to their clients' needs. At the same time, despite this element of therapeutic bias, Ifá remains a largely nondirective form of counseling. Even when the diviners select particular verses as a result of their personal bias, it is still the clients who select and interpret the meaning of those verses which they feel most directly apply to their own personal situations. In this way, the clients are really being encouraged to act on their intuition, to trust their own instincts, and are once again being validated through candomblé. Maclean (1978) has said that in Nigeria the Yoruba diviner priests function in a manner equivalent to psychotherapists, helping their patients in dealing with relationship problems. The divination of the palm nuts or cowrie shells is really a projective technique and has been compared to the Rorschach test of Western psychotherapy, in which the subjects see in the ink blots only that which they project onto otherwise neutral stimuli. As in the Rorschach testing situation, clients in consultation with Ifá diviners project onto the verses that which they feel or need in their lives, and "its interpretation depends on clients' motivations and other psychological factors" (Ribeiro, 1956).

Music and Spirit Possession

Returning to the period of initiation in candomblé, music is constantly present during the weeks of seclusion, through the singing of the appropriate songs and chants throughout the day. These particular songs are not connected to possession, and when possession does occur it is in response to music made by others on their behalf (Rouget, 1985).

There is an entire repertoire of possession music which includes very specific music (songs and drum rhythms) for summoning each of the orixas. The transition from the eré to the santo state is initially triggered only by the sound of the adja, the sacred bell. However, when in the santo state, the drum rhythms and songs of the orixas stimulate and sustain the initiates in their deep trance. The general intensity of the sonic environment, characterized by repetitive drumming, has some similarities to shamanic drumming, and certainly blocks left brain attention and encourages right brain exploration. In response to the music of their orixas, the initiates dance and act out their roles, the characteristic movements and behaviors of the spirits by whom they are possessed. However, to "act out" is really a misleading term, because in the candomblé belief system the initiates are not consciously creating roles: rather they are no longer in conscious control and have become the living incarnations of their orixas.

Dramatic Empowerment through Candomblé

The initiates are empowered in many ways when they are possessed, and this provides an interesting comparison with psychodrama therapy. In psychodrama, the protagonist can act out various roles to explore life possibilities through direct group experience, with the group members playing the roles of significant others in his or her life constellation. The psychodrama director might sometimes allow the protagonist to play the role of God, in this way providing the ultimate empowerment to be creative in taking control of one's life. But, as Figge (1989) has pointed out, even with the suspension of disbelief that occurs in psychodrama, the participants remain partially aware that the protagonist is not truly God, but is only temporarily playing that role. In candomblé, the initiate is not playing the role of God, rather he is a god, the embodiment of an orixa. This experience must inevitably be deeply empowering for the initiate, and, in fact, the concept of acquiring and developing one's axé (spiritual power), is basic to candomblé. At the same time, when possessed (and this is particularly the case in the more eclectic and syncretic candomblé—derived umbanda religion), the possessed person can offer direct consultations to other group members. Such possessed individuals have moved from their primary identification with the self to internalizing the second consciousness of their orixas, and finally, when consulting, to sanctioning on a third level of the original ego state that is so complete that it can happen that a possessed person can talk about their former selves as of a different individual. This ability to personally disassociate is reminiscent of the psychodramatic technique of role reversal. Through totally assuming the role of the orixa, the possessed person is then able to see himself more objectively, and this is exemplified in a fascinating example reported by Figge (1989, p. 449). In this case, during an umbanda session, a man possessed by an orixa told the observers "to advise his own medium not to drink so much in order not to destroy himself." Consulting with the possessed initiates creates another wonderful dimension of therapy for those who seek their counsel. That is, rather than trying to reach God's intermediaries on earth—the ministers and priests as in so many world religions—in candomblé one has the possibility to bypass all half-way measures and finally speak to God in person, face to face.

In a further comparison with psychodrama, the orixas can also be seen as parallel with the technique of the psychodramatic double, in which a member of the group doubles the role of the protagonist. The doubles function to assist protagonists on getting more directly in touch with different parts of themselves and in liberating their intuitive expression and spontaneity. The orixas can similarly be seen as extensions or doubles of the initiates' personality that aid the initiates in gaining in self-understanding and expression. Finally, the candomblé ritual of appeasing Exu, a potentially harmful spirit, in the early stages of the xiré ceremony can be seen as comparable in function to the psychodramatic warm up. In psychodrama, the warm-up period takes place before the group has developed a specific therapeutic focus, and serves to energize the group and establish connections between group members. In candomblé, the ceremony for Exu may also serve to warm up the group, to connect the participants to the beginnings of the ritual process, and help them to prepare and focus for the emotional intensity of the experiences that will follow.

Trance and Social Realities

Trance is defined by Rouget (1985) as an altered state of consciousness conforming to a cultural mode. Although the role of music in trance induction is inseparable from the totality of the ritual in candomblé, it still plays a very prominent and critical role. Specific songs and drum patterns trigger the public possession of the initiates in the xiré ceremony. Music pervades the world of candomblé, and the musical conditioning that occurs in the initiation period retains powerful associations. Although much of the possession repertoire may have been generically familiar to the new initiates before their first possession, the initiation period can also be seen as a period of specialized music education, in which conditioned responses are established between music and trance.

An important question is the consideration of just what trance means in Afro-Brazilian culture. Brazil, although superficially integrated, in reality functions with very pronounced social and economical divisions, with those of African descent at the very bottom of the socioeconomic scale. Poverty and the lack of real opportunities of escaping the privations of their class result in a life characterized by a great deal of stress for the Afro-Brazilian segment of the population. By contrast, association within candomblé provides its adherents with an alternative social context in which they can aspire to achieve levels of status and recognition far beyond what they could ever hope to achieve in the mainstream of Brazilian society. Therefore, the group membership and social support provided through candomblé are very effective stress coping mechanisms.

Trance, which has implications that extend far beyond mere social reinforcement, provides a place for total escape from the internal pressures of the self. It makes accessible a form of psychic retreat that may serve (in a far more benign way) something of the same purpose that electric shock therapy procedures have served in psychiatric therapy. Trance provides a retreat that is always available, and is certainly a profound technique for escaping from and thereby coping with stress.

A recent study of spirit possession in the town of Ambanja in northern Madagascar (Sharp, 1990) focuses on outbreaks of mass possession by Njarininsky spirits of school children between the ages of thirteen and seventeen. These group possessions seemed to have clearly served as stress coping mechanisms for the affected students who were primarily young women, school migrants from the villages to the cities, and pregnant and unmarried at the time of possession.

These Njarininsky spirits cause a form of possession sickness, evil spirits that need to be exorcised by traditional healers. Njarininsky have been sent by enemies who use magic-fanafody to cause harm. The affected girls, who become sexually active at an early age, compete for men for whom they become mistresses. This leads to rivalry between girls who then bring about the fanafody that leads to possession. More pragmatically, the possessed girls are then removed from school and the stresses of city life, and are returned to their villages and the care of their families until the harmful spirits have been removed. Further, during the period of possession, the girls have no memory of their former selves. This is a clear, if only temporary, stress coping mechanism for Malagasy girls.

In candomblé, the trance state is not only a response to a temporary crisis. Rather, it has become a fully sanctioned and institutionalized practice that provides an ongoing and lifetime coping mechanism for "resolving tensions" (Bastide, 1978), for people whose entire lives are characterized by continued socioeconomic stress. Brazilian psychotherapy, even when available to Afro-Brazilians to a limited degree through the social services, is dominated by therapists who are trained strictly in the European and American therapy models, with no connection to the belief system of Afro-Brazilian culture (Santos-Subbe and Stubbe, 1989). It is therefore no wonder that Brazilians of African descent would prefer to seek guidance from their own mae or pae de santo, and retreat regularly into trance, rather than experience the additional stress and essential rejection of a Eurocentric therapist who has no relationship to their world view and social reality. Candomblé supports a socially viable belief system. Even in the field of incurable diseases like AIDS (which is a major problem in Brazil), the belief system of candomblé can be of value. By consulting with their cult leaders, Afro-Brazilian AIDS patients can receive the spiritual strength that they need from the orixas. Although AIDS remains fatal in nearly all cases, some recent research in Kenya has demonstrated that AIDS patients who *believe* that they are being effectively treated by traditional healers have a better life expectancy than those who do not have this supportive belief system (Mulindi, 1989). There is ample evidence that positive imagery can activate the immune system in disease control (Achterberg, 1985). Furthermore, music therapy research has demonstrated that music can enhance relaxation and imagery, and that in combination with a wellness-directed belief system can effect positive change in a variety of disease conditions (Rider, 1987).

Modern medicine and candomblé are not contradictory, but complementary, and can function together in a mutually supportive way. Candomblé cult leaders in Bahia are counseling AIDS patients and thereby reinforcing the spiritual strength the patients need in order to most efficiently combat the disease, and at the same time candomblé cult leaders are cooperating with Bahian healthcare workers in AIDS prevention.

The powerful belief system in candomblé, with its unquestioning faith in the protective power of the orixas, maximizes the individual's ability to cope with illness. In the practice of music therapy, the use of music and imagery techniques that lead to an altered state of consciousness provides an effective therapeutic procedure in the Eurocentric world, but they are not supported by the unquestioning belief system that pervades the Afrocentric world of candomblé. However, the singing and drumming trance-induction techniques of candomblé provide interesting models for reaching an altered state that have possibilities for adaptation into music therapy clinical practice.

Candomblé and Modern Healthcare

The counseling practiced by cult leaders (cura) provides a form of healing which conforms to the holistic concept of health as defined by the World Health Organization (WHO) (Tiller, 1979, p. 257). The WHO defines health as "a state of complete physical, mental, and social well being and not merely the absence of disease or infirmity." As Tiller has further pointed out, patients in Brazilian hospitals often try to augment their standard medical treatment by leaving the hospital when possible to attend cult sessions, and some Brazilian psychiatrists have begun to study the psychological phenomena that occur in cult centers and their effects on patients. The umbanda spiritists have established many hospitals in Brazil that involve weekly cult sessions as a part of the medical treatment plan. Mediums possessed by their spirit guides remain in separate rooms, and clients go to seek direct guidance from their personal orixas, in the same way that Eurocentric clients may select their personal physicians or therapists.

Candomblé, with its energizing song, dance, and dramatic expression, provides a socially sanctioned opportunity for open expression and the release of inhibitions. Even the sides of oneself that would be normally repressed can be fully expressed and displayed to the group through the outlet provided by spirit possession. Yet, even the trance state has its boundaries and expectations for appropriate behaviors. Thus, like the structures built into play therapy for children, or the structures inherent in the expressive therapies such as music, art, dance, and drama when used with adults, the trance provides for freedom of expression, yet within a structured setting. In candomblé, freedom of individual expression is encouraged through the integration of music, art, dance, and dramatic action but still retains some behavioral boundaries. In therapy, self-expression is important, but limits are always essential and uncontrolled expression which is chaotic would be contraindicated for persons with emotional problems. Candomblé is the most holistic of therapies, in which music, dance, artistic expression through the costumes of the orixas and their symbolic paraphernalia, and the drama of spirit possession are taken to the highest levels of aesthetic as well as emotional and therapeutic expression.

Candomblé and Music as Therapy

As discussed previously, the drum rhythms and songs of the orixas are the primary mechanisms for triggering the initiates into the state of trance. These highly conditioned responses between specific musics and trance induction certainly suggest that Brazilian music therapists should be well versed in the music of candomblé if they ever hope to work effectively with Afro-Brazilian clients. Of course, the same principle holds true for music therapists in any culture. That is, music therapists must have a basic knowledge of the musics of the representative ethnic groups that appear in their client populations if they hope to be effective in establishing musical communication and rapport (Moreno, 1988).

For example, when Afro-Brazilian clients are encountered in the clinical setting, the music therapist familiar with the basic candomblé song repertoire, and the songs of the client's orixa, could sing a song of the client's orixa to, or with, them. Although hearing these songs outside the context of a cult house would be a very unfamiliar experience for candomblé initiates, at the very least these songs would elicit very strong and positive associative memories (Béhague, 1991). This kind of associative recall could be of great value, for example, in assisting hysterical clients in restoring their sense of identity and group connections, and provide a very calming and reassuring experience. It is also very possible that the musical associations and conditioning between this music and spirit possession could be so strong with some clients that in response to the songs of their orixa they would enter into the eré state, the mild trance-like state that could be of great value in the immediate stages of coping with emotional crisis. Another approach along these lines would be for the music therapist to invite a cult leader into the hospital setting to sing to, and with, the client. This kind of procedure has a precedent in some hospitals in the American Southwest, where traditional Navajo medicine men are invited directly into the hospital setting to work with Native American clients, along with the Anglo medical doctors. Certainly, this kind of interdisciplinary approach to healing, involving both traditional and modern medically trained practitioners, is an integration of the best of the Eurocentric and Afrocentric worlds of healthcare.

The richly elaborated musical structure of candomblé provides an enviable model of music as therapy, with its hundreds of songs and rhythms that serve as guideposts on the path to wellness, as well as its cohesive belief system and trance induction mechanisms that are all intrinsically connected to specific music stimuli. In the mainstream of music therapy we can see many parallels to the role of music in candomblé.

For example, it is commonplace in music therapy to make use of music for which a client has previously conditioned responses, or to utilize music that is conditioned during the therapeutic process to have a variety of specific associations. Music can be used for eliciting associative recall reminiscence, for its stimulating or calming effects, or music can be conditioned to bring about altered states leading to the exploration of the unconscious as in the techniques of music and imagery. In candomblé, music is similarly utilized to establish and later elicit conditioned trance and dance responses in association with the orixas, to stimulate or calm the initiates in their transitions between the santo and the eré state, and generally to trigger and sustain trance. Certainly, both the concepts of the "unconscious" and "trance" are culturally laden terms. Perhaps to the extent that we can find a continuum between these concepts, and between music therapy practice and music and ritual in candomblé, we can begin to fully appreciate, as well as learn from and apply the healing wisdom of candomblé into the world of modern psychotherapy.

References

Achterberg, J. (1985). *Imagery in Healing: Shamanism and Modern Medicine*. Boston: Shambhala Publications.

Bascom, W. (1969). *Ifá Divination: Communication between Gods and Men in West Africa*. Indiana University Press, Bloomington.

Bastide, R. (1978). *The African Religions of Brazil: Toward a Sociology of the Interpenetration of Civilizations*. The Johns Hopkins Press, Baltimore.

Béhague, G. (1984). Patterns of Candomblé Music Performance: An Afro-Brazilian Religious Setting (pp. 222-254). In G. Béhague (ed.) *Performance Practice: Ethnomusicological Perspectives*. Westport, Connecticut, Greenwood Press.

Béhague, G. (1991). Private communication. University of Texas, Austin, Texas.

Cossard, G. (1970). Contribution a l'etude des candomblés au Brasil. Le candomblés angola. Paris: Faculte des lettres et sciences humaine de Paris, 2 vols. ronetypes. In Rouget, G. (1985). *Music and Trance: A Theory of the Relations between Music and Possession*. Chicago: University of Chicago Press.

Figge, H. (1989). Controlled Spirit-Possession as a Form of Group Psychotherapy (the Umbanda Religion of Brasil) (pp. 445-450). In Peltzer,

K., and P. Ebigbo (1989). *Clinical Psychology in Africa*. University of Nigeria, Enugu.

Gonzalez-Wippler, M. (1989). *Santeria: The Religion. A Legacy of Faith, Rites and Magic*. Harmony Books, New York.

Hughes, C. (1968). In *Encyclopedia of the Social Sciences*. New York: The Macmillan Co.

Maclean, U. (1978). Choices of Treatment among the Yoruba (pp. 152-167). In *Culture and Curing: Anthropological Perspectives on Traditional Medical Beliefs and Practices*. University of Pittsburgh Press.

Moreno, J. (1988). Multicultural Music Therapy: The World Music Connection. *Journal of Music Therapy* XXV (I).

Mulindi, S. (1989). Western and Traditional Practices in the Healthcare Delivery System in Kenya. Unpublished lecture. Nairobi, Kenya.

Ribiero, R. (1956). Projective Mechanisms and the Structuralization of Perception in Afrobrazilian Divination. *Revue Internationale d'Ethnopsychologie Normal et Pathologique* I (2), pp. 3-23. In Bascom, W. *Ifá Divination: Communication between Gods and Men in West Africa*. Indiana University Press, Bloomington.

Rider, M. S. (1987). Treating Chronic Disease and Pain with Music-mediated Imagery (pp. 113-120). *The Arts in Psychotherapy* 14 (2).

Rouget, G. (1985). *Music and Trance: A Theory of the Relations between Music and Possession*. Chicago: University of Chicago Press.

Santos-Stubbe, C., and H. Stubbe (1989). Afrobrazilian Culture and Clinical Psychology (pp. 68-78). In Peltzer, K., and P. Ebigbo (1989). *Clinical Psychology in Africa*. University of Nigeria, Enugu.

Sharp, L. A. (1990). Possessed and Dispossessed Youth: Spirit Possession of School Children in Northwest Madagascar (pp. 339-364). *Culture, Medicine and Psychiatry* 14.

Tiller, A. G. (1979). The Brazilian Cult as a Healing Alternative (pp. 255-272). *Journal of Latin-American Lore* 5, p. 2.

21

An Aesthetic Foundation of Clinical Theory:
An Underlying Basis of Creative Music Therapy

Kenneth Aigen

Prelude to Kenneth Aigen

When I first met Ken, he was a graduate student in the master's degree Music Therapy program at New York University. He was assisting Barbara Hesser in the coordination of the 1982 Symposium: Music in the Life of Man at NYU. From the beginning, he struck me as a very serious man.

Later I got to know Ken better when he was working at the Creative Arts Rehabilitation Center in New York City. He phoned me up one day when I was in New York and asked if he could take me to lunch. As he formulated his burning questions and revealed himself as a person through this initial encounter, I began to realize that Ken was the kind of person who could make a difference in the music therapy world. He was sincere, extremely bright, passionate about his work, and dedicated to an intellectual approach. Initially, he was interested in learning more about the work I had developed in *The Mythic Artery*. Quickly our conversation turned from the historical and clinical aspects covered in the text to shared theoretical interests and concerns. As I savored the depth of Ken's thought processes about our work, I came to realize that he had the potential for making a unique and essential contribution to our field. He had a philosophical mind—one which could view the big picture and one which did not shun complexity.

Since this initial meeting, Ken and I have had opportunities to brainstorm about our work in a philosophical way. This "philosophy" is not the type of abstract endeavor which separates us from the human condition, but one which connects—because it is alive with the context of our shared work—the beautiful moments of music therapy practice with clients.

Ken subsequently completed his doctoral work at New York University and continued his interest in philosophy and theory of science, asking burning questions to us all about our work.

Over the course of the last five years, Ken has begun to develop a body of written work which I believe will serve music therapy in ways which are critical if our work is to endure through the necessary formulation of grounded theory. In his dissertation, Ken explores "indigenous theory," a theoretical orientation which challenges us to speak clearly and directly about our experience in music therapy from grassroots, unmediated by pre-designed theoretical constructs.

Presently he serves as the coordinator of research at the Nordoff-Robbins Music Therapy Clinic at New York University. Within the context of the Nordoff-Robbins approach, he examines the possibility of grounded theory, based on observation of thousands of hours of clinical work and many hours of dialog with members of clinical staff. He also serves as the current president of the American Association for Music Therapy and is thus in a position to bring the depth and substance of his approach to the political realm.

Of himself, Ken writes: "I came to music therapy through my interests in psychology, philosophy of science, and the improvisational rock and roll of bands like the Grateful Dead and the Allman Brothers. As a music therapist, I have worked with emotionally handicapped children in the New York City public schools and with children and adults at the Creative Arts Rehabilitation Center, Inc. In my current position, my interest lies in applying the tenets and values of qualitative research to illuminate the underlying processes of Creative Music Therapy."

Ken is married to Benedikte Scheiby, also a contributor in this collection. They live with their daughter Sara in New York City.

> As the painter places pigment upon the canvas . . . his ideas and feeling are also ordered. . . . The work is artistic in the degree in which the two functions of transformation are effected by a single operation. (Dewey, 1934, p. 75)

> These children order their being as they order their beating, realizing order and purpose in themselves as they find these qualities in the music. (Nordoff & Robbins, 1971, p. 53)

A Role for Aesthetics in Clinical Theory

Music is one of the avenues through which we appreciate sound. The aesthetic properties of music play an important role in establishing our affinity to various sounds and represent that dimension which transforms sound into music.

Given the primacy of aesthetic experience in framing our experience of sound into a musical one, it is surprising that the aesthetic dimension of music in music therapy has not been researched extensively.[1] Although it is probably the case that clinicians have implicitly recognized the importance of aesthetic factors, the paradigm of traditional research in music therapy has not lent itself to investigations of these aspects of human experience. The belief that aesthetic judgments are subjective and therefore beyond the pale of science has certainly contributed to the paucity of research in this area.

In recent years, however, there has been a growing body of published literature detailing the inadequacies of traditional research in music therapy.[2] Although there are a variety of criticisms of traditional research, a common element is the observation that through the methods of traditional research what is lost is nothing less than the music. As a profession we are finally recognizing that the very tool we use—music—is not being adequately represented in our research literature. Hence David Aldridge's citation of "a need for a phenomenological understanding that is isomophoric with the medium of music itself" (1989, p. 92), and Michele Forinash and David Gonzales's call for a research method "which allows for a more complete representation of the music therapy process: one which goes beyond analyzing musical behaviors and juxtaposing musical experience onto non-musical models of human life" (1989, p. 36).

But what is it to say that clinical theories and models do not represent music adequately if not that it is the aesthetic dimension of sound that is being ignored? Further, unless this aesthetic dimension is of primary clinical significance, its absence in the research literature would not be noteworthy. By calling for more attention to be paid to representing musical experience, music therapists are giving tacit recognition to the clinical salience of aesthetic factors.[3]

Perhaps it can be instructive to speculate on why music therapists have not drawn upon aesthetics either as a field for investigation or as a foundation for clinical theory. If we can examine the underlying bases of our avoidance here, and we find these bases wanting, then contrasting positions that support the importance of aesthetic experience are strengthened.

One reason that music therapists have been reluctant to discuss the role of aesthetic considerations in their work may be due to an overly limited conception of aesthetic experience. Clinicians may think that because they are not concerned with producing music that necessarily sounds pleasing or because their music is to be judged on standards other than those present in the concert hall, they are eschewing aesthetic considerations. Because clinical music is not necessarily appreciated outside of the clinical context, therapists may think that this music either lacks aesthetic import or only contains it incidentally.

Essential to this chapter, however, is the idea that aesthetic considerations are central to clinical music therapy process. Carolyn Kenny (1987)—in her discussion of the seven essential elements of music therapy process—suggests that, as a primary element, "the aesthetic is a field of beauty which is the human person. As one moves toward beauty, one moves toward wholeness, or the fullest potential of what one can be in the world" (pp. 93-94). I read the preceding as saying that there is a beauty to the process of human development and that efficacious music therapy is determined by the degree to which the therapist can facilitate the development of musical forms and experiences whose aesthetic partakes in this developmental process.

An important task for theorists for whom aesthetic considerations are primary is to develop an expansive notion of beauty—as Kenny does—broad enough to embrace the creative and expressive activities characteristic of music therapy process.[4] If our belief as therapists is that aesthetic factors play an important role in clinical practice, we can investigate these determinants by basing our work on an appropriately broad aesthetic theory.[5] One important function of the present article is to point the way toward just such an expansive theory.

Similarly, therapists may recognize the aesthetic content of clinical music, yet minimize the therapeutic importance of these factors in an attempt to differentiate their work from nonclinical uses of music. There is a long tradition in music therapy of seeking validation by extrinsic bodies, particularly the medical profession (Aigen, 1991). One way to acquire the sanction of the medical community has been to portray music therapy practice as akin to that of medical practice, where specific "prescriptions," that is, various musical interventions, are selected to remediate pathological conditions. Involvement in music—and the attendant aesthetic rewards thereby gained—is not seen as a valid clinical justification in this view; instead, music is used merely as a means toward an end, an end which might be approached through alternate paths.

It is not hard to imagine that, in the struggle to gain recognition as legitimate health-care professionals, it may have been counterproductive for music therapists to acknowledge that aesthetic considerations play a role in guiding their clinical interventions. This would come about for one of two reasons. Aesthetic considerations are either seen by the wider community (both academic as well as medical) as completely subjective without an objective basis, or as not essential for health and well-being. Whereas it has been traditionally acceptable for artists to appeal to subjective factors in explaining their creative decisions, therapists' judgments should presumably be grounded in more objective criteria.

So, there are a few challenges to these therapists committed to accounting for the contribution of aesthetic factors in the therapeutic process. First among these is to develop a notion of an integral component of facilitating the accomplishment of a wide range of common goals in music therapy. We also need to be able to discuss how therapists can be sensitive to the aesthetic content of a piece of music (or body movement, verbal utterance, etc.) where this sensitivity is rooted in empirical content. That is, we need to offer a notion of aesthetic experience where the judgments of therapists in this domain are seen as neither arbitrary nor purely subjective. Because of the broad perspective that he takes on the importance of aesthetic experience, John Dewey's ideas dovetail with many of the clinical considerations I have been discussing. It is these connections that I would like to explore in the balance of this paper.

John Dewey's Aesthetic[6] Theory and its
Relevance to Music Therapy

The Function of an Aesthetic Theory: Means, Ends, and Media

The artistic shaping of materials yields aesthetic experience. A hallmark of aesthetic experience is a high degree of integration and meaning, aspects which enhance personality development, cognitive functioning, and social interaction, which are, not incidentally, important clinical goals.

As was said earlier, any clinical theory in music therapy (or any arts therapy for that matter) must address the connection between aesthetic experience and these common goals of therapy. Another way of saying this is that in order to determine the value of whatever is experienced within the music therapy session, one must examine its relationship to the client's life outside of the session. Our task is then more finely tuned to this: What are the connections between aesthetic experience and the rest of human life, particularly those dimensions not typically considered to have an aesthetic quality?

In setting out to create an aesthetic theory, John Dewey (1934) has formulated his purpose in remarkably similar terms: "This task is to restore continuity between the refined and intensified forms of experience that are works of art and the everyday events, doings, and sufferings that . . . constitute experience" (p. 3). In Dewey's view, aesthetic experience has a common ground with ordinary, non-aesthetic experience because the aesthetic aspects of works of art function to "idealize qualities found in common experience" (p. 11).

In order to understand the context of Dewey's position, it should be realized that much of Dewey's social philosophy was directed toward addressing (and correcting) the divorcing of means from ends which he considered to be a destructive component of modern society. Dewey saw this artificial separation in (1) the evolution of work from that which is appreciated as intrinsically rewarding to that which is experienced solely as a means of securing the necessities of life; (2) the removal of the arts from being a "part of the significant life of an organized community" to exclusive residence in concert halls, theaters, and museums (p. 7); and (3) the maintenance of an arbitrary (and incorrect) distinction between fine arts and useful arts (p. 26). Regarding this last distinction, Dewey says that even "fine art *consciously* undertaken as such is peculiarly instrumental in quality . . . It exists for the sake of a specialized use, use being a new training of modes of perception" (1958, p. 392).

We can now look at the previously mentioned conception of clinical music as akin to medical prescriptions in light of this distinction between means and ends. The position that maintains the distinction between fine and useful arts is reflected in that body of thought in music therapy which distinguishes music making for its own sake from music making oriented toward clinical ends. This distinction is only tenable if one believes that music making for its own sake is the correct characterization of music experienced for its aesthetic qualities. Dewey maintains that this is a degenerative view because music appreciated for its aesthetic qualities is a music connected to the basic processes of life and nature. Its end is contained in the way in which it serves to enrich the life of listener and performer alike through its capacity to add meaning to life.

I am in agreement with Dewey here and believe that clinical and nonclinical music do not differ as described above. I acknowledge that clinical and nonclinical music may differ in some ways, but it is not along the dimension of nonclinical music existing merely for its own appreciation, while clinical music exists purely as a means toward an end without aesthetic content as a necessary property. Whereas music can be used as a means toward many different ends, when it is the aesthetic dimension of music that is of importance relative to a certain end, it is more accurate to talk about music as what Dewey describes as a *medium*.

Dewey observes that there are two kinds of means: those that are external to what is accomplished and those that are incorporated in the outcome. When we travel just to get to a desired location our trip is a mere means that we would just as well do without; alternately, when we travel for the pleasure inherent in the experience, our trip becomes a *medium* for aesthetic enjoyment. In this latter example, it does not make sense to say that we would just as well do without the trip in accomplishing our goal because our goal *is* the trip. When we characterize something as a medium it is because we observe a certain identity or unity of means with ends and this, to Dewey, is a defining characteristic of aesthetic value (1934, p. 197-198). Some traditional clinical theories maintain that music is a "mere" de facto means, by not addressing their aesthetic component.

In music therapy, we can see this unity of means and ends when we adopt a dynamic conception of the purpose of clinical process. Client outcome is not a static state of being achieved at the end of therapy, but is instead something that unfolds within the clinical process itself. A deep level of involvement in music therapy process—incorporating enhanced expressive freedom, confidence, insight, and personal power—is simultaneously the vehicle and goal of the process. The medical analogy discussed previously is invalid because music therapy treatment, unlike medication or other medical procedure, is not something offered or engaged in as a means toward some completely autonomous end. Instead, facilitating the ability of clients to *live in* the music is simultaneously the means and goal of Creative Music Therapy. And in "living in the emotional character of music, recognizing the elements of structure on which it is formed, and expressing his responses freely in his beating, [a child] has an important experience: his whole personality is vividly activated and working harmoniously" (Nordoff and Robbins, 1971, p. 50). Aesthetic properties are integral to organizing the ongoing flow of life into the discreet units—known as "experiences"—like the one just described. It is this process which we will now examine.

The Role of the Aesthetic in Defining an Experience

For Dewey, the aesthetic is that quality of existence that provides unity, completion, and wholeness to our experience. It is present in everyday acts that may have utilitarian purposes as well as in the products and activities of the museum and concert hall. "Any practical activity will, provided that it is integrated and moves by its own urge to fulfillment, have aesthetic quality" (1934, p. 39).

Consider these additional statements:

The enemies of the aesthetic . . . are deviations . . . from the unity of an experience. (1934, p. 40)

The aesthetic . . . is the clarified and intensified development of traits that belong to every normally complete experience. (1934, p. 46)

Dewey's ideas here are intriguing for music therapists. Many clinical goals can be framed in his terms: We often seek for higher level of personality *integration* for our clients; we hope to provide a sense of meaning and *wholeness* to their lives (as well as our own!); and we seek to engender feelings of *unity* in therapy groups to facilitate constructive conflict and resolution. If we can develop or apply Dewey's conceptions in this area, then it becomes possible to create an epistemological foundation for empirical investigations into the clinical importance of aesthetic experience.

Although people often have experience of things, these transient states are not always composed into having an experience. Some of our experience is fractured, not integrated into meaningful units, and begins and ends in arbitrary places: this is an unaesthetic experience. At other times—such as in working on a project to its end, solving a puzzle, eating a satisfying meal, listening to a symphony—we have an experience whose aesthetic nature is expressed through its singular identity. An experience does not merely cease at some arbitrary point but instead reaches an organic ending or consummation. The elements of an experience exist in significant relationship with each other and this relationship creates the identity and defining quality of the experience (Dewey, 1934, pp. 35-39).

A memorable meal, an engaging conversation, a quarrel with a friend, and witnessing an intense storm on the ocean are all examples of what Dewey considers to be an experience. And all of these experiences possess and reveal the unity of structure and purpose, the integration of parts, and the organic beginning and ending, characteristic of a work of art. The work of art merely highlights the aesthetic properties that integrate undifferentiated experience into an experience. The aesthetic is revealed when one understands how the varied components of an experience or phenomenon "are linked to one another and do not merely succeed one another" (Dewey, 1934, p. 55).

What I think is striking here are the parallels between unaesthetic experience and the conditions that often bring an individual to therapy, whether this individual is relatively well functioning or extremely disabled: an autistic child may have difficulty in organizing discreet intra-personal events into a coherent sense of self; a normally functioning adult may have difficulties in forming satisfying social relationships that grow beyond a series of unconnected social contacts; and an individual pursuing self-actualization may have acquired the trappings of successful social adaptation, and yet still be seeking for a sense of purpose in life. The common ground in these examples is the inability of the individual to experience isolated or discreet contacts as components of a larger whole, the sense of which adds meaning and purpose to life.

This pattern is most clear when we look at disabled children. The inability to form a coherent sense of self, to allow repeated social contacts to develop into a relationship, and to integrate the raw units of experience into larger wholes to facilitate social and cognitive learning can all be seen as a deficit in the ability to have an experience, as Dewey uses this term. It is the mastery of the integrative processes—whether seen in the social, emotional, artistic, spiritual, or intellectual sphere—that allows for growth and development in these realms.

The important implication for the current paper is that the aesthetic properties of music—incorporating the inherent dynamisms of melodic, harmonic, and rhythmic structures—have the ability to frame raw experience into a whole experience. The child whose random pecking at the keyboard evolves into musical phrases, whose vocal play expresses a cognizance of an A-B-A tempo and dynamics to interact conversationally with the therapist's piano playing, is developing these integrative processes through gaining mastery over the aesthetic components of musical expression. And the child's experiential and expressive capacities are inextricably linked:

> This is a dual process: the child's apprehending of the experience a form of activity can mediate depends upon his *ability to participate in it*, and this ability depends for its development, upon the *musical perception the experience engenders as it becomes apprehended*. Therefore, the capacity to participate experientially and the ability to participate actively in music . . . develop together. (Nordoff and Robbins, unpublished manuscript)

Experience in this aesthetic realm is not peripheral to the therapy but *is* the therapy. It is only the degree to which clinical music progresses in aesthetic quality—a quality that reflects increasing degrees of personality integration—that it can be considered an indication of growth.

The Origins and Importance of Aesthetic Experience

Dewey observes that it is inevitable that the relationship between an organism and its environment constantly changes. This change is characterized by the organism temporarily falling out of balance with the environment and then finding ways to restore this equilibrium or balance. Organisms that cannot adapt in this way die, those whose existence is not enhanced by this process manage to subsist. Yet "life grows when a temporary falling out is a transition to a more extensive balance of the energies of the organism with those of the conditions under which it lives" (1934, p. 14). In other words, those organisms that flourish, develop, and evolve can learn to benefit from the resolution of the tension caused by the ever-changing demands of the organism/environment relationship.

The musical metaphor is taken one step further by Dewey. These changes in the relationship between the organism and its environment have a rhythmic character. Development that occurs through the creative resolution of tension is characterized by expansion of the active organism, not by passive accommodation or withdrawal. Thus, in the most basic processes of our biological adaptation we see that states of balance and harmony are achieved through the mastery of rhythms of tension and resolution (Dewey, 1934, p. 14).

This description of an organism's biological relationship with the environment is applicable to one's social and emotional sphere. Personality development is characterized by a similar rhythm of stasis and valence succeeded by periods of tension which are then resolved into a higher level of integration. As we move through the stages of life we consolidate our functioning into a distinct self-image. The processes of maturity and growth present a new set of demands as when an infant first discovers his/her autonomy, a child first goes to school, and a young adult forms a new family. The individual's inner drives change so that previous relationships with the social environment must alter and transform to allow the individual to again be in harmony with this environment. Those individuals that cannot adapt may descend into pathology, those that reluctantly or passively adapt can function adequately but can lack fulfillment, and those whose beings grow and expand to meet the new demands flourish through the re-establishment of harmony with the environment.

This progressive reclaiming of balance and harmony after periods of tension and conflict contains a consummatory element that Dewey describes as being an essential feature of aesthetic experience. The significance of this for the current chapter is that the processes that represent the furtherance and development of life, on the biological, social, and emotional level, necessarily contain aesthetic features. The aesthetic is essential to our healthful embrace of life.

To bring an example from the clinic, consider a withdrawn, self-occupied autistic child of whom it might be said that he has reached a kind of balance with his environment. He may have reached a tacit agreement with his family members who no longer struggle to intrude on his preoccupation with the world of objects. The differences between the expectations of his social environment and his own inner limitations no longer create a tension for this child as his resistiveness has created a system where his fear or avoidance is not challenged.

To bring this child into a music therapy session is to set up an immediate tension. Now the child is in an environment where one goal is to bring about a higher level of emotional intercourse. The therapist is playing music which can be seen as an intrusion on the child's desire for withdrawal and isolation. Moreover, the therapist may be actively countering this desire through actions like establishing physical proximity or eye contact and by coaching the child on the use of objects, such as drum beaters, as tools of expression rather than as items to be compulsively manipulated. It would not be inaccurate to say that the therapist is increasing the level of tension the child experiences between his inner (pathological) needs and the environment.

However, this tension is not a bad thing and may in fact be a necessary precursor to any type of growth or development. The viewpoint that logically follows from Dewey is that this tension—between either the person and the environment, or between one's inner life and current functioning level—is a precursor of growth. Without this tension there is no motivation for change.

The music therapist's art consists of creating a musical environment whose demands do not exceed those which can be productively engaged in by the child and yet still be adequately challenging and thereby engaging. The great advantage that music provides is the inherent gratification produced by the rewards of the aesthetic consummation of musical experiences. This aesthetic gratification has a two-fold function. First, it provides the motivation for the child to endure and embrace this tension rather than shy away from it. The accommodation is then a productive one that enhances the child's functioning, rather than a passive or withdrawing accommodation that mirrors the child's inability to make use of the tension inherent in his relationship with the environment to further his development. Second, through learning to appreciate the gratification inherent in aesthetic consummation, the child has an experience, in Dewey's sense of the word. Musical interaction provides the effective/cognitive experience necessary for learning and emotional growth that is denied to the child outside of the musical milieu.

A concrete musical example of this process can be seen in a clinical improvisation in which the above-mentioned socially withdrawn child is beginning to allow deeper levels of contact with his therapist through musical improvisations that increase in duration over the course of the therapy. One possible musical intervention is for the therapist to build harmonic tension while the child beats a drum and to provide resolutions of this tension when the child engages in isolated cymbal crashes.

What is happening here is that the child is learning not just to tolerate, but to actually enjoy the tension produced by the interpersonal contact. By mirroring the child's internal tension through the choice of harmonies, the therapist evokes a higher level of interpersonal functioning. What is required of the child is to be able to experience his inner self as manifest in the music of the therapist/client dyad. This tension is resolved aesthetically as the child's cymbal crash indicates the appropriate harmonic movement for the therapist. The child thus controls the tension level of the session and the music and learns the most important lesson, that the experience of tension can be inherently pleasurable when this tension leads to an aesthetic consummation. And what is beautiful about the musical interaction is that the child does not leave the field of musical interaction with the therapist to resolve the tension but instead strengthens and deepens the musical interaction, as it is the musical movement to the cymbal that consummates the experience. Because it is the musical object—here, the beater and cymbal—that functions as the vehicle of consummation, the child becomes engaged in the world of objects as tools for expressive gratification and his obsession with their physical manipulation is lessened.

The artist cultivates moments of resistance and tension because of their potential for "bringing into living consciousness an experience that is unified and total" (Dewey, 1934, p. 15). Similarly, the artist within the child, that is, the music child,[7] learns to experience tension in a positive manner when his or her aesthetic sensitivity is engaged.

The Function of Aesthetic Tension

Understanding the nature of the relationship between emotions and music is an important component of clinical music therapy theory because it helps us to map out the various ways that music functions in the therapeutic setting. Although some may argue that one clinical function of music relates to its cathartic value, I believe (and subsequently support) the notion that pure catharsis does not really exist in a therapy session and, in any case, this function is not relevant in the aesthetic domain, the area that I am arguing is more fundamental in relation to clinical process.

I agree with Dewey when he said that "emotional discharge is a necessary but not a sufficient condition of expression" (1934, p. 61). A spontaneous shout of joy, a welling up of tears, and an angry tirade all discharge and reveal emotional or feeling states of the individual, yet effective content alone does not render them acts of expression with aesthetic import.

What is missing in these acts is the "administration of objective conditions [and] shaping of materials [without which] there is no expression" (Dewey, 1934, p. 62). These objective conditions can be an instrument, a musical form, or a therapeutic relationship or intervention. In any of these examples, it is important to see how the relationship, instrument, or aesthetic form provides both the *resistance to discharge* as well as the *vehicle for transformation* of the emotional energy that is otherwise dissipated through mere discharge. Instead, the clinically-aesthetic domain turns this energy to the service of growth, self-expression, and enhanced self-awareness. And in this way the client's inner development is fostered as "it is the aesthetic form—as opposed to social expectations of appropriate behavior or . . . the therapist's limits—that functions as the resistance to the client's . . . impulses" (Aigen, 1991b, p. 113)

The significance of these objective conditions is that they add something intrinsically vital to the therapeutic process: the potential for transformation of energy which is necessary for the growth characteristics of efficacious therapy. They do not function merely to provide an excuse or permission for a cathartic release. This context alters the meaning of such acts, much as a bicycle wheel becomes art (or at least an artistic statement) when displayed in a museum. I am not arguing that all acts—such as a sneeze, a cry of pain, etc.—become expressive merely by occurring in a therapy session. What I am saying is that as regards musical activity, there is always some external element in terms of which the discharge acquires communicative significance which voids its nature as pure discharge. To consider a musical act in a therapy session as pure catharsis is to ignore the ever-present clinical and relational context which orients all the activities taking place within it.

For the present discussion I would like to consider emotional expression to occur when the energy in emotional discharge manifests itself through an aesthetic context. It is probably true that expression requires inhibition of the raw emotion, although as Dewey notes, this inhibition is not suppression and *"restraint* is not, in art, identical with *constraint"* (1934, p. 97). I make this distinction because creative music therapy approaches—such as those of Nordoff and Robbins—are often differentiated from behavioral approaches by relying on, and trusting, the inherent rewards of the expressive, aesthetic experience in fostering growth. An otherwise hyperactive child expressing his/her inner experience via a gentle, reflective improvisation on the resonator bells is showing *restraint* through the materials; in a behavioral or other non-aesthetic scheme, the child must be coerced to engage in an act where the emotional energy is *constrained* by either the therapist's limits or by the promise of rewards external to the musical interaction.

In the aesthetic scheme, everything the child encounters in the therapy session can serve this double, seemingly paradoxical, function of providing resistance to discharge while being a vehicle for expression. This resistance to discharge does produce tension between the child and his (social or physical) environment, but as Dewey notes for the artist, "without internal tension . . . there would be nothing that could be called development and fulfillment" (1934, p. 138).

There are many types of tension in the music therapy session: foremost among these are "the tensions that lie between the old self and the new self" (Robbins and Robbins, 1991, p. 70) as the client explores new capacities for social expression and interaction; there is the inner tension in the instrument as a resistor to an impulse (imagine the function of a drum in stopping the arm movement of a player whose effective state first motivates the movement); and there is the tension in encountering the therapist as one who represents an alternative to the client's perceptions and pathological or more limited functioning.

Yet, "therapy can lie in resolving the conflicts between the old and the new selves" (Robbins and Robbins, 1991, p. 59) and the resolution of all these tensions are integral components of the music therapy process. It is primarily through the dissonance of harmony that these tensions become manifest in the music therapy session:

> Expressive dissonance helps to awaken [handicapped children] to the musical activity in which they are engaged [and] dissonances can set a child into movement, can increase his attention-span, and can give vitality to the harmonic accompaniment of the songs he sings. (Nordoff and Robbins, 1971, p. 45)

The degree of efficacy a particular musical intervention possesses is related to the degree to which these tensions (dissonances) are resolved aesthetically and at a pace and to a degree that truly reflects the client's genuine state of being. When these tensions are handled aesthetically—thus allowing for the re-integration of the tension-causing element into a wider or more expansive self-image—the goals of therapy are facilitated. In non-aesthetic resolution, the tension and resistance have not been managed in the service of the individual's growth.

A fine example of the manner in which clinical interventions can produce productive dissonances or tension when they run counter to a client's expectations is recounted in Nordoff and Robbins (1971). The authors describe a course of therapy where their clinical stance had been initially gentle and undemanding but which now required providing more of a challenge to the client. Sensing that there was sufficient trust in the relationship to adopt such a stance, the author's interventions nonetheless provoked a rageful reaction,

> but [the boy's] *new musical self* transformed rage into musical expression—he sang his rage, and [the therapist] could sing with him [his] understanding of it and [his] contending attitude toward it . . . Over a harmonic sequence of supporting chords [the] singing reached a climax. He clearly sang the melodic resolution and then became quiet. This expressed an *emotional resolution*—signifying the presence of some capability to accept a new direction of activity. (Nordoff and Robbins, 1971, pp. 108-109)

The tension in the therapeutic relationship introduced by the therapist expressing new expectations of the child was mirrored in the dissonance of the music. Rather than provoking a rageful reaction that could have resulted in a resistive or avoidant retreat, this child was instead able to express his tension musically, use it to move to a new level of tolerance of interpersonal contact, and take "hold of his old turbulent emotional reactions and [impress] upon them a responsive and organizing capacity" (Nordoff and Robbins, 1971, p. 109).

Resistance to discharge functions to rhythmically organize human emotional expression. When emotional energy is immediately discharged, "there is not enough resistance to create tension, and thereby a periodic accumulation and release" (Dewey, 1934, p. 155). It is this periodic—or rhythmic—character of its movement into the world that allows emotional energy to contribute to human development.

Through the use of effective Creative Music Therapy, the locus of resistance to discharge becomes the locus of aesthetic expression. Unrestrained discharge is only therapeutic in the extent to which it serves as precursor of further expressive and communicative development. It involves no other cognitive or expressive capacities and thereby does not facilitate self-awareness. Aesthetic considerations transform discharge into expression. Their manipulation provides the only possible rationale for music therapy treatment. Why else would we employ an artistic medium unless those factors that define it as such are integral in its application?

The Self as Manifest in Music[8]

The nature of the relationship between music and human emotions is a perennial topic in the philosophy of the arts. A common position is that music somehow *represents* the emotions as one or another type of symbol. Usually this claim goes unchallenged, although philosophers differ strongly on the nature of the logical or formal relationship between music (symbol) and human affect (thing symbolized).

This traditional approach is exemplified in the thought of Susanne Langer when she asserts that music is the logical expression of feelings and that if music "has an emotional content, it 'has' it in the same sense that language 'has' it symbolically" (1948, p. 176). It is the nature of the symbolic relationship between musical forms and human feelings that Langer addresses in saying that it is the morphology of feeling that music expresses, rather than evoking specific instances of particular feelings. The originality of Langer's conception is seen in her belief that music is a symbol whose "significance is not logically discriminated, but is felt as a quality rather than recognized as a function" (1953, p. 32). Langer applies the traditional dualistic perspective of symbol and thing symbolized to music because she believes that

> until symbolic forms are consciously abstracted, they are regularly confused with the things they symbolize. This is the same principle that causes myths to be believed and sacraments to be taken for efficacious acts. (1948, p. 199)

For Langer, it would seem that any theory that promotes an identification between actual feelings, emotions, or individuals and pieces of music would be guilty of an overly primitive and naive view. It would be analogous to arguing that a totem is a living god or that a flag is the nation it represents. And it is this view that is common in the psychotherapeutic literature when one looks at how dreams, pictures, and, of course, musical creations are considered. Most often these creative products are considered to be symbols that represent various intra-psychic structures or processes.

Yet this is not the only way to conceive of the nature of musical (or any other creative) expression. For example, the aspect of pure experience of music that allows us for the dramatic results of an approach such as Nordoff-Robbins Music Therapy has been described in the following manner:

> Our experience, as we live with [music], is defined by the character and iteration of its structural elements. Our mood is charged by its mood. Our emotions are tempered and held by the changing tensions of its harmony. When we live in the movement of a melody we become identified with it—as children do when they

sing it. When we live in the tonal and temporal structures of a musical composition—as children do when they play instruments in it—our participation integrates our responding faculties. It is out of this completeness of the relationship between music and the human being that music therapy in its truest sense arises. (Nordoff and Robbins, 1971, p. 17)

Consider also the following descriptions of clinical process by the present writer:

At the moment of creation what I am aware of is the music and feeling into what *it* needs. I respond to the client completely via the music . . . What is occurring is that I am becoming aware of the music as a unique manifestation of the client. The duality of act disintegrates and I experience the music as the person, not as a symbol or representation. I am living in my music in the same way as I am perceiving the client within his or her music. (Aigen, 1991a, pp. 235-236)

In Music Therapy, therapists allow the music into their beings, simultaneously extending their being through infusing their selves into the musical domain. In this way, tones function as an extension of one's being—indeed *are* extensions of our being—as they penetrate out psychological, social, and physical environment, much as a microscope or telescope provides biologists and astronomers with information and experiences otherwise unattainable. (Aigen, 1991a, pp. 255-256)

It is clear that, in both of these views, the traditional philosophic and psychodynamic conception of music as a symbol of various inner processes is inadequate. This traditional view maintains a triadic relationship between the symbol, the referent of the symbol, and the symbol user. Yet, as Dewey, rightly observes, this conceptualization

is a product of reflection upon direct phenomena [and is] not a description of what happens when so-called symbols are potent. For the feature which characterizes symbolism is precisely that the thing which later recollection calls a symbol is not a symbol, but a direct vehicle, a concrete embodiment, a vital incarnation. (Dewey, 1958, p. 82)

Understanding art as a mere symbol is then not to understand its deepest aesthetic significance. Instead, the uniquely distinguishing feature of aesthetic experience is . . . that no such distinction of self and object exists in it, since it is aesthetic in the degree in which organism and environment cooperate to institute an experience in which the two are so fully integrated that each disappears. (Dewey, 1934, p. 249)

What Dewey is saying, then, is that the traditional view does not maintain the experience of the participant in its analysis. If one's goal is to understand music therapy process as it is experienced, the traditional view is inadequate. And it is precisely this goal which contemporary critics of traditional research in music therapy are articulating as a crucial deficiency of traditional research and as a necessary component of research with a greater degree of clinical applicability.[9]

In music therapy process, a musical interaction occurs—whether of an intra- or inter-personal character—that is an example of a real and basic human encounter. One's values, fears, strengths, frailties, humanity, openness, communicativeness, and degree of caring for others is directly *expressed*; these personal qualities are not merely *represented* through an abstract symbol system. The power of music therapy lies in the capacity of the therapist to invest his/her own being into a living music that simultaneously engages the client in a living interaction where those client capacities that exist as potential outside of the music can be more fully realized.

Consider now the quotations at the head of this article referring to the simultaneity of the process of organization of materials and organization of the self. Dewey and Nordoff and Robbins each say that this is one and the same process. Yet this is actually what we should expect to occur if the characterization of client and therapist as living in their music is an accurate one. Since there is no fundamental distinction between one's being and one's music it is natural that changes in one should be linked to changes in the other.

When we facilitate the creation of music in the clinical setting we are simultaneously fostering the client's capacity to create and discover how to find meaning in life. As clients in music therapy integrate the materials of their medium into a unified whole, they gain the ability to experience themselves as a part of a greater whole and experience their relationship and connection to the social and physical environment. Thus, as they learn to express themselves through an artistic medium they gain a sense of their place in the world.

Like Dewey, I agree that works of art can inspire other valuable experiences that are not essentially connected to the work's aesthetic properties. This is very clear in the clinical domain when we consider how things like cathartic releases, images, memories, and feelings can be triggered by a piece of music without such an association being dependent upon the essential structure of the music. (I have in mind something like when a client hears a piece of music, is reminded that it was his or her father's favorite piece, and then proceeds to explore hitherto unexpressed feelings toward the father.) Although I do not want to deny the clinical relevance of such experiences just because they are not derived from the aesthetic character of music, I do not consider them to be essential components of music therapy process; instead, they are more like incidental (although occasionally clinically important) by-products. Each of these types of experiences can be occasioned in other ways (such as smelling a familiar scent from childhood and proceeding to discuss long-forgotten feelings toward a parent) and do not tap the unique characteristic of creative aesthetic process in furthering the goals of therapy. If we want to answer the question as to what music uniquely offers in the clinical realm we must look at the contribution of its aesthetic character.

The Objectivity of Aesthetic Perception

Now it may be correct to assert that aesthetic considerations play an important role in guiding music therapists' interventions and in facilitating the clients' growth. Yet, as I previously mentioned, it may be that clinicians have been reluctant to speculate on the importance of aesthetic factors from a belief that the evaluation of the aesthetic content of a piece of music results from subjective considerations antithetical to those employed by legitimate mental health professionals. In this view, these factors would then be incorrectly consigned to the artistic facet of music therapy and would not be considered valid subjects for any type of scientific or systematic investigation.

I would like to support the opposite notion that whereas the aesthetic properties of an entity[10] are not reducible to sensorially observable or material properties, it does not necessarily follow that aesthetic characterizations are therefore arbitrary or purely "subjective." In other words, the fact that we cannot formulate publicly observable criteria for evaluating aesthetic content—as we can when determining the key or idiom of a particular piece of music—does not reflect upon the objectivity of aesthetic judgments. If we can carve out a niche for the objectivity of such judgments, then the door remains open to incorporating our aesthetic capacities into theories of clinical music therapy process. It is the idea of the objectivity of aesthetic perception that I would now like to explore.

In appraisals of works of art, Virgil Aldrich (1963) observes that when one uses such terms as unified, delicate, warm, formal, and economical in their description, one is trying to be objective because the intent is to say something about the constituents of the work of art, not merely about one's experience of it (p. 6). These aesthetic properties are not inferred and do not arise from a process of interpretation; rather, these properties are perceived. Because there is a human capacity for aesthetic perception, Aldrich believes that the application of aesthetic terms has an objective basis.

Aesthetic perceptiveness—a conception that Aldrich attributes to Frank Sibley (1959)—is a "special ability to *notice* or *discern* things" (Sibley, p. 423). It is distinguished from the capacity to make statements of "mere subjective preference or liking on the one hand [and statements resulting] from the good eyesight of people with 20-20 vision on the other" (Aldrich, 1963, p. 20). Although I will not recount the details here, Aldrich presents a (convincing to me) argument that "the same material thing may be perceptually realized either as a physical or as an aesthetic object" (p. 21). The physical object is experienced through observation while the perceptual mode revealing aesthetic objects is called "prehension" (p. 22). And the important conclusion for the present discussion is that the mind "does not necessarily become subjective" in shifting between the various modes of perception (p. 23).

To make this distinction clear, when one comments that a particular piece of music was of 18 minutes duration or that its volume level reached 86 db it is the physical object being referred to; when one says that there was a vital interplay among the string sections or that a particular theme is poignant it is the aesthetic object being described. Neither observation, however, is inherently more objective than the other in this view.

Aldrich discusses how "an aesthetically insensitive . . . person may notice (observe) the arrangement of the materials in physical space—notes, colors, contours—without noticing their relationships as aesthetic elements of the *medium* of the art" (1963, pp. 43-44), because it is the manner in which the materials interact in the aesthetic space which determines their contribution to the object's aesthetic content. Thus, to the extent that one discusses properties of a piece of music that can be observed, one is excluding those aesthetic properties containing deeper levels of clinical significance.

Now this is not to say that the only clinically significant aspects of a client's music that are worth talking about are somehow mysteriously intuited by the music therapist and are not connected to the actual piece of music. It is to say that the piece of music—as a *clini-*

cally aesthetic object—results from a specialized prehension of the properties of the piece of music in question. It involves a first-order perception of the music's aesthetic character as well as an ability to further penetrate into the personal meaning and depth of involvement maintained by the client in this material in order to be able to work with it clinically.

In *Creative Music Therapy* "the clinical significance of a [musical] response [cannot] be determined by its *structural form* alone—the *degree of activation or engagement* expressed in it must be recognized as having *at least* equal importance" (Nordoff and Robbins, unpublished manuscript). Formal observations of music cannot reveal this depth of client involvement—it is available to those whose understanding of the personal meaning of the clinical music to the client is most developed: primarily the client's music therapist(s).

The ability to assess the clinical significance of a musical interaction, although dependent upon the perception of its general aesthetic properties, is not achieved simply by this perception. A lay person might be able to perceive aesthetic qualities in a piece of music from the clinic and yet still not be able to determine its clinical significance. It is not that one must know a client's personal history to experience the clinically-aesthetic object—although this can allow one to see the music in a certain light, just as knowing a composer's life history often provides a certain context for understanding his or her music. Rather, the significance of the clinically aesthetic object is something that one gains access to as a consequence of clinical training, much as one gains the capacity to perceive deeper levels of meaning in works of art as one's sophistication in aesthetic perceptiveness develops.

The deepest level of meaning of a particular client's music is open primarily to the clinician who has maintained the relationship in which the music has arisen. Nordoff and Robbins have characterized the essence of music therapy as involving the "improvisational creation of music as a language of communication between [the therapist] and an individual child" (1971, p. 143), and I have discussed elsewhere the implications for research of observing that music therapy involves the very establishment of a mutually understood musical language between client and therapist (Aigen, 1991a, p. 247). Understanding a client's music means being able to respond to the music in a manner that facilitates the client's growth; it does not necessarily mean being able to translate this music into verbal language. The client's and therapist's musical intelligence and awareness become attuned to each other's nuances and subtleties of meaning. That is why I say that it is the clinician contributing to the creation of a piece of clinical music who best understands this music, although this understanding may be resistant to verbal formalization.

Music therapists' perceptions of their client's music are objectively grounded in the music itself, much as the music lover's aesthetic appreciation of any piece of music is similarly grounded. There is a difference between the two, however, and it may relate to the type of aesthetic one is perceiving. Dewey has said that "nature is an artist that works from within instead of from without" (1958, p. 92). I understand this as meaning that while a human artist assembles materials and combines them into an aesthetic object, nature generates aesthetic objects that exist primarily and solely as aesthetic objects; they are not constructed as an after-thought from non-aesthetic materials.

In this sense, I see the aesthetic of human development as the goal and vehicle of clinical music therapy process. Because this is not the only type of possible aesthetic experience, perhaps we can say that it is the degree to which this process occurs in a musical interaction which distinguishes the clinical significance of a piece of music with aesthetic value from an aesthetic piece of music without this clinical value. And in Creative Music Therapy this process of development—in so far as it is a natural process, that is, one that occurs without the intent of creating an aesthetic object—is more akin to that of the aesthetic of nature than that of artist. I say this because "in creative music therapy, the child's self is developed from within—using inner resources" (Robbins and Robbins, 1991, p. 57). The music therapist can provide the conditions conducive to growth as much as a botanist can provide the correct nutritional conditions for a particular plant. Yet the process of growth in each case is a natural process that the human agency can facilitate, but cannot take credit for.

It is the degree to which the process of human development is aesthetically realized in a music therapy session that determines how deeply a session embodies the essence of music therapy practice. Aesthetic content is thus necessary, though not sufficient, to establish the clinical value of a music interaction as partaking of an essential element of music therapy process.

Closing Words

The relevance for the profession and discipline of music therapy of establishing the primacy of aesthetic considerations in determining clinical interventions has many dimensions: Foremost among these is to realize that the basis of efficacious therapy can never be conveyed through a system of rules for practice. General guidelines can create appropriate contexts for growth through musical interactions, yet the actual clinical intervention, the music, is something that is forever dependent on the therapist's creative, artistic abilities. Music therapists are artists, in the best sense of the word, and there is no need to either hide this fact or explain it away through clinical theory that does not account for the contribution of the therapist's—and the client's!—artistry in accomplishing clinical goals. Last, if it is correct that aesthetic factors play a prominent role in clinical process, then it becomes important for research and training to reflect this fact. Certainly the work of Kenny (1987, 1989), Salas (1990), and the present chapter all point toward possible directions for research. What is still to be addressed is the way in which the academic and post-academic training of music therapists can develop aesthetic awareness as well as direct this awareness to facilitating the goals of clinical practice.

There is one caveat that I would like to offer here. I cannot emphasize strongly enough that I am not advocating an abrogation of the clinician's responsibility to his/her client. When I aver that the actual music created in clinical improvisation springs from aesthetic, creative considerations, I am not minimizing the importance of preparation on the therapist's part. Elements of practice such as the professional relationship between client and therapist, treatment planning, and ethical considerations

> are the supportive edifice which allows and enables the transformative experience to emerge. By providing feelings of safety, regulation and a context of professional responsibility, this structure helps to ensure the integrity of Music Therapy treatment. What I am urging for is a recognition that the components of the enabling social structure are not themselves the agents of change (Aigen, 1991a, p. 245).

To conclude on a more personal note: I recognize that to infer that all music is generated from aesthetic considerations would render the term "aesthetic" meaningless, and this certainly is not the nature of my experience. Rather, I would say that through music therapy practice my capacity for aesthetic experience has been expanded to include that which I had formerly considered to be monotonous, ugly, dissonant, clashing, disorganized, unrefined, and aggressive. It is not that I no longer perceive these qualities in music, but that they have acquired aesthetic value for me through bringing to life the truth of an individual's existence and the struggle to give meaning to this existence.

Notes

1. Although in this chapter my clinical examples are limited to the theories of Nordoff-Robbins Music Therapy, in fact the conclusions are relevant for all of those music therapy techniques whose efficiency is determined by the therapist's creativity and ability to access the client's aesthetic sensitivity.

2. See (Aigen, 1990, 1991a) for a fuller account of these developments and for a detailed description of the differences between "traditional" research and "new" research in music therapy.

3. Jo Salas (1990)—who has recently written on the clinical importance of aesthetic experience—concludes that "searching questions on this subject have scarcely been asked, let alone answered" (p. 2). Salas recognizes the integral role of aesthetic experience in music therapy process and she identifies the role of aesthetic experience in art—as that which "creates an expansion in meaning from the personal to the ontological" (p. 5).

4. I am not certain that Kenny's conception of beauty is the same type traditionally referred to in discussion of works of art. What I would like to assert is that there are elements that both types of experiences share in common, and it is these elements that I would like to consider in the subsequent discussion. Here I have in mind properties like organic unity, balance, dynamism, intensity of expression, vitality, novelty, poignancy, warmth, and organization, whose presence can be assessed—or at least meaningfully discussed—in the clinical domain as well as in traditional works of art.

5. Salas recognizes as much and provides an expansive conception of beauty as referring not purely to "pleasing harmony," but to "any created form that in some satisfying way matches our experience" (1990, p. 14).

6. Dewey utilizes the spelling "esthetic." I have altered his spelling to maintain stylistic continuity for this paper.

7. "The Music Child is . . . the individualized musicality inborn in each child: the term has reference to the universality of musical sensitivity—the heritage of complex sensitivity to the ordering and relationship of tonal and rhythmic movement" (Nordoff and Robbins, 1971, p. 1).

8. The ideas presented under this subheading were originally presented in Aigen (1991a).

9. See (Aigen 1991a) for a description and analysis of traditional and contemporary trends in music therapy research.

10. I use "entity" rather than "thing" or "object" to make clear that I am referring to a piece of music as well as a sculpture, painting, dance, or anything else traditionally considered to be a candidate for the term "work of art."

References

Aigen, Kenneth (1990). Echoes of Silence. *Music Therapy* 9(1), pp. 44-61.

Aigen, Kenneth (1991a). *The Roots of Music Therapy: Towards an Indigenous Research Paradigm.* Unpublished dissertation for the Doctor of Arts. New York: New York University.

Aigen, Kenneth (1991b). Creative Fantasy, Music and Lyric Improvisation with a Gifted, Acting-Out Boy. In Kenneth E. Bruscia (ed.), *Case Studies in Music Therapy.* Phoenixville, PA: Barcelona Publishers.

Aldrich, Virgil C. (1963). *Philosophy of Art.* Englewood Cliffs, NJ: Prentice-Hall.

Aldridge, David (1989). A Phenomenological Comparison of the Organization of Music and the Self. *The Arts in Psychotherapy* 16, p. 917.

Dewey, John (1934). *Art as Experience.* New York: Wideview/Perigee.

Dewey, John (1958). *Experience and Nature.* New York: Dover.

Forinash, Michele, and David Gonzales (1989). A Phenomenological Perspective of Music Therapy. *Music Therapy* 8(1), pp. 35-46.

Kenny, Carolyn (1982). *The Mythic Artery: The Magic of Music Therapy.* Atascadero, CA: Ridgeview.

Kenny, Carolyn (1987). *The Field of Play: A Theoretical Study of Music Therapy Process.* Dissertation, The Fielding Institute.

Kenny, Carolyn (1989). *The Field of Play: A Guide of the Theory and Practice of Music Therapy.* Atascadero, CA: Ridgeview.

Langer, Susanne (1948). *Philosophy in a New Key.* New York: Mentor.

Langer, Susanne (1953). *Feeling and Form.* New York: Scribner.

Nordoff, Paul, and Clive Robbins (1971). *Therapy in Music for Handicapped Children.* London: Gollancz.

Nordoff, Paul, and Clive Robbins (1977). *Creative Music Therapy.* New York: John Day.

Nordoff, Paul, and Clive Robbins (unpublished manuscript). Musical Response Rating Scale.

Robbins, Carol, and Clive Robbins (1991). Self Communications in Creative Music Therapy. In Kenneth E. Bruscia (ed.), *Case Studies in Music Therapy,* pp. 55-71. Phoenixville, PA: Barcelona Publishers.

Salas, Jo (1990). Aesthetic Experience in Music Therapy. *Music Therapy* 9(1), pp. 1-15.

Sibley, Frank (1959). Aesthetic Concepts. *Philosophical Review* 67, pp. 421-450.

22

My Funeral Music

Jeremy J. Shapiro

Prelude to Jeremy Shapiro

In 1983 I began my doctoral studies at The Fielding Institute. My first mentor was Jeremy Shapiro. He was excited about a text he was composing, entitled *Zen Socialism*. He was also fascinated by Mozart and learning about computers. I still have the first letter Jeremy wrote to me from New York, suggesting certain readings which might be pertinent to my studies at Fielding.

This first letter was an indication of the astonishing range of his interests. For me Jeremy was an exemplary model of a contemporary Renaissance person. I remember thinking that Jeremy must be the kind of person Noam Chomsky had in mind when he said that the task of the intellectual is to translate the world of ideas into the contemporary social context for the benefit of all. Jeremy seemed to me to represent the essence of the socially responsible intellectual, yet he grounded his ideas in the heart and thus ultimately represented "the intelligence of the heart."

In the last ten years Jeremy has been a beacon of light to me. He is not afraid of depth and passion. His grasp of language and thought is phenomenal. He is simultaneously a seeker and a seer. And he is a man of the heart.

Of himself Jeremy says: "I am a critical theorist and have studied with Theodor W. Adorno. Currently I am writing a book entitled *Too Short A Life: An Introduction to Listening to Classical Music*. I am deeply concerned with the one-dimensionalization and trivialization of experience endangered by our society, which endangers the capacity to experience individuality and complexity. I deeply believe that listening to music can help restore this capacity. I teach philosophy, sociology, and information systems at The Fielding Institute in Santa Barbara, California, where I am on the Human and Organization Development faculty as well as director of academic networking and computing."

For a long time I have had strong, definite wishes about the music I would like to have played at my funeral. I think it is because, not believing in life after death, personal immortality, or reincarnation, I conceive of transcending mortality primarily through participation in spirit as it is manifested in works of art. I imagine that transcendence as attaining the universal dimension of experience of others outside of me, before me, and after me who similarly attain that dimension. To me attaining universality through art, philosophical and personal self-reflection, and moral action is the only way I can conceive of achieving an analog of immortality that does not depend on arbitrary acts of wishful thinking or what is called faith.

Periodically, especially at times when I feel desolate, isolated, misunderstood, or hopeless, I have felt something that I think of as "wanting to be encompassed": wanting to feel comprehended, cared for, and shared with in a solid, unshakable way, to feel linked to others by deep, intimate, and unquestionable bonds. Perhaps it is similar to what people want when they turn to God or feel God turning to them—or what people experience when they feel comfortably and happily ensconced in a nuclear family.

When I am feeling this desire, in the face of a kind of transcendental isolation, feeling locked into my finitude, in which it seems that no one can fully share my experience, I sometimes think about people who, sometime in the future, whether in a hundred years or a thousand, will be listening to some of my favorite pieces of music. I imagine their inner selves taking on the same shape that mine does when hearing this music, having perhaps very similar, and in some ways identical, aesthetic and spiritual experiences. And I think of some of them occasionally realizing that, at some time in the past, there was probably some other person, such as I, who listened to these same pieces and shared these experiences with them. With that thought, I imagine myself encompassed, understood, and relieved of the misery of isolation.

One way in which this transcendence of finitude is more satisfactory to me than the way I, at least, imagine religious transcendence, is in its concreteness and corporeality. That is, because music is individual and concrete, and inherently oriented to the physical existence of real human beings, the universality that I experience myself as attaining in listening to music and sharing it with other human beings, even nonexistent ones, is a concrete, living universality, not one that denies or overcomes concreteness, morality, and finitude. That is why for me music is the resurrection of the body and not just of the spirit. Because of the way in which music takes over one's body and in which one's embodied self takes on the shape of a piece of music, listening to music with someone else is a shared bodily experience—not sexual, but like sex in the communion of intimate and interior bodily experience.

Otto Rank wrote that because death is a consequence of life, a neurotic is a person who has an exaggerated fear of death and who believes that by avoiding life he can avoid death. Life and love and sexuality and music all have this in common, that they require abandonment. Only through abandoning one's self to them completely can one fully experience the ecstasy that they contain, and yet this abandonment leads precisely to death at the same time as it leads to the transcendence of the limits of mundane existence. That is why accepting the life of the spirit and accepting death are two sides of the same coin.

I decided to include here not only my list of funeral music but also my feelings about and reasons for including the pieces that I have chosen. Even though these are personal (and I certainly do not have a recommended list for other people's funerals), I thought that others might be interested in seeing the way in which music is meaningful to another person, since that is something not generally written about, and that this might indirectly contribute to another's relation to music.

My choices of funeral music are shaped in part by my beliefs about death. I cannot help but find death irrational and irredeemable, for three reasons. First, it is inconsistent with the transcendence of time inherent in human consciousness—so that one can argue that consciousness "is meant to be immortal"—and yet ineluctable given present biological and social circumstances. Second, it is inconsistent with the fundamental human drive for the "eternity of joy," which enables us to envision and yearn for personal immortality. Third, what seems most horrible about death is not what to the realist is just the disappearance within the universe of a particular existing being, but rather what to the idealist is the disappearance of the entire universe that has laboriously come to exist as refracted through the individual's consciousness. Thus, the death of an individual is at the same time the obliteration of the entire universe that exists as centered in and individuated through that individual and all of whose reality is saturated with its meaning for that individual. Finally, under a repressive social order in which much of our lives is spent in unnecessary suffering, obsolete forms of the struggle for existence, and coping with social irrationality, all of us die before our time, because so much of our time has been wasted, had not been available to us to realize our genuine potentialities.

I agree with Hegel that death is humanity's "original sickness," and I think it should be treated as a sickness—but one whose cure is not in sight. My personal belief is that facing death authentically involves accepting both the irrationality and undesirability of death on the one hand and its overwhelming irresistibility on the other. I find myself impatient with the denial of either side of this antithesis. And, in my view, this antithesis must be understood not merely as a timeless existential contradiction but one which takes place under conditions of societal repression that give it a particularly tragic and bitter quality.

It was hard to select the pieces to be played at my funeral. Mainly because not infrequently, when I am listening to a piece of particularly beautiful music, I hear its beauty in a way that makes me think, "I have to have that piece played at my funeral." It is a particular way of hearing or grasping the music. It is not as though the thought of having the music played at my funeral were a subjective response of mine to the objective beauty of the music. It is rather as though certain pieces of music contain within them their appropriateness to a funeral.

Introit: Bach, *Nun danket alle Gott* ("Now all thank God"), Leipzig Organ Chorale Prelude

Copland, *Appalacian Spring* (original version), Section I, ("Very Slowly")

Gesualdo, "Aestimatus Sum" ("I am reckoned") (from *Responsorio*)

Mahler, "Wo die schonen Trompeten blasen" ("Where the beautiful trumpets sound") (from *Des Knaben Wunderhorn*)

Mahler, "O Roeschen rot" ("Oh little red rose") (from 2d symphony)

Mahler, "O Mensch" ("Oh Man/Woman") (from 3d symphony)

Schubert, "Im Abendrot" ("At Sunset")

Monteverdi, "Pur ti miro," ("To gaze at you," from *The Coronation of Poppaea*)

Shapiro, "Amen" (from *Mini-Cantata*)

Mozart, "Der Welcher wandert diese Strassen voll Beschwerden" ("Whoever wanders these roads full of difficulties") (from *The Magic Flute*)

Ravel, Piano Trio, First movement

Liner Notes

I originally decided to annotate my selections for personal funeral music because I thought such a list would seem meaningless to people without some account of the reasons for my choices. After writing some of these annotations, it occurred to me that they, in turn, might seem vaporous without the music itself, so I decided to create an audio tape cassette containing all of the pieces annotated here, including the song texts in the original and in translation. (The cassettes of the complete Funeral Music for Jeremy Shapiro can be obtained by sending $10 for postage and handling to Funeral Music, Jeremy J. Shapiro, The Fielding Institute, 2112 Santa Barbara Street, Santa Barbara, CA 93105, U.S.A.)

After then going on with the annotation process, I realized that I was unintentionally creating the liner or program notes for this tape—in fact, the kind of notes that I would often have preferred to read over many of the useless ones I had encountered. I started to imagine, as part of an ideal of "hermeneutical democracy," that everyone would write her own program notes personally interpreting pieces of music, which would accumulate somewhere, perhaps in a large database file, that anyone interested in a piece of music could access to help him in the crystallization of his experience with that piece. So I offer my comments not as definitive interpretations, but as expressions of the subjective meaning of these works to me with regard to my death.

Introit: Bach, "Nun danket alle Gott" ("Now all thank God"),
Leipzig Organ Chorale Prelude

When I attune myself to my underlying feeling, the one that is at the bottom of my stomach beneath everything else that ever occurs in me, what I feel is gratitude—a simultaneously joyfully energetic and peacefully satisfied gratitude. When I visualize my underlying image of myself, I see a radiant center of energy streaming joyful energy out into the universe, like images I have seen of Jesus Pancrator or saints who are beaming spiritual and physical energy outward or creating the universe through the positive force of their being. Bach's Chorale Prelude "Nun danket alle Gott" captures these feelings precisely. Almost every time I hear it, I feel them in myself and in the music simultaneously, as though it were simply a manifestation of my inner state, but one that had the power to regenerate itself in me. Also, the deep physical vibrations of the organ emphasize this state as a concrete, material, embodied one. So I would like it to set the stage for my funeral both because it represents me and because I hoped it might generate some of this feeling in those who attend.

I often have this feeling of gratitude after having sex. It feels like a fountain that is going off in my stomach and sending waves of warmth throughout my body. It is always accompanied by a feeling of gratitude. Sometimes when I am in that post-coital state, I feel that I must have felt a form of this feeling as an infant. And it feels like the basic, underlying feeling that I have been alive. Also, when I am in love, I feel this feeling most of the time, both in general and, especially, toward the person with whom I am in love. I feel that there is no way that I could fully express the gratitude I feel both for the other person's being alive and for their loving me.

Copland, *Appalacian Spring*, Section I ("Very Slowly")

The opening section of *Appalacian Spring* begins with slow, drawn-out, suspended notes, chords, and fragments of simple melodies that evoke in me feelings of tenderness, infinite sadness, desolation, and material and earthly sorrow. A thick melancholy hovers over the land, even though the music suggests a sunrise. The sadness is that of people, but a sadness inherent in a landscape.

It is the loneliness of being an American. No one from other cultures knows how lonely Americans feel. The isolation and alienation felt by modern Europeans in their cities and expressed in their art of the avant garde is nothing compared to the loneliness that dwells in America, even in the midst of family closeness, celebrations, and camaraderie. It is what is symbolized by the Wild West, plains, canyons, mountains, and deserts. All of these are external representations of that essential American loneliness.

As someone who has lived in both Europe and America, I am particularly sensitive to this American loneliness. One of the consequences for me of having lived as a child in France is that forever after I was an outsider everywhere: as a European in America; as an American in Europe; and as a Jew in a fundamentally Christian culture. I can identify easily with Mahler's statement that he was thrice outcast: as a Czech among Austrians, as an Austrian among Germans, and as a Jew among the peoples of the world.

The forms of loneliness are culturally and historically and perhaps even geographically specific. The loneliness of a Jew is the loneliness of never fitting within what is taken for granted. The loneliness of a European, for at least a modern European, is that of reconciling contradictions, the loneliness of irony; of living out a particular blend of enlightenment and tradition, industrialism and pre-industrialism, or urban and agricultural existence, of bourgeois and anti-bourgeois values. The loneliness of Americans is entirely different. It is the loneliness of people who do not know that they are lonely but bear it constantly upon their faces. It is the loneliness of people lost in space, projected out of history, condemned to naivete, forced to combine smiles and panic, white curtains and the smell of alcoholism. I am very much an American. Like many of my compatriots, I discovered that even when immersed in European culture, I think and feel as an American. I share in that distinctive American loneliness, that beautiful, poignant, tender loneliness of this nation of children.

Although I did not do it on purpose, it seems appropriate that this musical funeral service begins and ends with compositions by Americans; because I have identified with being a European and being a Jew, America was the horizon of this identification. Just as it is characteristic that *Appalacian Spring*, that quintessential American music, was composed by a Jew who studied in Europe, as though only those who have one foot outside of American loneliness can capture and express it.

This music conveys a sense of the infinite beauty and tenderness of the Earth and existence upon it, of how physical that existence is and, hence, how sad, as in Mahler's Song of the Earth. It sounds like a hovering, dawning first moment of creation, as seen from the perspective of someone who knows it to be only temporary.

Pascal's "silence of those infinite spaces [that] terrifies me" is most true of existence as experienced by looking out over vast American plains and mountains.

Gesualdo, "Aestimatus Sum" from
Tenebrae Responsories for Holy Saturday

I was reckoned among those who go down to the pit;
I am become like a man standing alone,
Free among the dead.
They placed me in the lowest pit,
In darkness and in the shadow of death.
I am become like a man standing alone,
Free among the dead.

"Aestimatus sum," whose text was adapted from Psalm 88, conveys the intensity, morbidity, and mystery of the realm of death as well as the mysterious ecstasy of the moment of piercing transcendence of death. The pit is supposed to be the place of the dead. The idea of being "free among the dead" (inter mortuos liber) that concludes this piece is to me one of the central symbolic themes of my life. I have always felt that I have intimately known the experience of wandering around among bones and corpses in the realm of death, and it has always seemed to me that part of my feeling of ecstasy at being alive is the feeling of having magically escaped the sentence of death that has been pronounced and executed upon my human and physical environment, and that within it I am free, although intimately aware of death. This comes partly from the way in which World War II and Nazism affected my childhood, partly from my experience of the alienated character (Reich's "emotional plague") of normal existence that comes to me from my conception of societal and psychic repression, partly from my psychotherapeutic experience of recovering myself and the richness of internal and external life from a state of banishment and psychic numbness, partly from the way I have experienced art, primarily music, as granting imaginative liberation from distorted and falsified experience. I had a dream several years ago in which I was in a concentration camp where everyone was being tortured, but I was walking around in a bathrobe and no one was bothering me, it was as though I was invisible to the agents of death and torture. I think people who like me do so because they sense that in me, that element of inner freedom from the death in life that our society spreads over so much of experience.

I was fascinated to discover recently, after knowing the Gesualdo piece for years, that the Latin translation of the psalm is already a particularly Christian interpretation of the original, one that emphasizes the overcoming of death. Psalm 88 is actually a plea to God from a person in a state of abject and hopeless misery, and it contains no element of redemption or salvation. In the original Hebrew, the words rendered in Latin as "free among the dead" are actually "forsaken among the dead" and do not have the transcendent implication emphasized in the music, which is part of the Holy Saturday service focused on Christ's passage from Crucifixion to Resurrection. Nevertheless, Gesualdo's music to the words "They placed me in the Pit, in the nether regions, and in the shadow of death" captures horribly the state of being forsaken among the dead, even though it is portrayed as the prelude to liberation rather than, as in the original psalm, part of a state of hopelessness.

Mahler, *Wenn Dein Muetterlein* (from *Kindertotenlieder*)

> When your mommy
> Comes in at the door
> And I turn my head
> To look towards her,
> My gaze does not fall
> First upon her face
> But on the place
> Near the threshold

Where your dear little face
Used to be,
When you, bright with joy,
Would enter, too,
As you used to, my little daughter!

When your mommy
Comes in at the door
In the candlelight
It seems to me as if
You come flitting after her,
As you used to,
Into the room!
Oh you, of your father's cell
The, alas, too soon,
Too soon extinguished light of joy!

This is my favorite of the *Kindertotenlieder*, the songs about the death of children. I think it is because it is not only about the death of a child but addressed to a (no longer living) child and written musically in the style of a nursery rhyme (with its echo, in a minor key, of "Twinkle, Twinkle Little Star"). The combination of the feeling of sad parental tenderness with the survival in memory of the child's naivete and loveliness create a sense of the intimate bonding that is interrupted by death, especially because of the irony that the nursery-rhyme music makes it seem as though the song, whose words are the parents', were being sung by the child, thus producing a sense of the child's simultaneous presence and absence. The result is that, unlike the last of the *Kindertotenlieder*, which begins in an angry protest against the death that ends in resignation to a higher power, this song protests to the end the injustice of death in the soft voice of the child who had not yet experienced either injustice or protest.

In the second strophe of each verse, while the original melody returns in a higher key, it is accompanied by a figure in the flute that conveys a sense of painful tenderness and has the physical feeling of fingers softly caressing a face, as though the father were touching, lovingly and for the last time, his daughter's countenance.

I think, too, that I would like people to remember me, after I die, in the way the singer remembers the child in this song. Mahler, "Wo die schoenen Trompeten blasen" (from des Knaben Wunderhorn)

Who then is out there and who is knocking at the door?
Who can so softly, so softly wake me?

It is your heart's best-beloved,
Get up and let me come in!
Why should I stand here any longer?
I see the dawn come up,
The dawn, two bright stars,
With my sweetheart I would like to be!
With my heart's best beloved!
The girl got up and let him in,
She bids him welcome, too.
Welcome, dear boy of mine!
So long you have been standing!
She gives him also her snow white hand.
From far away sang the nightingale.
The girl then began to cry.
Oh do not cry, you love of mine,
Oh do not cry, you love of mine!
Next year you shall be all my own.
My own you shall be for certain,
Like no-one else on earth!
Oh love on the green earth.
I go to war on the green heath;
The green heath, it is so far!
It is there where the beautiful trumpets are sounding,
there is my house of green turf.

The song "Wo die schonen Trompeten blasen" is a quintessentially Mahlerian song: because of the lush, material tenderness expressed in the love of music; because it sets this love in a concrete material context as well as the finite context of death, hope, promise, and foolish waste; because of the way Mahler's principle of excess expresses the intensity and tenderness of love by having the words "welcome dear boy of mine" begin with a rich, new love theme that outdoes the one used previously for the words "It is your heart's best beloved"; because of the way in which the trumpet calls announce both the grim sentence of death and the seductive promise of ideological death; and because of the way in which the music expresses not only the feelings of the young lovers, but also Mahler's maternal compassion toward them.

The songs set love in the context of death. It shows the charm, naivete, and foolishness of heroic death—of those who would reject the material happiness of romantic love for some "higher," ideal value such as patriotism, national glory, or military honor. In this it resembles

Brecht's poem "Lasst euch nicht verfuehren" ("Don't let yourself be seduced/misled"), with its recurrent injunction not to sacrifice material happiness and the joy of the present, because "Nothing comes afterwards." The love music has the melting tenderness of the first adolescent love, the reminder of all of the promise that is the reality of love but that is never completely fulfilled except, as Herbert Marcuse writes in *Eros and Civilization*, in the remembrance that preserves the happiness without the anxiety over its potential loss.

This piece protests the tremendous social pressure to betray the hope and promise of youthful love by capturing the latter in such a palpable manner (and emphasizing it by framing it with death). I wanted it played at my funeral because I feel that in my life I have similarly refused to abandon or betray a core feeling of optimistic, naive abandonment to the initial, giddy joy of love that has pervaded my feelings of romance all the way back to and forward from my early childhood. I remember having these feelings at least from the time I was seven years old, and I have them still. It is largely because these feelings have remained central to me that I "forgot" to take on the socially expected roles of unromantic family life.

Mahler, Solo Voice Movements from 2d and 3d Symphonies

Part of Mahler's greatness was that his music breaks with music as ideology in the sense of art as a separate realm completely cut off from the world of concrete, material human existence and desire. Instead, Mahler gives voice to the material and utopian longings that in classical music are subliminated and transfigured into a world of separate spiritual values. Music becomes prophecy, even propaganda, to deny the element of illusion, reconciliation with an oppressive world, and hence propaganda contained in the message of classical music and art in general. Beethoven started this, at the height of the classical period, with his 9th Symphony, in which the spoken prophecy of joy and fraternity is presented as overcoming the deficiencies of self-contained, absolute music. Mahler takes it up again, at the culmination of the romantic period.

I have always thought of the solo voice movements of Mahler's 2d and 3d symphonies as counterparts expressing the two halves of what I see as Mahler's world view. One half takes literally, materialistically, the Judeo-Christian promise of redemption and unification with God as release from the miseries of earthly life; the other half takes literally, existentially, the Enlightenment promise of the redemption of the earth, of nature, and of finite, moral existence through the liberation of human nature and its capacity for joy and ecstasy. These are precisely the two halves of my world view also. I could say that these two movements from Mahler's second and third symphonies express the underlying theme of my intellectual and personal world view since I was seventeen years old and which I still hold today.

Mahler, "O Roeschen rot" (from 2d symphony)

> Oh little red rose
> Man lives in greatest need!
> Man lives in greatest woe!
> I would rather be in heaven.
> I came upon a broad road;
> There an angel and wanted to turn me away;
> Oh no, I would not be turned away.
> I am of God and want to return to God!
> Dear God will give me a little light
> To light my way into eternal blissful life!

In the last movement of Mahler's Resurrection Symphony, trumpet fanfares accompany the opening of the graves from which the dead are resurrected. The music suggests the resurrection as both a ghastly and terrifying physical reality, as well as a spiritual journey. In the present movement, which precedes it, a brass choir sounds ceremoniously as the soul pursues its way with simultaneous trepidation and resolution toward unification with God. After giving voice to the soul's complaint about the present misery of humankind, Mahler utters with tenderness the soul's impassioned wish to be in Heaven and its faith and hope that God will help light the way.

There is something childlike in this expression of faith and hope: the feeling of wanting these things to be true takes precedence over the element of knowing them to be true. It is a bit like children who no longer fully believe in Santa Claus, but want him to exist. Mahler captures the religious soul at the point where it is still in touch with its underlying yearnings and before it has taken on the rigidity of religious dogma. He captures the utopian longing that is the radical element in Judaism and Christianity.

I do not believe in God, yet I resonate with many aspects of religious sentiment, especially the desires expressed here for a better world than this one and for mystical union with God. I was named after the prophet Jeremiah and the prophetic yearning for a better world are part of me. It is actually these truths that I personally hold to be self-evident.

Mahler, "O Mensch" (from 3d Symphony)

> O Man, take heed!
> What does the deep midnight say?
> I slept! From deep dreaming I was woken!
> The world is deep,
> And deeper than the day imagined!
> Deep is its grief!
> Pleasure, deeper still than heartache!
> Grief says: Expire!
> But all pleasure craves eternity,
> Craves deep, deep eternity.

To me, one of the most exciting moments in the history of music, even in the history of Western culture, is the succession of mysterious, dark trombone chords that follow upon the opening fanfare of Mahler's Third Symphony. When I hear this music, I feel as though I were an eyewitness to the creation of the world, because to me they and their accompanying drum rolls capture the sense of pulsation, groaning, rumbling, and yawning that I imagine must have occurred at the beginning of the Universe and that which correspond to the sense that I have had of Genesis' description of the universe before God created the world, when everything was unformed and darkness floated above the face of the waters.

Whenever I hear this passage I feel as though the bottom of my stomach were about to fall out, as I experience the awe and mystery of this primal state of being. It feels as though the bottom dropping out of my stomach is attuned to the bottom having dropped out of the universe or not yet having been provided to the universe. To me, this third movement of Mahler's Third Symphony, which begins with a repetition of those chords of pulsating, grumbling, groaning, and yawning, expresses the predicament and ecstasy of being-in-the-world and reverses Western culture's existential definition of suffering, misery, and sorrow as the human fate in civilization.

The Nietzsche quotation that Mahler uses here parallels the one chosen by Marcuse in *Eros and Civilization*, representing the foundations of his projection of the possibility of a civilization without repression. This is the materialistic and humanistic version of the religious utopianism of the Second Symphony. As I understand this thought, at this present historical turning point of consciousness, it becomes possible to recognize that joy is deeper than sorrow and that experiencing this world as suffering and heartache is part of a historical fate that has been imposed on Western civilization—but one that it is possible to escape. However, there is a price to be paid for this escape, and that is accepting finitude and mortality. So the victory of the pleasure principle is bought at the price of abandoning religion's hope for permanence and immortality in the other world. To me, this music expresses beautifully and with dignity this humanistic, existential, tragic view of life. Tragic, however, in the modern sense of accepting finitude rather than of being vanquished by moral laws built into the universe.

One attains ecstasy by freely accepting grief, including the grief at one's own finitude. In my own life, to the extent that I have done this, it has been through choosing or learning to tolerate the catharsis of crying and laughing and emotionally confronting anguish and grief about loss and limitation, ranging from the loss of specific persons through grief at social and historical injustices, like the Holocaust and the war in Vietnam, to grieving at my own morality and the morality of those I care about.

I feel that the hours I have spent crying about these and other things have contributed to an ecstatic relationship to life, to other people, and to myself, and I am grateful to those who have accepted from me the tears I have shed and who have thereby allied themselves with my own joy and ecstasy.

During the period of writing this essay, I experienced one of the most painful and devastating losses of a loved one that I had experienced in my life. It was the closest that I came to having my faith in this world view shaken, and indeed, it was shaken on and off for a period of several months. What healed me was the love of two special friends. But part of what made it possible for me to accept that love and reciprocate it were the tears that I shed in remembering the feeling of bliss and ecstasy that I had had previously, with the idea that, even in its brevity, bliss had in some way outweighed and redeemed all of the suffering I was experiencing—admittedly an idea that was difficult to sustain continuously.

To me, greatness of this third movement of the Third Symphony consists primarily of two things: first, Mahler's linking of the human predicament of joy versus sorrow with the primal rumbling and pulsating of the universe; second, the sudden intensification and melodic rise that occurs when the words "yet all pleasure wants eternity" are sung. Until then, it is as though the voice were like a spirit hovering over a formless void at the beginning of the universe and, when it sings the words, "but all pleasure craves eternity," it is as though that hovering and formlessness crystalized into an ascent of joy and construction of it in their work has contributed to my own belief in its validity.

Schubert, "Im Abendrot"

Oh how beautiful is your world,
Father, when it streams with gold!
When your radiance descends hither,
And paints the dust with glitter,
When the red that gleams in the cloud
Sinks into my quiet window!

Could I complain, could I hesitate?
Be confused about you and me?
No, I want my breast already
To bear your heaven in this very place.
And this heart, before it succumbs,
Still drinks the glow and consumes the light.

This song captures in an unusual way the experience of being in a mystical, bliss trance state.

In the summer of 1965, in Frankfurt, I took a long walk with some new friends in the Westend neighborhood. On our walk we discussed animatedly philosophy, art, politics, and personal experience. We walked and talked until almost dawn. Our conversation and the meeting of minds and selves that occurred was so exciting to me that I was thrown into a state of ecstasy that verged on trance. They left me standing on a square in Frankfurt, under some large trees. It was so late at night that birds had started to chirp and fly around in the trees in preparation for morning. I stared up at the trees in the period before dawn and went into a bliss trance. I stood motionless for at least twenty minutes, staring at the trees, the birds, and the sky and feeling the intense excitement of being alive and having such a rich experience.

I often feel that this state of bliss trance is my most basic state, and I have experienced it many times in my life. I also experience gradations of it, so that it can range from an extreme bliss trance to a state of mild delight at being alive in the world that can come over me as I am walking down a city street.

I have also experienced forms of this state that have been induced by drugs, in particular mescaline, which I took several times in the 1960s and early 1970s. Under the influence of mescaline, I experienced classic states of being overwhelmed by and enamored of simple perceptions of things in the world and inside myself that seemed completely enchanting and deserving of infinite ecstatic wonder.

I once told my friend Hannah that she did not fully know me because she had never seen me in my characteristic state of having bliss while walking by myself in the streets of New York.

I have included this Schubert song in my funeral music because it not only describes this state, but also, to my mind, reproduces it. When I hear this song that describes ecstatic appreciation and ecstatic experience of heaven on earth manifested in simple perception, I start to feel it, regardless of my prior state. A number of Schubert's compositions capture states of bliss. This one does so in a short, pure, and self-conscious form.

I have a photograph of myself at age five months, in which I am staring out into space with an expression that I still identify with, and which I take to be one of mystical, blissful appreciation of the world. Perhaps it is what Freud called "oceanic feeling." When I read descriptions of mystical experience, I usually think, "Oh, I have experienced that for ages."

Monteverdi, "Pur ti miro" (from the Coronation of Poppaea)

> Let me gaze on you, let me enjoy you,
> Let me embrace you, let me enfold you.
> No more strife, no more death,
> Oh my life, Oh my treasure.
> I am yours, you are mine, my hope,
> Tell me so and tell me again.
> You are my idol, my joy,
> My heart, my life.
> Let me gaze on you, let me enjoy you,
> Let me embrace you, let me enfold you.
> No more strife, no more death,
> Oh my life, Oh my treasure.

A close friend of mine once said to her husband, while I was sitting in their kitchen, "Isn't it too bad that people can't get paid for what they're really good at? The main thing Jeremy is good at is falling in love. Isn't it a pity that he can't make a living from that?" Sexual, romantic ecstasy has always seemed to me to be the main point of life and my life seems meaningful and rich and happy when I am having it and tends to seem meaningless when it is absent from my life. I know that I have felt this way at least since I was six years old. Often it is hard for me to remember that there are all of these other things that many people want to be doing with their lives. Actually, there are other things that I want to do with my life too, but they seem more like side-lines than like primary activities. I can imagine that there must be many people who feel the way I do. I think that I sometimes express it in more extreme ways or give myself more license to pursue it as a primary activity.

An old girlfriend once reminded me of something that I did many years ago. After we had made love, I was so manic and happy that I ran into the kitchen, took a jar of cinnamon, and started sprinkling cinnamon all over myself out of the sheer feeling of ecstasy and overflowing energy. Often in the context of love and sex, I experience a feeling of pouring out, occurring in my stomach, as though there were a fountain there that kept bubbling and overflowing. That feeling is close to the core of what sexual, romantic ecstasy is like for me. I also experience a melting feeling in my chest that sometimes is so strong that I feel that I can barely tolerate it, and that too, for me is part of romantic ecstasy.

Monteverdi's song "Pur ti miro," which concludes the opera of *The Coronation of Poppaea*, is for me the most perfect musical expression of sexual, romantic love and ecstasy. To my mind, Monteverdi's music surpasses all later romantic music, because he captures an element of sensuality and concreteness and physicalness that is essential to romantic experience, but that I find lacking in most later romantic music, for example, that of Mozart, Wagner, or Strauss. I find the love and passion music from this opera to be the only healthy erotic music that I know. Compared with it, eighteenth- and nineteenth-century erotic music sounds bowdlerized and repressed.

When I first saw *The Coronation of Poppaea*, I was literally shocked, because in it sexual passion and naked acquisitiveness triumphed over morality and reason. I believe that initial shock was an appropriate reaction to such uninhibited music. Several years ago, the opera was shown on television and an elderly aunt of my mother called her up and told her that she could not watch it because the opera was getting her too aroused. This, too, seemed an appropriate reaction.

Shapiro, "Amen" (from Mini-Cantata)

Amen!

This short student piece of mine, the conclusion of a musical setting of some verses of the Book of Revelation, is the last thing I included in my list of funeral music. I hesitated to include it, because I did not have the same feeling of conviction about its relation to my funeral as I did with the other pieces. What decided me in favor of it was partly just the idea of having something that I wrote, and that (I admit) I find piercingly beautiful, played at my funeral, as though I had created in the world something of that special reality called music that enhanced my right to die.

More important, however, is an experience that it has afforded me that exemplifies something fundamental about music in general. At times, when I listen to music by the "masters," I hear passages that sound so uncannily beautiful to me that my reaction always includes shaking my head in amazement and thinking, "How did he do it? How did he do it?" These passages, which often combine intense, concentrated beauty with intellectual complexity, seem to defy what I can comprehend as the product of a finite human mind, of deliberate human skill. They come from the point where the personal and more-than-personal merge.

One of my reasons for studying music theory and harmony was in order to better understand things about music that seemed mysterious to me. I believed that by knowing about the harmonic and contrapuntal and formal structures of music, I would be able to penetrate into both musical works and the process of creating them in a way that would make my mind more congruent with music and its composition. I think that I imagined, after doing this, some disturbingly mysterious aspect of music which I associated with my own ignorance would disappear. Especially I thought that things could be learned and taught, things that I believed to be manifestations of skill would seem intuitively comprehensible to me in a way that they previously had not been. At some level I subscribed to that particular hermeneutic view that one could understand subjective meaning by being able to reproduce in one's own mind the process of its creation.

When I took a college-level harmony course, I discovered that I could compose. And I composed several pieces that are quite beautiful. But when I listen to them, I do not hear them with that inner understanding I had fantasized. Instead, when I hear a particularly beautiful part, the words that come to my mind, unbidden, are "How did he do it? How did he do it?"

Mozart, "Der Welcher wandert diese
Strassen voll Beschwerden" (from *The Magic Flute*)

He who wanders these streets full of trouble
becomes pure through water, fire, air, and earth.
If he can overcome the fear of death
Then he will soar from the earth into the heavens.

Illuminated, he will then be in condition
To devote himself wholly to the mysteries of Isis.

I sometimes think of the greatest composers as adventurers who have had the courage to expose themselves to humanly, almost intolerable limit conditions of terror, anxiety, disintegration, misery, the abyss, annihilating transcendence, cosmic rupture, primal unity, meaninglessness, and experiential saturation and returned from these states to make them at least partially accessible to other human beings. I believe that Mozart was one of those who descended most deeply into these realms. And this passage of *The Magic Flute* grasps the ungraspable limit condition of passing into and transcending death.

Anyone who has awakened screaming from a nightmare or covered their eyes in a horror movie knows that there are things too terrifying to contemplate or experience fully. Probably most of us live our lives held in tighter rein than we realize by terrors too horrible to be aware of. The terrors we have experienced are not the worst of what we have to fear. It is possible to imagine an ideal limiting case of enlightened and spiritually evolved humanity, in which everyone would face these terrors and somehow integrate them into consciousness and because of having so integrated them leading a wiser, more aware, more humble, and more ethical life. And it is also possible to imagine a limiting case of a "successfully psychoanalyzed" humanity for all of whom Freud's dictum would have come true, that is, of having their hysterical misery transformed into ordinary everyday unhappiness. Personally, I consider the realization of these limiting cases to be extremely unlikely, and, because of this, I think that we would all be advised to be humble in awareness of the narrow straits within which we walk and live. And, within them, it is to the arts, particularly music, that we can look to get a glimpse of those things that are too terrifying for us to experience fully.

Ravel, Piano Trio, First movement

I imagine that most people are like me in wishing that, when they died, people would know what it was like for them to have been alive. Of course, most people, like me, would like people to know what it is like for them to be alive while they are living, which is already a difficult proposition. And I do not know why, in fact, it should be any easier for people to know what it was like for you to be alive right after you died. In fact, it is more unlikely, unless you leave behind some great secret memoir or journal that suddenly reveals what things were really like for you. But it does seem, in some way that makes intuitive sense, that when you die, at least then, at least for a few minutes, somebody should know what it was like for you to be alive in this unique, non-reproducible, little stretch of time which you inhabited, created, and underwent in the universe. Even though a number of the pieces that are chosen for my funeral express or capture some of the deep meanings to me of existence, none of them captures what it was actually like because of the tendency toward idealization and sublimation in classical premodernist art and music.

I suppose that there is a certain sense in which Bach's life was like his music, just as I imagine that there is a certain sense in which the life of some ancient Egyptians was in some way like the paintings in their tombs. But because music and art are often not intended to express the texture of everyday lived experience, I think that often there is little relationship between music and the nature of everyday lived experience. Certainly when I myself composed some pieces of music in a romantic style, I did not experience that the music captured, in any immediate way, what my life was like either in general or at the moment I was composing those pieces. In fact, I was quite aware, while composing them, of going into an "altered state" in which my attention was completely absorbed in an ideal, imaginary, aesthetic state shaped by the musical ideas themselves, that had nothing observable to do with what it was like for me, at that point in my life, to be sitting late at night, in the basement of an empty university office building, excitedly exploring the process of composition.

I say all this because there is some music which for me captures to a significant degree what being alive and being in the world was really like for me, and Ravel's Piano Trio, especially its first movement, is perhaps the main one. Many years ago I noticed that, a lot of the time, I experience an ongoing undertone of buzzing or scintillating accompanying my consciousness of being in the world. It is like a kind of Brownian movement of consciousness accompanied by a slight crawling sensation in my stomach, as though my stomach were at all times receiving a kind of electric current from being alive and exposed to the world. Sometimes this sensation is intensified and when it is, it feels like ecstasy. It is a two-fold ecstasy. Partly it is just an internal sensation; partly it is an experience of direct response to the world and its existence and aliveness. I experience that this is not just one single sensation or quality of experience. It takes on various forms in different contexts. There is for me an ecstasy of walking in the street and feeling the excitement of being not only in the world in general, but in an urban world in particular, of being exposed to the intensity, novelty, and unpredictability of urban events.

There is another kind of ecstasy for me, one that is almost unbearable, that I have experienced in taking long walks through the French countryside and feeling the earth come up at me under my steps as though each step were occurring directly on the crust of this earth and as if the earth were coming back at me with every step, sort of like playing pattycake, pattycake with the earth. And there is another ecstasy of being inside in the rain, looking out into the gray day and experiencing how everything in the room—the furniture, curtains, the lamps, the books on the table and in shelves—arrange themselves specially as comforts for living that rainy day, as though the house were suddenly a doll's house with all the furniture as doll's furniture. And there is something so peculiar about the particular combination of sadness and elation that accompanies that rainy day, as though it were impossible for these two emotions to co-exist and yet they belong together—a kind of tender, warm sadness, as though the sadness was there just as an excuse to be comforted, as though that rainy day caused consciousness to suddenly be aware of its own infinity, of its own transcendence of everything natural, and yet completely at home in the world in that moment of lonely transcendence.

Whenever I hear the first movement of Ravel's Piano Trio, I feel all those things. And because that feeling is so much like what it was for me to be alive, to be in the world with a physical body and have that being in the world under one's skin and in the pit of one's stomach, I hear this music as music to be played at my funeral, for capturing what it was like for me to be alive, concretely alive in this world at this one point in time, with this body and this culture and this history.

Reference

Marcuse, H. (1955). *Eros and Civilization: A Philosophical Inquiry into Freud.* Boston: Beacon Press.

23

The Listener: Dreaming the Soundscape with Howard Broomfield

Robin Ridington and Jillian Ridington

Prelude to Robin and Jillian Ridington

Robin and Jillian are perhaps the best example of the relationship between love and work contained in this collection. For them it seems that there is no difference between the two. For two decades, they have shared a work, sometimes difficult and demanding, which hurled them into unknown worlds. They learned to endure and to love the people they came to study, and to represent the people of these worlds with integrity and honor.

My first connection with Robin and Jillian came when I began my interdisciplinary studies at the University of British Columbia in 1976. Robin was one of my professors in the Department of Anthropology. He was also a poet and a musician.

Robin taught his students about what he had learned from the Indian people of the North, the Beaver or Dunne-za. I came to understand that Robin had put the sense of community he had learned form the Dunne-za to practice when, after the birth of my son, Josh, he agreed to hold our graduate seminar meetings in my home, so that I could be near my nursing child. This did not fit my stereotyped image of a Harvard University Ph.D. and professor at a provincial university in Canada that took its institutional culture and traditions very seriously. These meetings in front of the fire will remain an inspiring example of community and learning and connection. Several students in my group were attracted to the lifestyle of the Senoi, the dream people. Robin was in the process of struggling to integrate his poet/musician self with his social science training. He knew that his own integration of his anthropological training with his artistic sensibility would determine how faithfully he could communicate his experience with the Dunne-za. The harvest of his deep struggle is documented in his beautiful work, *Trail to Heaven*, the story of his life with the Dunne-za.

We also shared a friendship with Howard Broomfield, the subject of Robin and Jillian's contribution to this volume. When I was working with the

Children's Spontaneous Music Workshops, R. Murray Schaefer was at the height of his interest in the soundscape, and through Murray, we met Howard, one of the team for the soundscape. Many years after the soundscape project, Howard interviewed me about music therapy on Vancouver's co-operative radio's "Pigeon Park Review," on which he was working with Robin and Jillian. That interview was a great high because of Howard's listening and sense of sound. It was a vocal improvisation, which I remember shifted my mode of consciousness into describing and exploring new realms of music therapy—all inspired by Howard. The funny thing was that, because of some technical difficulty, the show did not get recorded. Howard and I laughed. We knew that the best things never get on tape, after all. They are immediate.

Because of our connection with Howard, Robin and Jillian and I share the tragedy of his death. Although Howard was not a Native American man, in the formal sense, he was Native in some true sense, because of his capacity to listen. In truth, he was the Soundman.

In the Indian way, it is often said that we can be closer to people once they have died. Robin and Jillian's essay here is an example of how they continue to learn and grow from their relationship with Howard, to ponder and appreciate their experience with him. His friendship enriches their lives, even today.

Jillian is a writer/researcher/ethnographer living on Retreat Island near Galiano Island, British Columbia, where she is learning the joys of living in a small community. She has worked with women victims of abuse and written extensively on women's issues. Since 1978, she has learned from the Dunne-za. With Robin, she co-authored *People of the Trail* and *People of the Longhouse*, and she is now working on a children's book about the history of First Nations people and newcomers to Canada. As a director of the Galiano Conservancy Association, Jillian is working to preserve Galiano's fragile ecology and rural way of life from the pressures of development. Both she and Robin have come to value their community greatly, and are committed to speaking out in support of communities, including their own, that are threatened by impersonal outside forces.

Robin is professor of anthropology and the University of British Columbia and lives on Retreat Island with Jillian. He has studied with elders of the Dunne-za. His books include *Trail to Heaven: Knowledge and Narrative in a Northern Native Community*, and *Little Bit Know Something: Stories in a Language of Anthropology*. He also writes about the Omaha Tribe of Nebraska. With Jillian, he learned to listen from Howard Broomfield.

Introduction

English is one of the languages that habitually nominalizes experiences into things. We speak of "sound" when what we really mean is listening to the vibrations of a physical medium. Sounds are what we hear of these vibrations. They are the interpretations and meanings we give to the limited range of frequencies that we experience. Sounds are meaningful because we know how to contextualize them. Listening is an act of creative intelligence. We receive sound from "out there" and take it into the deepest reaches of our being. In so doing we make it our own. We hear the frequencies we are physically equipped to receive, but we listen through cultural and spiritual and personal equipment that is even more finely tuned.

Sounds express movement within the physical world. Sound waves are physical phenomena. They have shape, frequency, harmonic overtone, speed of propagation, amplitude. Sound is physical, but it does not belong exclusively to the world of physics any more than do written words because they are traditionally propagated through a physical medium of ink and paper. To say, "I hear a sound" could also be expressed as, "There is listening within me." Sound is not just "out there." It is also within us as we bring it into being. It is at once objective and experiential. Sound is alive as we are alive. It is alive as music is alive. It is the substance of which music is the singing.

This essay is about sound, but it is also about a dear friend of ours, Howard Broomfield, who died in 1986. Howard was one of those special people for whom language never quite achieved dominion over experience. Sound was always reflexive for Howard. It was always an act of listening. His relationship to the world of sound, the world he learned from R. Murray Schafer to call the soundscape, maintained the primacy of listening that most of us retrieve from the child-world only in dreams. Howard was a talented ethnographer and audio documentarian. He "took sounds" from wherever he found himself. He recorded cultural soundscapes with the same intelligence and respect that he gave to those of the natural environment. People and frogs spoke to him with equal facility. Even radio and television called with the cries of living creatures to his inquiring ear. He recognized a spirit of life within every acoustic event to which he was witness. To the Beaver Indians, or Dunne-za, who introduced Howard to the sounds of their northern life, Howard was the man who "took sound"—Soundman. But always and above all, Howard was a listener. Between 1984 and 1986 he co-hosted a show with Don Druick on Vancouver's Co-operative radio, CFRO. It was called simply, *The Listener*.

A year after Howard died, we collaborated with Howard's wife, Morgan Ashbridge, to present a collection of his audio work in a series called *Soundcarvings* at the Vancouver Community Arts Council Gallery. We called the presentation simply, *Soundman*. Our introduction is presented below:

Howard—"The Listener"

Howard Broomfield was a *Soundman,* a listener, and a composer. He experienced the world as music. His tapework compositions were his way of sharing that gift with others. Howard heard conversations as parts in a composition above and beyond their literal meanings as texts. He listened to the timbre of sounds as keynotes for his compositions. He listened to the rhythms that exist beyond meter. He listened for inner meanings that lie between the lines. He listened for delicate harmonics and resonances that reveal personality and define situation. He used audio actualities as other composers use scored instrumentation.

Howard's genius was not simply his mastery of an "experimental" compositional medium. Although he was influenced by Glen Gould's radio compositions and by his work with R. Murray Schafer on the World Soundscape Project, Howard's great gift was his intuitively creative way of listening. "Clean your ears," he would say to us. He was not telling us to get rid of waxy buildup, but urging us to sharpen our awareness, to clean out the sludge that most of us carry as insulation against the noise of the world—insulation that prevents us from distinguishing such noise from the beauty of the sounds it may be concealing. His compositions reflect the many voices he heard in the world around him. They have a sound that is distinctively his own. Howard was always in the world he recorded. He recorded people and animals, wind and waters, junk collections and drunks. Howard was able to have a *personal* connection with all of them. His work was a kind of reflexive ethnography of the soundscape.

Howard's world is distinctive, yet familiar. His works turn us all into listeners. They bring out a musical dimension that we all experience, but cannot always select out from the din of events we are conditioned to believe are real. Howard lived in the world of a different reality, a musical reality. He lived in the world of a listener. His works generously share that sound with us all.

Howard gave his recordings names to indicate that each one was a story. Each one documented an encounter. For instance, Howard called a recording he and Robin made of rain falling on their camp at the Doig River reserve "Sammy Says" because Sammy Acko had told us how nice it is to listen to rain on the roof of a tent. At Howard's suggestion, our camp became "Monias City" complete with a sign that said, "Population five." Monias is the Cree word that the Dunne-za have borrowed to refer to white people. Following in Howard's tradition, we named each piece for its keynote image or sound signature.

Soundman

Field Recordings, Performances, and Compositions by Howard Broomfield.
Presented in the Vancouver Community Arts Council series—
Soundcarvings—June 14, 1987
by Morgan Ashbridge, Jillian Ridington, Robin Ridington

Order of Pieces

1. Ambience Overture
    dawn chorus from Wikanninish (20:00)
    slow cross fade between recordings
    frog chorus and train whistles from Ft. Langley (11:00)
2. Listener Theme∏Howard Broomfield and Don Druick (4:00)
3. Introduction to "A Radio Program about Radio" presented on CBC *Ideas* series, "Soundscapes of Canada" (2:20)
4. Howard's Greatest Hits—A pastiche of sounds and songs recorded in northeastern B.C. by Howard Broomfield (11:00)
    "Sammy Says"—rain symphony at Doig River Reserve
    Debbie, Shirley, Dolly, Colleen, Iain, Howard—"Who Stole the Cookie from the Cookie Jar"
    Debbie Apsassin singing—"Where Could I Go but to the Lord?"
    "Why Baby Why"—tape collage by Hank Snow, Tommy Attachie, and Sally Tokola
    Lodgepole String Band—"Mansion on the Hill"
    "Tommy Sings the Blues"—Tommy Attachie, Robert Dominic
5. Field Broomfield: A tape collage of excerpts from the "fieldnotes" tapes, recorded by and with Howard in northeastern B.C. (16:00)
6. Old Time Religion—Howard Broomfield and Robin Ridington
    talking field notes, narrated story, actualities (5:45)
    final passage (1:20)—(total time 7:05)
7. Musique du Nord (6:20)
    timbre of timber—Howard and Robin playing a "found xylophone" of freshly cut tamarack fenceposts with Tommy Attachie on power saw
    metal on metal—Howard, Robin, Amber, and kids from Prophet River Reserve playing abandoned gas station at mile 233, Alaska Highway
8. Post-Literate Music (11:35)
    Improv: Al Neil, Howard Broomfield
    Blue Mule Band (Roy Kiyooka, Trudi Rosenfield, Howard Broomfield)

Improv solo at the Ontario College of Art: Howard Broomfield
with Don Druick, Diana Kemble, October 10, 1981
The Great Spandini—Howard Broomfield, Al Neil, Spandini

Short Break

Tapework Compositions—selected excerpts from:
9.   A Birth Narrative (with Pat Tait and Ariel)—1983 (4:28)
10. Suffering Me Slowly (With Jillian Ridington, for CBC: The Hornby
     Collection)—1981 (5:28)
11. In Doig People's Ears—1984 (11:00)
12. Radio on Radio—CBC *Ideas* (18:00)
13. Blessing for a Long Time to Come
     Omaha Pow-wow music—1985 (6:00)

Listening To Soundman—January, 1992

In order to talk about Howard's work, we decided to renew our
contact with it by listening. Four and a half years have passed since we
put the *Soundman* program together from work Howard left behind.
The distance is such that we are now able to approach it as listeners
ourselves. The sounds that he recorded and we edited remain the same,
but their meaning has changed as we have changed. We are listening to
them now in the quiet of our home on Galiano Island. Howard was
thirty-nine years old when he died. We are now in our fifties. Howard's
place in our lives has now changed with the passage of time. He has
become more legendary. He is still thirty-nine. Some of the sounds
Howard recorded have also become legendary as the people and places
and events they documented have changed. The baby born as Howard's
tape recorder caught her first breath is in grade four, and the children he
played games with are getting their driver's licenses or starting families.
Some of the adults he "took tape" from have become elders, while others have joined Howard on the trail to heaven. But like photographs
which "take pictures" and preserve in an instant as an unchanging
image, so Howard's tapes "take sound" and crystallize it as constant
through time.

Recorded sounds as physical vibrations remain constant as long as
the medium on which they are stored does not deteriorate, but their
meaning as listening experiences changes each time they are played.
Like a photograph of the written word, audio documents may be understood as texts whose meaning changes with each new context in which
they are played. We originally presented *Soundman* less than a year
after Howard's tragic departure. It was a tribute to his memory and a

means of releasing his spirit. It was our way of saying goodbye. Now that five years have passed since he left us, the anguish is further from the surface of our waking consciences. Still, the gifts of awareness he gave us and the memories of the work we shared retain the clarity of etched images. Our voices are part of the document that is *Soundman*. Now we have come to it as listeners. What follows is a new reading of Howard's texts.

The acoustic space that *Soundman* created in the Community Arts Council Gallery on Vancouver's Robson Street began even before the audience had entered the building. It began with the sound of wind-driven waves at Wikanninish beach on Vancouver Island, one of Howard's last recordings of a natural soundscape. People came into the gallery and settled down gently. Many of them were Howard's friends. Many had worked with him and performed with him at other times and places. Their voices blended with the murmur of water breaking and reforming at the edge of a continent. Our playing of Howard's recording created another soundscape, an acoustic ambience into which the people settled their minds and spirits. It was frogs that brought them from that dreamspace to attention. They were, of course, Howard's frogs, the last of many he recorded over the years. Frogs have a curious way of starting and stopping their chorus. They usually stop when a human enters their soundspace and places a microphone on the ground. We found a place on Howard's tape where the frogs were beginning to reclaim their space from the invasion of an alien being in their midst. As their voices grew louder, those of the audience subsided. Without knowing it, waves, people, and frogs had settled into sympathetic patterns of vibration. Then, in a moment of heartbreaking beauty and poignancy, we faded up "The Listener" theme, played by Howard on percussion and Don Druick on clay flute. This piece had always been the introduction to their program on CFRO. We spoke brief words of introduction through our tears. The listening began. The listening began to show us Howard's experience of the world as music.

As we listen again, we think about the ways in which sound is meaningful and beautiful. The act of "taking sound," like the act of listening itself, constitutes a form of authorship. Frogs sing for other frogs, not for us. Winds sing simply because it is their nature to do so. We encounter them as characters in our stories, not as what they really are. Frogs' songs are acoustic releasers of an amphibian mating program. Winds are the sighing of atmospheric thermal clines. They move according to their own devices. It is we who give them storied lives. It is we who poetize them. We read them as signs. We take them as signs for what it is that moves us, not for what it is that moves them.

Every listener is a composer of the soundscape he or she hears, but not every listener composes music that can reach out to touch another person. A composer of music is a signer rather than a sign. He or she is closer to us than to the frog, and more delicate in his or her way of touching us. Howard was a composer. He created music in the medium of audio actualities. He was an author of work with the power to move the listener within us. He knew how to play us as his instrument. We listen to his work with closer attention than to a frog and wind. We recognize in it a mind and spirit akin to our own. We listen with more of a response. We listen with greater responsibility. The composer and the one who receives his songs make up a sympathy. We compose a world we know together. Sometimes sounds come to us from the intelligence of other humans. In these cases, the authorship may be shared. Listening to music composed by a human is a romance, a mirroring of sympathetic experiences.

Listening to *Soundman* again is a rush of memory for us; it takes us back to times and places we remember. We hear the voices and songs of people we know or knew, and we hear the sound signatures that recall the smell of moosemeat and poplar smoke, the sound of rain on the roof of a tent. Howard was like a poet. He was able to focus your attention on the little things that would otherwise seem mundane. He made us really listen to the little things that are real. His work helps us clean our ears. We think about how completely tuned in to sound Howard was. Those ears were out there. We called one of the sections of *Soundman* "Field Broomfield" because it was made up of recordings that documented Howard's own voice in the field. We have transcribed it here because it evokes Howard's spirit well, and demonstrates his commitment to the audio experience, the fact that wherever he was, "those ears were out there," turned on and cleaned out, alert for the perfect world, as a photographer's eye anticipates the moment when the light will hit her subject in the way that best delineates it. Jillian put the pieces together and introduced it as follows:

> I composed this piece during and after a three-day stint listening to the "X-rated" series—the field tapes which chronicle the adventures of the small team of us who worked with the people of the Doig River Band of Beaver Indians from 1979-1985. Sometimes the "team" was very small—Howard and Robin alone—often I was there, and/or Morgan, and a variety of offspring—Amanda, Amber, Juniper, Eric—were with us from time to time.

The field tapes were usually made late at night, after we had returned from our various expeditions on and around Doig. They were our way of creating a journal, filling each other in on our observations, and exchanging ideas and suggestions. The talk was usually thoughtful and analytical, and at the same time the mood was relaxed, comradely, often tired, and generally full of humor. I listened to the field tapes because I thought they would be the best place to find the essential Howard, the best source of quotes in Howard's own words about his work, his concerns, his reflexive approach to being a documentarian. They also proved to be a good source of clips demonstrating how completely tuned in to sound Howard was. No matter how involved he was in the conversation, Howard's antennae always picked up sounds like those in "Good Dogs Barking." He never missed a chance to take the sound of car wheels on a northern road, nor an opportunity to enjoy fellowship with a kindred spirit, or to revel in enjoyment when he learned that his most critical audience—the people he had documented—understood and appreciated his work.

This piece is gentle, for the most part, as Howard was gentle, and passionate about his work. There is mourning in it, and celebration. The units are named, in Howard's tradition; that is one of the many things he taught me to do. Each one tells a story, whether it consists of one sentence, or a five-minute segment. The piece is sometimes rough, as the conditions we lived and recorded in were rough. Unlike many other documentarians, Howard, and the rest of us, often worked with bottom-line equipment and relied on talent—Howard's talent mostly—and the luck of the cosmos, or whoever, to help us come up with good results. Here is Howard in the field—"Field Broomfield."

Segment One, *Dawn Chorus and The Mighty Doig*, rose under Jillian's introduction. It consists of bird songs; there is no dialogue. We had named the second segment *People in Mourning/Real Life Movies*. It begins with Robin and Howard talking in the car late at night: Howard's voice is heard over the car radio, which is giving a station ID.

Howard: I've seen the police treat people who were in mourning as being drunk . . .
Robin: God Damn! . . . So much has happened.
Howard: It's just that the same existential bullshit web that we live in in our own lives is very exciting here.

Robin: Boy, it's been complex, what's going on—the movie that we walked into.

Howard: It's not a movie; it's just real life. Yeah, some of the guys were just pleasantly afternoon drunk . . . normal afternoon sunshine.

In Segment Three, *The Star Likes It,* Howard and Robin are talking about Gerry Davis's reaction to "Suffering Me Slowly," a program Howard and Jillian did for the CBC.

Robin: Gerry was just beautiful. He probably had a little bit, but—

Howard: Yeah, he was very warm.

R: He has such a nice voice, doesn't he? It purrs.

H: He must have listened to that tape really closely.

R: I'll bet—'cos he was really very impressed at what you guys had done with it. 'Cos he knew what happened, so you can't con him about it . . . if you don't know what happened you would sort of hear the thing as a piece, as being "Oh, well, they just recorded what happened." But he knew that all those sounds were coming from 1001 different sources, times, and places.

H: That's true.

R: And being smart enough, you know, he's a trained Beaver Indian and all.

H: But he would have known what they were really saying. I wouldn't even know what people were talking about.

R: Yeah, he knows the story. He knows what happened.

H: He knows the surrealism.

R: I think he really liked the fact that he made up the title. He was really happy at that. That's good. That makes that piece worthwhile, doesn't it?

H: Yeah, it sure does . . . when the star likes it . . . what the hell.

In Segment Four, called *Working With Gerry,* Howard is telling Robin about his car trip with Gerry Attachie, the Chief of the Doig River Band. They had been recording sounds that were significant—not necessarily to Howard, but to Gerry. He recognized it as a means to enter the world that we were documenting; to experience it *In Doig People's Ears.*

Howard: In the course of driving today, although there was a lot of conversation that went on, it seemed like I was mostly recording what Gerry asked me to record. And—there were a couple of country songs, and the rodeo reports—were the things that he thought of as significant.

Robin: Oh, you were recording off the radio.

H: Well, Gerry and I went into the mode that we, yeah, that we got into last time, which was where I decided that I would just record what he asked me to record. I would let him be the director and I would be the technician, 'cos that's the role I know the best. And, you know, he would tell me when the radio came on to record certain things, and . . .

R: Oh, that's great.

H: Today I kind of reacted—I did some wrong things, 'cos I didn't . . . couple of times I said, "Na, you've got to tell me before the song starts or else I'm not going to touch it."

R: Ooh.

H: And things like that. So I should wise up. But we should get Gerry to do something very specific for the tape, and interview with someone else, I think.

There is no definitive marker between this section and Segment Five, *Grasshopper Stew*, but the subject changes.

Howard: Yeah, we just gravitate towards different . . . you gravitate more towards older people . . .

Robin: Yeah, I gravitate to older people.

H: And I gravitate to kids, where I get to be a little bit looser. They are good kids. Kids are another thing.

Kid 1:   What's that for?

H: Take the sound.

H: So, how many? You kids got grasshoppers, huh?

Kid 1:   I got a whole bunch.

H: How many you got?

Kid 1:   I don't know, I can't even count them. Two thousand, ha ha.

H: Two thousand grasshoppers. I think that's enough for dinner. We should make a fire here, and we'll cook the grasshoppers.

Kid 2:   I'm not goin' to eat nuttin', yuck!!

H: It's grasshopper stew.

Kids: (moans and giggles, giggles, and groans)

Kid 3:   I got one groundhog.

Kid 2:   Groundhog?

H: Got what? Groundhog?

All kids: (giggles)
Kid 2:   "I got one Greehnog." You say that.
Kid 1:   What's that for?
H: It takes sounds . . .
Kid 1:   With that?
H: Yeah—Listen!!

Segment Six, *Taking Stories*, is another conversation between Howard and Robin.

Howard: I wrote the note to Chesher Babcock for Tommy. I wonder what Tommy told him about us. I mean I assume that he mentioned us because he didn't seem to take any surprise at our being there.
Robin: Yeah—I don't know.
H: Tommy must have said who we were, I mean described us to him. Yeah, "These two guys from Vancouver come to visit me."
R: "Take lots of . . ."
H: "To hear me tell stories."
R: "They take my stories."
H: Yeah, tape of stories, take tapes of my stories, take my tape. Like, "take my picture, take my tape."
R: Yeah, but we say, they've heard us say "tape"—we "tape" things, and they translate that as . . .
H: I don't think they've heard us say it, I think it's from . . .
R: It's just a transfer from . . .
H: From photography. Because everybody uses it. Yeah! It's the same as taking a picture, it's the same level of mediation that's going on.

Segment Seven, *Good Dogs Barking*, begins when the conversation is interrupted by Howard saying "Good dogs barking." Robin responds, "Do you want to put it out?—contexted discourse for inquiring whether Howard wanted to roll the car window down and put the microphone outside the car to more effectively record the sounds. With this accomplished, the barking grows louder and dominates the quiet northern night.

Segment Eight is called *Mud on the Microphone*.

Howard: We got a lot of car trips going on. We got a really nice recording of an engine being tuned . . .

Robin: Oh, yeah
H: . . . carburetor being set, cows getting their little balls cut off.
[radio music up, then loud sound of a diesel car motor, sounds of car
door opening, wheels churning through mud and snow]
H: Yuck! Lots of mud on the microphone, man! Yuck!

Jillian chose Segment Nine, *Saviour*, because it illustrates
Howard's capacity for intimacy with adults, just as *Grasshopper Stew*
shows his rapport with kids. Howard did not strive for objectivity;
he got involved, and let you know what it sounded like to be
involved.

Howard: Well, we interviewed Saviour a little about his new house
           which he said was no good, he liked the old one better,
           because the furnace worked, the fireplace worked, and the
           furnace doesn't work in the new house. Ummm . . .
Robin: He didn't have to sweep the floor in the old one.
H: That's right! And Tommy talked about how his house was
           going to be renovated, and he talked about how he'd
           worked all winter and was doing real good. And Saviour
           said that he had an ulcer and couldn't drink whiskey—so
           Tommy pulled out a bottle of wine for him. And then we
           drank that, and talked, kind of did a lot of affirmation of
           fellowship and toasted each other, and held each other's
           hands and stuff. Said how glad we were that we were all
           still alive. Saviour said he would probably be the first to go.
           But he's not that much older than anybody else. He was
           born in 1938.

Segment Ten, *Laser Blades*, is another section that shows Howard's
constant awareness of sound. In it, Howard, Jillian, and Robin are com-
paring notes on Johnny Chipesia's story-telling session.

Howard: I was thinking while I was watching him today, tell the
           story, that you could start TV programs just with him sitting
           in the chair, with that spitcan, maybe start out with the spit,
           and then have him start a story and then kind of have it dis-
           solve into . . .
Jillian: Yes.
H: . . . into the actual story, and occasionally it comes back to the
           chair . . .
J: Just like Alistair Cooke. (laughs)

H: He just seems like such a pro! He was beautiful, the hand movements and stuff.

Robin: You got some pictures, didn't you Jillian?

J: Just a couple.

H: I got nervous because I was hearing clicks loudly on the tape, so I got nervous, in case we wanted to use the tape.

J: I doubt it, that you would hear it that loud . . .

H: 'Cos it was dead in there, it was *so* silent. Except you could always use slides, and have them timed to the clicks. Or put background sound in at that point . . .

R: Actually, you could probably cut it if you wanted to cut it out.

H: With a laser blade, you could cut it out, yeah.

J: Yeah, you could cut it out if it was important.

H: With a laser blade.

J: Yeah, laser blade. Hey, that's an idea!

Segment Eleven, *Saturday at the Fort*, involves Howard, Robin, and Jillian.

Howard: Summer is more gentle. If you want to go to Fort St. John, sit in the Fort (hotel) and just have a nice afternoon.

Robin: Yeah. The door kept coming open, and this golden shaft of light and a beautiful strong wind, the west wind, kept coming in.

J: Which was great, because I was trying to take pictures. We were both trying to take pictures.

H: It was almost as though we were in church. I mean I really felt like Marshall [the local Missionary]. Like it was another, it was a more civil translation of a religious get-together. Like people really liked each other, a lot of touching and people changing tables and sitting with one another. I broke my glass and the beer broke and the guy next to me bought me a glass of beer.

R: It was one of the times that in times of turmoil you know you will look back and say, "Oh boy!"

H: "Remember the good old days at the Fort?"

J: Yeah.

H: Well, try it again next Saturday.

The last segment, *Existential Doubt*, shows Howard's essential honesty. It did not always matter whether or not the sounds he used for a production were ones that were recorded at that time and place; what mattered was capturing the experience, making the tape tell the truth about what it was like to be there.

Howard: Why do it when they are going to blow us up soon? There's nothing else to do at the moment.

Robin: Remember about writing down the information—that it was recorded in mono in Albert Askoty's cabin, and you said, "We'll remember," and I said, "This is for posterity, a thousand years from now. We'll be dead. And if anybody wants to know where it was recorded, they won't remember."

H: No, but I mean we'll remember by next week, next month, or two years from now. A year from now we'll still remember every scene of recording almost. I think. With a little bit of luck.

R: Probably some. Some of them you won't.

H: But the distortions'll be the truth. Otherwise it's just a bunch of lies.

R: Well isn't it?

H: What?

R: What we are doing.

H: What?

R: Bunch of lies

H: No, I don't think so.

When Robin said that what we were doing was a "bunch of lies," he was playing on the Dunne-za translation of their word for "stories" as "lies" in English. Working with Howard was always storied, but it was never "a bunch of lies." Howard probed to find the essential truth. Poets do this in words. Howard did it with sound. His work has the same quality of getting at the essence, of distilling the quality of an experience to a few evocative phrases that the best poets also capture.

Howard once said, "We created the environment and then played it." His compositions were often sound sculptures as well as sounds. He quite literally created environments and then played them. For a series of performances that Howard and fellow artists Al Neil, Roy Kiyooka, Trudi Rosenfeld, Greg Simpson, Don Druick, and Diana Kemple referred to as "post-literate music," Howard constructed a sort of sound cage within which he created a world of percussive sounds. *Soundman* presented a selection of tapes that document these remarkable group improvisations, usually performed at the Western Front, that were part of the Vancouver music scene during the mid 1980s. In a less formal setting, Howard improvised on sound sculpture wherever he found it. A piece he whimsically called "Musique du Nord," for instance, consisted of freshly cut tamarack fenceposts, and with Robin and Dunne-za kids on the tanks and pipes of an abandoned gas station at Mile 233 on the Alaska Highway.

Our writing about listening to Howard's work would not be complete without a few words to describe his remarkable tapework compositions. One of the first and perhaps the most ambitious of these was Howard's piece, *Radio on Radio: A Radio Program about Radio Programs*, which he completed while a graduate student in the Communications Department of Simon Fraser University. Aired somewhat hesitantly on the Canadian Broadcasting Corporation's *Ideas* series on Halloween evening of 1974, the piece is a varied tape collage of radio and live actualities that begins with the voice of veteran CBC staff announcer, Doug Campbell, and then the following dialog between Howard and the host of the series, which was called "Soundscapes of Canada."

Host (whispering to Howard—sound of mike switch):   Stay fairly close to the mike, eh.

Host (in his "radio voice"):   Actually, listening to your program I did find it rather inconsistent in places. It is a very strange program, isn't it?

To which Howard replies: I, um, aah, the kind of program that I make.

Host: I know, uh, we had a lot of discussion before we, uh, decided to accept it for broadcast as to whether it was suitable for broadcast . . . whether it came up to the CBC's high standards.

Howard: Um.

Host (in his off-air voice):   Let me cut that because that's too, that's too much. Um.

Howard (laughing amiably):   All right.

Host (in his radio voice):   Actually, we did have a lot of discussion, uh, about these programs as we discussed them all. Um, as to whether it was suitable for broadcast. Uh, we thought perhaps it would be a bit too "far out" for many listeners.

Howard: Ah, it seems to be the kind of thing that I hear on the radio all the time, uh, someone said it was a radio program, so I just tried to make a radio program about, the same way that radio programs are made . . .

Host (brightly to the point of being manic):   So, it's a radio program . . .

Howard (genially co-operative):   . . . about radio programs.

This piece continues with nearly sixty minutes of astonishing and brilliant juxtapositions of sounds and devices recorded off air, on air, and sometimes seemingly out of the poetics of thin air. Howard obviously delighted in trying out every editing device he could think of, but his purpose was always artistic, not merely technical wizardry. Sometimes they blow like woodwinds and brasses, as in a passage that blends a charismatic preacher's story of the battle of Jericho and the brash blowing of a horn that becomes a radio speaker's many voices. The passage ends with a compelling tape-poem made from loops of the words, "now just let me tell you."

Radio on Radio concludes with its own beginning, a reprise of the CBC announcer and a conversation between Howard and host.

Host: The next sixty minutes consists of a radio program about radio. In fact, that's what it is called. And it was prepared by Howard Broomfield, an associate to the World Soundscape Project. Howard's here, uh, to explain it to you before you listen to it.

Howard (earnestly): What I've tried to do in the program is to take the stuff of radio, the stuff that radio has been throughout its lifetime, since about 1920 for commercial radio, well, for broadcast radio . . . I've tried to take that lifetime and compress it into an hour. I've begun in the first part by just finding out what people think about radio now. I've kind of done a social survey of radio. And throughout the song, "Turn the Radio On," which was written when radio first came out, it was an expression of the people's first thoughts about radio. Throughout that song, I've put in the clips of what people are thinking about radio now. And in the second part, I try to demonstrate how the sound of radio affected history.

Host: You've used a lot of historical material in this program, haven't you?

Howard: Uh hum.

Host: Historical tapes, and also as you just mentioned, material that you collected down on street corners and places like that.

Howard: Ummm.

Host: You've produced several radio programs, rather surrealistic programs of which this is the latest. I've always thought that you were the sort of composer that collects a lot of material out of the trash can.

Howard: There are some quotes from certain of the radio personalities in Vancouver, and there are pieces of music that you people have done that have been on the CBC in the past. And um, I'm not sure what their fate was there.

Host: Well, shall we just . . . Do you want to say anything more about it or shall we just listen to it?

Howard: Let's listen to it.

Doug Campbell: *Ideas: On Soundscapes of Canada.* This is the ninth program in our current series, and here to introduce it is Murray Schafer. (30 seconds of Schafer's—and Canada's—soundscape signature, a loon calling at dawn on a lake in Ontario)

Host (excited and in a conversational tone):   That'll be nice.

Howard (with dawning understanding and joy):   To come at the end! (laughs with joy)

Host (with great enthusiasm):   See what I mean? Let's listen to it! And then we go on to the, you know . . .

Howard: Beautiful! (two minute, 35 second reprise of Schafer as loon— sounds of splashing—dawn chorus—cow mooing—silence)

Conclusion

In "Field Broomfield," Howard and Robin had the following conversation.

H: No, but I mean we'll remember by next week, next month, or two years from now. A year from now we'll still remember every scene of a recording, almost. I think. With a little bit of luck.

R: Probably, some. Some of them you won't.

H: But the distortions'll be the truth. Otherwise it's just a bunch of lies.

Howard listened to ordinary reality with an extraordinary ear. The sounds he put together may sound unbelievable because of their unusual juxtaposition, but they are all real. In Howard's work, the distortions become the truth. They become the story. Listening to Howard's work now is like remembering our Saturday afternoons at the Fort Hotel.

R: It was one of the times that in times of turmoil you know you will look back at and say, "Oh, boy!"

H: "Remember the good old days at the Fort?"

J: Yeah.

H: Well, try it again next Saturday.

On July 6, 1986, we took a canoe ride with Robin's daughter, Amber Ridington, on Fairview Lake in New Jersey. We were there to celebrate the 50th wedding anniversary of Robin's parents. The call telling us of Howard's death had come the day before. As we paddled, cried, and listened to frogs that seemed to be commemorating the occasion with their most exhuberant cacophony, Amber said, "Howard is part of the noise now." She was almost right. Howard distinguished noise from sound. For him, noise was extraneous, an impediment blocking the exquisite world of sound in which he gloried. Sound was pure, desirable, and full of meaning—even if it was as common as the sound of a diesel Rabbit motor or "good dogs barking." Howard was never extraneous. Howard is not part of the noise; he is part of the sound.

List of Completed Audio Documentary Pieces by Howard Broomfield

Audio Documentaries about the Dunne-za

Soundwalk To Heaven (50 min). Howard Broomfield and Robin Ridington. CFRO Vancouver 1979.

Trails of the Dunne-za: A Suite of Four Radio Pieces (Four 5-minute pieces). Howard Broomfield, Jillian Ridington, Robin Ridington. CBC "Our Native Land" 1980.

Suffering Me Slowly (60 min). Howard Broomfield, Jillian Ridington. CBC "The Hornby Collection" 1981.

Next door Neighbors (30 min). Howard Broomfield and Robin Ridington. CFRO Vancouver 1981.

Old Time Religion (60 min). Howard Broomfield and Robin Ridington. 1982. Presented as a slide-tape "docu-drama" at the 1982 Canadian Ethnology Society meetings.

In Doig People's Ears (42 min). Howard Broomfield. 1983. Composed for a conference on *The Sociology of Music: An Exploration of Issues.* Trent University: August, 1983.

Video of slide-tape piece—In Doig People's Ears: Portrait of a Changing Native Community (30 min).

Partial List of Other Audio Documentaries

Radio on Radio
(composed at SFU Department of Communications—presented on CBC "Ideas" October 31, 1974)

A Birth Narrative
   (produced for *Newsounds Gallery* CFRO-FM—material recorded February
   24, 1983—Ariel's birthday)

Blessing for a Long Time to Come
   (based on field recording of 1985 Omaha pow-wow by Robin and Jillian
   Ridington—produced September, 1985)

When the Circus Came to Town
   (an exposé of Expo produces for CFRO "The Listener"—June, 1986)

Location Marker
   (produced for CFRO "The Listener"—1986)

   In addition to the above pieces, there are a number of as yet uncataloged
performance tapes, "Listener" programs, and tapework compositions.

Published Work Relevant to *Soundman*

Ridington, Robin
   1988 Trail to Heaven: Knowledge and Narrative in a Northern Native
      Community. Iowa City: University of Iowa Press. (Douglas and
      McIntyre in Canada).
   1990 Little Bit Know Something: Stories in a Language of Anthropology.
      Iowa City: University of Iowa Press. (Douglas and McIntyre in
      Canada).

Schafer, R. Murray
   1977 The Tuning of the World. Toronto: McClelland and Stewart.

24

The PowWow

Carolyn Bereznak Kenny

Prelude to Carolyn Kenny

My connection to Carolyn Kenny is probably briefer than that of any of the contributors in the book.

We are colleagues at Antioch Southern California (Santa Barbara) where Carolyn is the Earth Mother of cross cultural studies (and affairs), quietly needling and cajoling sophisticated graduate students and faculty into granting they know even less about their ethnic and class orientations and biases than they do about their sexuality. This is hard work.

I fill this page for symmetry. All the other pieces here are being introduced quite personally by Carolyn, her sense of balance and proportion is disturbed at the last minute and she tells me it is only fair to have someone say something about her and that I will do, since I volunteer and can do my own typing. Actually, my filling up this page is a measure of Carolyn Kenny's humility. She genuinely does not care what is on this page and has agreed to print any damn thing I write at this late hour.

I have known her about two years and only learned she was a music therapist when she asked me to take a look at the manuscript for this book for typos. I got sucked into reading it rather closely. "You seem to be the Earth Mother of the left wing of music therapy," I told her reverently after reading.

"Now, now," she retorted, changing the subject to the federal conspiracy to stamp out Indian Health Clinics.

She cuts through life like a maple leaf in the heavy fall air, landing gently here and there, scarcely leaving a karmic trace. A gentle soul with moral muscle, looking pretense and pomposity in the eye and making it laugh at itself for having been such an ass.

Other vitals: at Antioch she also teaches "Dialogues: Explorations in the Socratic Method," and "Ceremony, Ritual, and Play: Anthropological Perspectives on Healing." She's an "interdisciplinary multiculturalist," a mystic and a poet, a thorn in the paw of complacency and a nurturer of budding therapists, writers, and artists (this my description, not hers), and, according to the high school yearbook she does not know I stumbled onto, senior class president and editor of the yearbook.

I think the field is a sweeter place for having Carolyn Kenny, the yearbook editor and Earth Mother.

Jack Crane
Antioch Southern California

Many years passed before I found myself at the Pow Wow.[1] It was something about almost-forgotten roots or ones barely remembered. Then all of a sudden they were felt and found. The sights and sounds of the Pow Wow were exhilarating. Yet the moment was a quiet one.

It was at day's end. I was curled up in my tent, close to the Earth. And then I felt. Some would say I heard. But no, I felt the sounds of the drums across the camp—consistent, enduring, quiet drums and quieter chants, long into the night. They were the heart in me. They went on through the night.

Some throw hot words and power about Indian things. I only knew the melting of sorrow and the continuity of all things. The drums and the Earth. I was safe. I was home.

Sounds held me. Hundreds of mocassins dancing at the Pow Wow—a quiet, constant sound. Feet were touching the Earth through soft mocs, hundreds of soft, beaded mocs worn by women and men and children. There were elders. There were young men—fancy dancers with the flora and fauna of the wild. There were stately women who barely moved. I heard their breath. They stayed close to the Earth. The men often flew. And I heard the sound of their flight. They were really birds, you know. And there were zephyrs whispering through thousands of feathers there—another soft sound. And it was a sight as well.

The sound of hot bubbling oil as the women stood for hours in the kitchen making Indian fry bread. The soft pats of throwing dough from heel of hand to heel of hand continues now. We women made hundreds of fry bread. There was laughter there. Madeleine was always giggling from tickling spirits coming out of all those hot bubbles on the stove. It's one of the things that happens at the Pow Wow. The laughter held me. When Reggie came to the window and made a joke, Linda said: "What would we have done without the humor of Indian men?" "We probably would have died," I said. "We would have all died." And what of the endurance of Indian women? The fry bread kept coming.

Grandfather spoke and told us that the minute we are born, we are dead. "So," he said, "what is race, what is tribe? We're all dead. So it doesn't matter anyway. We're dead. Together, we are all dead."

Then there were delicate sounds of the crane, the dolphin, dances of the Chumash—little clicks and whistles. And even the movements were sounds—so soft, less than the wind. Shells on buckskin—tinkling sounds. Sounds even shine, you know.

I found my soul there.

There was the sound of the great fire. Mark was looking for his grandmother. He was calling people up in the hills. They were trying to remember. She was Cherokee. Although my grandmother was Choctaw, Mark and I are still related. We are all related. Around a fire one knows about these things and then there is the sound of words, words which come easy, like the day and sometimes like the night. Words even sound of dusk and at times like dawn, like the sun, like the beginnings of things.

Often many tribes dance together in the same circle these days. Drums and singers come from near and far. People dance and sing and with them they bring the animals and all of the sounds of the Earth. The drum never stops. And we dance. And then we sleep. We share food. Lots of jokes and tricks. And the drum goes on. I feel the sound of the drum. With every beat I'm born. And I also die. It's like Grandfather says: "The minute we are born, we're dead." The drum reminds us. This is the continuity of all things. This is how we are together in one place.

I found myself at the Pow Wow. And the Earth rose up to greet me. It was a sweet embrace. The drum told the tale. "Grandmother, are you there? Can you see from your place in the sky? Can you hear me dancing now? Does the wind carry me to you?"

We are born again and we die.

At the Pow Wow I found my way. It was a sound and many sounds on those days. They surrounded me and held me. They held the soft tears which came from my eyes. They held laughter. The sound held the dance. And the sound held the animals as well. And each feather, too. They were all there. We have the Earth and the drum. I was home. Home found me at the Pow Wow that night. The drums and the Earth. I was held. I was held by the sound of existence itself on that simple night. The drums, the Earth, I was held. I was home.

Note

1. This story is in the oral tradition. Recreate with your voice.

Part V

LISTENING, PLAYING, CREATING:
THE POWER OF SOUND

Introduction to Part Five

Music: you stranger. You feeling space, growing
away from us. The deepest thing in us, that, rising above us,
    forces its way out . . .
a holy goodbye:
when the innermost point in us stands
outside, as amazing space, as the other side of the air:
pure,
immense, not for us to live in now.

—Rainer Maria Rilke
excerpt from poem "On Music"
translated by Robert Bly

For much of my life I have been alone. I have been in a yearning state because I am captivated by a sense of anticipation. I am always waiting on the edge. Music is this to me. It is the place in between. And because it gives us our yearning and it gives us our becoming, it gives us hope, even in the face of despair.

Between the lines of many of these works, in the song, you might hear a kind of crying out for existence itself, and a coming into being through the sound. Many of us have heard this sound of existence emanating from those who find themselves on the edge, or seemingly lost. It is a state we know. There is a profundity in the expression of our human condition through sound.

Perhaps yearning is fundamentally a spiritual state.

The music tells.

Late one night, that first year in the Catskill Mountains, in Phoenecia, we began a wild chant, holding on to each other in a circle, moving to the rhythm of the stars. All of the words in our song ended in "ing." Our humour was dark and light, black and white and gold. We were not alone. We held on.

"Ing" was the place we wanted to be because it was immediate—in the act of creating. We dismissed the old and heralded the new. We appreciated the old and made fun of the new. We made fun of ourselves. We prayed. We played. "Ing" music seemed to keep us in the place "in between." It kept us in the sound.

I broke apart my theory, you know, because it was not really like the sound—not ambiguous enough, not free to hold and let go—even with opening and closing and such. It turned into three ings and friends with whom I have walked along the way.

Listening

In listening we can find the silent source, an unbidden song, the body, change, Beauty, intuition, a sacred act.

So many of these authors have mentioned silence and meditation in their work. This kind of listening has to do with something other than what we can perceive in the mundane. In this listening, we can sense—a new pattern, a new thought, a feeling quivering in the recesses of our soul. But this kind of listening takes a shift from our normal state. Music therapists are required to listen in this way. Listening is the pathway to change. When things are quiet, perhaps we can more easily hear the Sound. Soundman knows. Healing knows. And the people who walked this way also have known, those who have been connected to the Earth. Know your home. Listen to home.

Playing

When could we remember how to listen? Perhaps early, when we played. In our early times, even in our mother's womb, before words, before even thought, maybe we listened to the sound. Then we lived in a world of ambiguity. Form and formlessness ebbed and flowed. We drifted from one to the other. We could be in a state of flux.

Now in our work-a-day world, in our society, we speak of consciousness. We need some rituals to hold us for change. Can we still be free? Or must we be bound and to what? We have language and speech as well as sound. We have ceremonies too. We dwell in a land—Nature is our home. We even go to stores and hear sound. We suffer and we sing. We become who we can be when we play.

Creating

We seek Beauty on our way. And for humans, beauty can mean death, loss, letting go. Often it is death. Then it can also be birth once again. It can be anticipating and yearning and then moving beyond the edge into the unknown.

We hear this in the breath, in the sound. We see it in an image. We know it as a wailing cry. Beauty is food without which we will die. It is our hope. It is our light. It is the way we can reveal ourselves to one another and sing: "Now I am found."

Contributors

Kenneth Aigen
Nordoff-Robbins Music Therapy Clinic
New York University
26 Washington Place
4th Floor
New York, New York 10003

Dorit Amir
Bar-Ilan University
Department of Musicology
29900 Ramat-Gan
Israel

Kenneth E. Bruscia
Temple University
Esther Boyer College of Music
Philadelphia, Pennsylvania 19122

David Burrows
511 West 232, East 52nd St.
Bronx, New York 10463

Joanne Crandall
547 Pala Dr.
Ojai, California 93023

Michael Fles
530 Warren Creek Rd.
Arcata, California 95521

Francis Smith Goldberg
155 Beacon St.
San Francisco, California 94131

Barbara Hesser
Department of Music
New York University
35 West 4th St.
Room 777
New York, New York 10003

Connie Isenberg-Grzeda
Département de Musique
Université du Québec à Montréal
Case postale 8888
Succursle A
Montréal, Québec
Canada
H3C 3P8

Carolyn Bereznak Kenny
P.O. Box 4500
Blaine, Washington 98231-4500

Gillian Stephens Langdon
Creative Arts Therapies Department
Bronx Psychiatric Center
1500 Waters Place
Bronx, New York 10461

Paul Lauzon
155 Vaughan Rd., Apt. 2
Toronto, Ontario
Canada
M6C 2L9

David Marcus
2350 Broadway
New York, New York 10024

John Marcus
13630 Bradley Ave.
Sylmar, California 91342

Nancy McMaster
Music Therapy Program
2055 Purcell Way
North Vancouver, British Columbia
Canada
V7J 3H5

Joseph J. Moreno
Music Therapy Department
Maryville University
13550 Conway Rd.
St. Louis, Missouri 63141

Penelope Nichols-Rothe
c/o KTD Monestary
352 Meads Mountain Rd.
Woodstock, New York 12498

Peter O'Loughlin
4464 James St.
Vancouver, British Columbia
Canada
V5V 3J1

Robin and Jillian Ridington
Retreat Island
Galiano Island, British Columbia
Canada
V0N 1P0

Even Ruud
Institutt for Musik og Teater
Universitetet 1 Oslo
Postboks 1017 Blindern
0315 Oslo 3, Norway

Benedikte Barth Scheiby
38 Montgomery Place
Brooklyn, New York 11215

Jeremy J. Shapiro
The Fielding Institute
2112 Santa Barbara St.
Santa Barbara, California 93105

Lisa Summer
The Bonny Foundation
2020 Simmons St.
Salina, KS 67401

Christopher Tree
c/o L'Arbre à Musique
Le Grand Moulin
53270 Ste. Suzanne
France

Index